UNDER A NEW SKY

Books by Olga Andreyev Carlisle

Voices in the Snow

Poets on Street Corners

Solzhenitsyn and the Secret Circle

Island in Time

Under a New Sky

Under a New Sky

A REUNION WITH RUSSIA

Olga Andreyev Carlisle

TICKNOR & FIELDS NEW YORK 1993

Copyright © 1993 by Olga Andreyev Carlisle
All rights reserved
For information about permission to reproduce selections
from this book, write to Permissions, Ticknor & Fields,
Houghton Mifflin Company, 215 Park Avenue South, New York, NY 10003.

Library of Congress Cataloging-in-Publication Data
Carlisle, Olga Andreyev.
Under a new sky : a reunion with Russia / Olga Andreyev Carlisle.
p.   cm.
ISBN 0-89919-957-7
1. Soviet Union — Intellectual life.   2. Russian literature —
20th century — History and criticism.   3. Carlisle, Olga Andreyev —
Journeys — Soviet Union.   I. Title.
DK287.C37   1993   92-33469
947.085'4 — DC20   CIP

"Lot's Wife" and "All is despoiled, abandoned, sold" by Anna Akhmatova,
translated by Richard Wilbur, reprinted by permission of the translator.
"To Alexander Blok" was reprinted from *Poems of Akhmatova*, selected, translated and introduced by Stanley Kunitz with Max Hayward. Copyright © 1973
by Stanley Kunitz and Max Hayward. First appeared in American Poetry Review. By permission of Little, Brown and Company.

All unacknowledged translations are by Olga Andreyev Carlisle.
Chapter 23, "Two Friends," first appeared, in different form, in *Vogue*.

Printed in the United States of America

HAD 10 9 8 7 6 5 4 3 2 1

For Gloria Loomis,
the best of friends

Acknowledgments

I want to thank friends Russian and American who have helped with this book, notably my editor John Herman and Cindy Spiegel of Ticknor & Fields. I extend my special thanks to Nancy Hamilton, whose typing and editorial advice have been invaluable. I am also grateful to my husband, Henry Carlisle, whose love and professional guidance have sustained me through the writing of *Under a New Sky*.

No, the lost Russia will not be silenced.
On all sides the rot feeds a wild courage.
SERGEI YESSENIN
(Translated by W. S. Merwin with OAC)

CONTENTS

Contents

Preface

NO POLITICAL TRANSFORMATION that Russia has undergone to date was quite as dramatic and yet as bloodless as the one that unfolded at the Russian Parliament building, the so-called Moscow White House, in August 1991. For some months a climate of fear had been spreading through the Soviet Union. There were government troops ready to strike in various republics, threats of pogroms, KGB intimidations. There may even have been some measure of connivance on the part of Mikhail Gorbachev. His efforts to restructure the Soviet Union had greatly accelerated its breakup. Now he seemed in terror of his more orthodox Communist colleagues, unable to face the fact that the vast multinational country was at last escaping the grip of Marxist-Leninist ideology.

When the moment of truth came, though it might have had support in some KGB quarters, it was a clear victory for youth and decency. Russian soldiers would not shoot at Russians. An obsolete political order that had tyrannized its subjects and threatened other nations for some seventy years was collapsing. When the cellist-conductor Mstislav Rostropovich appeared arm-in-arm with Boris Yeltsin on the balcony of the White House, it was a celebration for Russia and for her culture. A democratically elected leader and a musician long exiled were proclaiming that freedom was possible in Russia, that art would bring people together, and not only Russians. The rejuvenated face of Eduard Shevernadze, a Georgian who had been Gorbachev's foreign minister, came next on the screen. He had last been seen warning the world darkly about an imminent return to dictatorship, but now he looked elated.

In San Francisco my husband and I watched the events on CNN. The removing of Dzerzhinsky's statue from its pedestal left us breathless. The grim monument to the founder of the Cheka, who in 1919 on Lenin's orders had conducted a relentless hunt for my grandfather Victor Chernov, was being toppled. Russia was entering a new age.

I remembered walking by Dzerzhinsky's black, oversized statue with my cousin Aliosha one day in 1989. Stepping out of the Lubyanka beyond it, a detachment of KGB officers was filing up toward the monument, eight or ten men carrying an enormous wreath of red carnations. Evidently they were celebrating some secret police anniversary. All around us in that busy part of town, Muscovites were hurrying by, pointedly ignoring the ceremony that was enacted in their midst. But now Muscovites had taken matters into their hands. On screen we could see the faces of KGB officials peering out of the Lubyanka windows, anxiously studying an eerie sight — their patron saint's statue floating horizontally above its pedestal.

We will not know for a time whether these images were in fact moments of truth for Russia or simply exalted photo opportunities. But it just might be that the country has found its face for the twenty-first century, symbolized by that of Rostropovich, a great artist now living abroad, surrounded by a sea of youthful faces — people coming into their own under the sign of their culture, the one value that has endured through the violent reincarnations of the Russian empire in the last three hundred years.

There are different ways of numbering Russian revolutions depending on whether the abortive 1905 revolution is included and whether February and October are considered separately or together. However, since the middle of the sixteenth century, when Moscow shook off the Tartar yoke — St. Basil on Red Square commemorates that event — there have been precisely four radical political upheavals in Russia.

Moscow had been its first full-fledged incarnation, gaining ascendancy over the adjacent principalities through its willingness to act as the Tartar invaders' tax levier. Medieval Russia, deeply religious, closed to the rest of the world yet aggressive toward its neighbors, with its small fortress-towns scattered across a boundless wooded plain, disintegrated in the seventeenth century as a result of dynastic strife and invasions from the west.

A second Russia was born in the beginning of the eighteenth century. It was created on a European model by Russia's first emperor, Peter the Great, ruthless and yet inspired, who willed a modern empire into existence and endeavored to make it part of Europe. This was the Russia of Alexander Pushkin, the author of *The Bronze Horseman,* a visionary poem about the crushing of the individual by the state. St. Petersburg remains to this day an emblem of that empire.

Some two hundred years later, Peter's Russia dissolved in turn as a result of the blows inflicted on the country by World War I. In 1917 a third Russia was created by Lenin, which released for a time the underprivileged classes of society and gave them a share of political power. This new Russia, a police state, was atheistic, nationalistic, imperial. Its symbol became the gulag, a system of labor camps where millions worked and died in the service of the Communist state. It too collapsed, ostensibly because of mismanagement and of the impact on its subjects of modern-day communications.

In August 1991 a fourth Russia was born. The birth of

this non-state, an inadvertent result of Mikhail Gorbachev's efforts to humanize and modernize the Soviet Union, took only a few days — the lifting of censorship two years before had helped bring it about. Its emergence is a vindication for the Russian intelligentsia, whose spirit lived on through the Soviet years, sustained by the example of a few intrepid, talented individuals like Boris Pasternak, Anna Akhmatova, and Andrey Sakharov.

Despite decades of fierce literary and political censorship, Russian intellectuals and artists survived in part because the state allowed many classics, whether Russian or foreign, to be read — these were regarded as innocuous. The Soviet citizens of Rostropovich's generation turned out to be better educated than was generally supposed in the West. Despite their lack of experience in matters of self-government, they are now working to map a democratic future for their country.

The huge funerals honoring Pushkin in St. Petersburg in 1837 and Pasternak in Peredelkino in 1960 were spontaneous yet solemn rituals demonstrating the Russians' enduring love of their writers. Andrey Sakharov, a scientist who became a democratic activist under extremely unlikely circumstances, was given a similar funeral in December 1990. That winter, crowds several hundred thousand strong came out into the streets of Moscow and Leningrad to demonstrate their support for democracy. After the attempted coup, the official ceremony honoring the three young men killed by the government's tanks, one of whom was Jewish, inaugurated what one may hope will be a new era in Russian public life.

The deep-seated causes of the emergence of the fourth Russia are still hard to assess. Perhaps because its history has been so harsh, compassion has traditionally been the country's most cherished virtue, expressed by the ancient legend of the Virgin unwilling to remain on her heavenly throne while the damned burn in hell. It is a glimmer of that compassion, unexpected in a Party official, which people all over the world recognized in Gorbachev as he dismantled the gulag, hoping to establish "Communism with a human face" in his country.

In 1987 Gorbachev brought Sakharov back to Moscow from a seven-year exile. Sakharov, the father of the Soviet H-bomb, had been the first in the Soviet Union to declare openly that it could one day become a democracy, that unilateral nuclear disarmament was a key to world stability. By 1989 Sakharov had become the dynamic leader of the anti-Communist opposition, which grew, like Pushkin's Tzarevich in the *Tale of Tzar Saltan,* not with each day but with each hour. At that time many Russians came to believe that perhaps there could be a democratic future for their country.

Since then, Sakharov's virtues of courage and humility have become legendary in Russia. So has his love of Russia: the leader who is revered as the hero of glasnost is not Gorbachev, who defeated a fearsome Party structure, but Sakharov. We have here a traditional Russian shift: over the years a humble Moscow saint, St. Basil, overshadowed the Holy Intercessor, the Virgin, who was said to have helped Ivan the Terrible defeat the Tartars at Kazan. It was St. Basil who gave his name to Moscow's most patriotic church.

In Boris Yeltsin, the man who succeeded Gorbachev as the country's leader, another Russian homespun virtue came forth — the willingness to repent. Russians remember how Boris Nicolaevich resigned from the Party, stalking out of the Soviet Parliament, walking away from the podium, from Gorbachev and a row of glowering Party bosses. Yeltsin repented openly — and then promptly outlawed the Party. Now, earnest though often clumsy efforts are being made to try to solve humanely some of Russia's huge economic and social ills, and to give a new constitution to the Confederation of Independent States, the Soviet

Union's replacement. Sakharov's constitutional draft, composed in the last months of his life, is no longer appropriate, now that the former Soviet empire has lost its ruling center in the Kremlin. The outlying republics are understandably reluctant to regard the new Russia as the Soviet Union's legal heir.

No significant purges have yet taken place in Russia: Communists can still be found in all the branches and at all levels of government. The plundering of the Soviet state has made many among them quite wealthy. Often they are reluctant to give up their managerial posts and turn property or land over to the citizenry. From them we hear about the need for protecting the newborn state from corrupting Western influences, from unscrupulous entrepreneurs and greedy investors, who actually do present a threat to the devastated ecology of the country. However, the invocations to the Almighty by these former Communists are suspect. In their voices we hear echoes of old Soviet propaganda slogans mixed with currently fashionable *ancien régime* kitsch.

Not that the widespread return to Russian Orthodoxy in Russia is anything but heartfelt. The Soviet people were trained to believe. The urge to repent, to find new spiritual guidelines, is genuine, yet the separation of church and state voted in during Gorbachev's tenure must be maintained if Russia is to become a modern state. To try to convert Communism into Russian Orthodox dogma would be catastrophic. Recently reformed Marxist-Leninists would be all too happy to step forth as church elders. Given the Russian penchant for extremism, Russian Orthodox ayatollahs would soon be running the country.

However, in the political debate now going on at all levels of the Russian government, we do hear also the echoes of Sakharov's voice. His injunction to dismantle the Soviet nuclear arsenal is heeded, as is his plea for the complete release of the non-Russian republics. It is to be hoped for the world's stability that economic necessity might keep them within a loose federation with Russia, particularly the Muslim ones, which may be tempted to follow Islamic fundamentalist models.

The lifting of censorship in 1989 has already proven to be one of the crucial events in Russian history. For the first time since 1917, when it was allowed for only six months, the citizens of the former empire have freedom of speech. However, because former Communists still control most of the country's resources, the shift in social and political orders has put much of Russia on the verge of starvation. Publishing houses and museums are collapsing for lack of funding. After decades of stagnation Russian cultural life is in a state of ferment. We can only speculate as to its future. Still, we can detect two tendencies at odds with each other — the humanistic legacy of Sakharov and Pasternak, challenged by Solzhenitsyn's isolationist, fundamentalist stand. But Andrey Sinyavsky, one of the finest Russian literary minds today, a writer who is an expert on contemporary poetry and has written brilliantly about modern art, is optimistic. He says that he is expecting "an unprecedented flowering of Russian culture, even if Russia remains within the borders of the ancient Moscow principality."

However, should chaos and hunger spread throughout the country, the followers of Alexander Solzhenitsyn's precepts of retrenchment and strict moral discipline are likely to come to power. Censorship would be reinstated and hopes for a liberal Russia lost. An authoritarian government would be running Russia, one which might or might not tolerate Jews on its territory, and the reading of classics.

At this time Russian neo-fascists are relentless, skillful propagandists. They control dozens of publishing houses, newspapers and magazines. Known now as the "Red Browns" — for the Communist flag taking on the hue of

Hitler's Brown Shirts — they are not chastised by the failure of the 1991 coup. Their mood is militant; they make no mystery of their efforts to overthrow the present government. Their methods of subversion are Lenin's, while the racist ideology they promote is Hitler's. Here is a random sampling from articles published recently in Russian far-right newspapers:

> *Pravda* (no. 81, June 16, 1992): We call on all patriots to form grass-roots organizations at enterprises and in residential areas. We call on army officers to remember the traditions and honor of Russian officers. — Alexander Sterligov

> *Den* (no. 24, June 14–20, 1992): We'll talk to our people in a simple and easy-to-understand language and will direct their industry, intellect, and talent to the salvation of their great country. This is what patriots, now in opposition to the antipopular regime, think about when they see how this regime is rottening and falling apart. — General Albert Makashov

> *Russkoye Voskreseniye* (no. 7, 1992): Russians should be ruled by Russians! This, I assure you, is neither fascism nor racism. It's common sense. You can build any state system you want, if because of some Yid-inspired principles you don't like the Russian Orthodox monarchy. You can call it Leninism, Stalinism, socialism, communism, KGBism, or whatever you like. But it should be free from Yids.

Because of the nature of the Red Brown ideology, the establishment of a democracy in Russia has become a matter of urgency, much as the preservation of the Union at the time of the American civil war was essential to the survival, in the United States, of the republican experiment and of the nation itself. The alternatives are terrifying, and not only for Russia. Yeltsin and his followers appear to understand this. Last spring the first elected president of Russia solemnly declared, "In our country democracy and patriotism are inseparable." And indeed Russia could be saved from fascism only by a government that would know how to demonstrate to the disaffected, frightened citizens its fidelity to a tradition of national pride. Historically, love of Russia has not been the prerogative of reactionaries. Patriotism has been abused by them — by the pre-Revolutionary Black Hundred, as it is now by the "dark people," Communists and KGB operatives turned chauvinists, who exploit it deliberately for demagogical reasons. Through adversity, Russians as diverse as Pushkin, Tolstoy, Pasternak, Babel, and Akhmatova remained patriotic. Akhmatova wrote:

I wasn't under a new sky,
its birds were the old familiar birds.
They still spoke Russian.

In this book I relate my experiences in the heart of this Russia that does not yet know its name nor its future, a country locked in an age-old conflict between two aspects of herself, nationalism and a humanistic tradition that are both deeply rooted in her past. As a Paris-born Russian, brought up in the tolerant world of Parisian emigration, I write as a witness to a great and decisive struggle.

UNDER A NEW SKY

Introduction

BEFORE WORLD WAR II, as a child, I lived with my parents in a small, modern apartment in a remote suburb of Paris. My father's study, with its single window overlooking well-tended vegetable gardens, was a sunny, quiet room, walled with books and journals. The thin, light-colored ones were collections of contemporary poetry in French and Russian. There were heavier books in dark bindings, among them four identical volumes bound in violet cloth. My father told me these were the works of his father, my grandfather, which I would read when I was older. In the meantime I could look at pictures of him and of my father as a young boy. He showed me tasseled, tooled-leather albums containing sepia photographs, and glass color plates kept in small, carefully crafted boxes labeled in a round hand. These opened for me the world my father had known when he was a child.

My grandfather, Leonid Andreyev, was the man with the black eyes who never smiled at the camera. Though he had died in Finland eleven years before I was born, his presence dominated my early childhood. Besides his photographs, there were his paintings and the massive possessions that my father put to daily use: a tall Remington typewriter, a gigantic wooden German camera, and (my favorite) a monumental bronze Empire inkstand that stood on the desk in the study and that I often drew in still lifes.

These objects spoke of Andreyev; they suggested that the arts to which he had devoted his life — writing, painting, and photography — had the power to bring the past to bear on the present. When my father, Vadim, an émigré poet then in his early thirties, assumed the artistic legacy of his once celebrated father, Leonid Andreyev was all but suppressed in the Soviet Union and — outside of a small theatrical milieu — unknown in France. Before the October revolution he had been one of the most successful and controversial of Russian writers. He and Alexander Blok, the playwright and poet, were the most charismatic literary figures of that era, foretelling as they did an ominous future for Russia and for Europe. Andreyev died at the age of forty-eight in 1919, during the civil war, at the time of the collapse of a whole culture, which had engulfed him as it swept Russia into an unknown future.

The new society developing in place of the old was my parents' central concern. My father was possessed by a longing to return to Russia. But when would the time be right? We read Blok's *The Twelve* aloud. The poet's vision of Christ crowned with roses leading the twelve men of the Revolutionary Army through frozen Petrograd seemed holy. I understood that my father embraced Blok's view. But even as a child I discovered that Andreyev had not shared the vision of the Bolsheviks' ultimate vindication. Political editorials he had written at the time of the October coup d'état had culminated in *SOS,* his appeal to the Allies to intervene in Russia and drive the Bolsheviks out. I knew that this publication dismayed my parents. They detested the Bolsheviks, but they found the notion of calling for foreign intervention against one's own country unacceptable.

I was born in peacetime in Paris and had a happy childhood, yet I felt an overpowering involvement in the catastrophic events that had marked my family's past — World War I, the Russian Revolution, the civil war. My parents as adolescents had had extraordinary adventures. After his father's death, my father had fought in the civil war in the Caucasus. My mother, Olga Chernov, had been born into a family of revolutionaries with populist roots. They were non-Marxist socialists to whom Leonid Andreyev had been close and had participated in the moderate February revolution, only to be destroyed by Lenin as he seized power. The Socialist Revolutionaries (SRs) were in the majority in Russia. They had been especially threatening to Lenin because their party had had a wide popular appeal which the Bolsheviks lacked and envied.

My maternal grandmother, Olga Kolbassin Chernov, and her three daughters, my mother and her two sisters, were arrested and imprisoned. They would have perished, as did most of the SRs, had it not been for a miracle. That miracle — permission to leave Soviet Russia — was wrought by a man who played a unique role in the lives of both the Andreyevs and the Chernovs. He was Maxim Gorky, foremost among the Russian writers who aligned themselves in the early years with the Social Democrats, many of whom later became Bolsheviks.

There were several photographs of Gorky in our apartment — some in the company of Andreyev, one with my father as a young boy in Capri. He had wide cheekbones, bushy eyebrows, an air of informality that contrasted with Andreyev's solemnity. Gorky had been my grandfather's closest friend for many years; he had helped launch Andreyev's literary career, and he was my father's godfather. But the two older writers had become estranged over philosophical and political issues — issues that were still very much alive, ardently debated in my family.

Gorky had wanted to believe that a radical revolution would bring social justice to Russia and free mankind from oppression. In contrast, Andreyev had spoken for freedom and individual responsibility, for a moderate revolution and a constitutional government. Many years later certain Russians who came to be known as dissenters — among them the poet Boris Pasternak, the physicist Andrey Sakharov, and the writer Lydia Chukovskaya — were to embrace the same ideals, having come face to face with the consequences of the Bolshevik revolution. As Andreyev had foreseen, the reform of the social order by Lenin and his followers soon turned into a tyranny beyond Dostoyevsky's darkest imaginings. Nonetheless, in the thirties, before the existence of the gulag was revealed, the Soviet Union seemed to many liberals in the West (and most poignantly to many of the Russians who, like my parents, had been forced into emigration) to be a land of promise that would one day emerge from the storms of the revolution. This was the Soviet Union as it appeared not in Andreyev's forebodings but in the dreams of Maxim Gorky.

Ever since the turn of the century, Gorky had been a beloved public figure in liberal circles. His charm, his decency, his legendary kindness vouched for his convictions, even if these were somewhat naïve. It was heartening to know that he was alive and well in Russia. From time to time we had news of him through his first wife, Yekaterina Peshkova, who on occasion came from the USSR to Paris, or through the writer Isaac Babel, a friend of my father's who visited us twice in those years before he disappeared in the Terror of the late thirties. Babel encouraged the publication of my father's first prose work, *Childhood,* which came out in Paris in 1938. During that time in Moscow my father's younger brother, Daniel, also became a writer, but the contacts between the two brothers, who shared a mystic love for their country, were almost nonexistent.

In 1928 Gorky returned in triumph from self-imposed exile on Capri to be glorified as the father of Soviet literature. Once or twice, in messages passed on by friends, he

urged my parents to return to Russia. Then came the news
of his death. Two years later, during the last of Stalin's
great show trials, it was alleged that Maxim Gorky had
been poisoned by his doctors. Photographs of his kindly
face again appeared in the newspapers. There was no
longer any question of our going to live in Russia in the
immediate future. The Russo-German pact and the German invasion of France followed soon thereafter.

We left our apartment for a summer vacation in 1939,
expecting to return in the fall. The war kept us away for
five years. During that time my grandfather's books, his
pictures, and the great Empire inkstand stood undisturbed
in our apartment. I was nine when we left Paris for the Ile
d'Oléron, and during those years of the German Occupation, Andreyev's spell over our family lost some of its power.

We settled in a stone house in a windblown seaside village, surrounded by vineyards and pine woods. We had
very few books with us, but Russian literature sustained us
nonetheless — Russian poetry rather than prose, because
every adult in our extended family knew a great deal by
heart. My aunt Ariadne remembered most of Tsvetayeva's
and Akhmatova's verse, and *Evgeny Onegin* from beginning to end. My mother's favorite was Mandelstam;
Tyutchev, Blok, and Pasternak were my father's. We had
with us a volume of Pasternak's *Themes and Variations*. In
the evening my father sometimes read from it. My love for
Pasternak's poetry was born then, though it never occurred to me that Pasternak himself existed somewhere on
earth. Like Pushkin's, to whom *Themes and Variations* is
dedicated, his was a voice out of that ideal Russia which
one day would be ours again.

And indeed, many years later, during the "Thaw" that
followed Stalin's death, my parents and I were permitted
to go to the USSR for visits. By then I was married to an
American man of letters, Henry Carlisle, and lived in the
United States. Later on, after the fall of Khrushchev, from

1967 to 1989, I was no longer given a visa to the Soviet Union because of my literary activities on behalf of Russian dissenters, and especially Solzhenitsyn.

During the twenty-two years that I was not allowed into Russia I had a recurrent dream. It came in two parts, at dawn, when sleep and waking states are hard to tell apart. First it was winter and I was in Moscow, shut up in a telephone booth half buried in snow. I was trying to call a friend who was my contact with Alexander Solzhenitsyn in the matter of the publication of *The Gulag Archipelago*. But it was growing dark and very cold, and my gloved hands were clumsy. I could not manage to dial my friend's number though I knew it by heart. The cold was slowly putting me to sleep.

In the second part of the dream it was summer and I had tumbled back in time and space from Russia to my Parisian childhood — such warmth and brilliant sunshine, such fullness of summer had existed only then. It was midday and I was crossing the beautiful old park in Le Plessis, where I grew up. I was looking for a public telephone to make a reservation to fly to Russia. At the edge of the park was a small, decrepit café. It seemed abandoned but in fact it was open. Inside elderly waitresses were cleaning up after lunch. They spoke Russian. They let me inside a back room where there was a telephone and a shelf above it laden with telephone books. But as I opened these one after another I discovered they were yellowed Russian dictionaries, ancient volumes of the etymological Dahl dictionary. I would not be able to reach a travel agent or to go to Russia ever again.

For many years I reconciled myself to never returning. Then in the mid-1980s, as the spirit of glasnost was awakening in Russia, I felt exhilaration and at the same time sadness that I would not be a witness to the events that my parents had dreamed of seeing in their lifetimes. At long last, in the fall of 1988, at a cocktail party in San Francisco, I was introduced to the Soviet consul general there. Evidently he was aware of the fact that I wasn't allowed into the Soviet Union. In a lighthearted tone, the consul said that of course I'd get a visa if I asked for one. "Why not," he added. "I'll take your application to Moscow myself when I go there next week. In June of next year the Writers' Union is organizing a conference celebrating Anna Akhmatova's centenary. Didn't you know her in the sixties? This would be a fine occasion to return — a celebration honoring one of Russia's great poets."

ONE

Remembering the Sixties

~ I ~

Pasternak's Mission

MY FIRST TRIP to Russia, in the winter of 1960, had unfolded like a fairy tale. The year before, in New York, where my husband worked as an editor at Alfred A. Knopf, the publication of *Doctor Zhivago* had raised a storm in literary circles. Here was an epic novel by a Russian author almost totally unknown in the West. *Doctor Zhivago* suggested that treasures were buried beyond the Iron Curtain, that astounding works were being written there in the freer atmosphere following Stalin's death.

That summer, Harold Humes and George Plimpton, two editors of *The Paris Review,* asked me to go to Moscow to interview Boris Pasternak. *The Paris Review,* founded in the early fifties in Paris but now settled in New York, specialized (and still does) in interviews on the theme of "Writers at Work." It had never occurred to me that I could one day call on the poet I admired above all others. *The Paris Review*'s offer was amazing. In those years the *Review* was decidedly male-oriented. Its editors drew inspiration from Ernest Hemingway, who had once granted George Plimpton a memorable interview. It seldom gave assignments to women — at the *Review,* women were employed as typists or volunteer readers of manuscripts.

It had been our friend Harold Humes's idea. An eccentric, adventuresome novelist, the author of *The Underground City,* Humes was acquainted with my father, who had known Pasternak in Berlin in the twenties. My parents had been warmly received by the poet at his home in Peredelkino in 1957, on their first visit to Russia in more than thirty years. Not adverse to the notion of international intrigue, Humes became convinced that, though I was a painter and not a writer, I could nonetheless obtain an interview that would be a journalistic scoop for the *Review.*

Pasternak's scandalous treatment at the hands of the Writers' Union was known throughout the world by then. Though he was under orders to avoid contact with visiting foreigners, he would make an exception for Vadim Andreyev's daughter. My husband, passionate about literary matters, encouraged me, and so did my parents, who offered to care for our young son while I was away. George Plimpton did not quite share Humes's enthusiasm for the undertaking, but he allowed himself to be persuaded. He stressed the fact that interviews with other, unspecified important Soviet writers might also be welcomed by *The Paris Review.* But the most desirable would indeed be an in-depth interview with the winner of the 1958 Nobel Prize.

Half a year later, I found myself in Moscow, where the atmosphere was full of hope. The intellectuals I met believed that in a matter of a few years the USSR would be liberalized from within by a spontaneous political process still largely undefined. Stalin's portraits were being removed from public places. Two days after I checked into the Hotel Metropole, a painting of the mustachioed dictator studiously reading a book, pipe in hand, disappeared from the stairway of the hotel. The five weeks I spent in the USSR were filled with recognitions. Books I had read made Moscow and Leningrad familiar to me at once. A yet undiscovered part of me had come home for the first time.

In 1960 a number of people who had known Leonid

Andreyev were still alive in Moscow and Leningrad. The writer Kornei Ivanovich Chukovsky and Gorky's first wife, Peshkova, treated me as a family member and arranged introductions for me — to Ilya Ehrenburg, to Mikhail Sholokhov, to the young writers and artists of Moscow. They also wanted to tell me in private all that had happened to the Russian intelligentsia during Stalin's Terror.

Peshkova confirmed that Gorky had been killed by his doctors on Stalin's orders. Chukovsky described how the scheme worked: "Entrapping writers within a cocoon of comforts, surrounding them with a network of spies." In a hushed voice he told me that in 1928 Gorky, returning from exile on Capri, was isolated by the secret police, and that through their manipulations, members of his family intermarried with those of Stalin's chief of secret police, Beria. A distinguished critic and scholar at work on a study of the nineteenth-century poet Nikolay Nekrasov, Chukovsky had survived by becoming a children's author but was threatened at any moment by arrest.

Of all my Moscow encounters the most extraordinary was with Boris Pasternak. Unannounced, following Chukovsky's directions, I called on him at his home in Peredelkino; trying to telephone him would have been dangerous. The first visit went well, and Pasternak asked me to come back afterward. During the brief walks I took in his company in Peredelkino, the Russian countryside came to life for me — the country air, the snow, the dark fir trees, a frozen brook. Pasternak held my arm lightly to help me across a narrow wooden bridge. I remember thinking, Here is Russia at last, landscape and artist joining in perfect harmony. The poet was willing to speak at leisure about literature and life with a visitor brought up on his poems. Although he seemed youthful and in good health, Pasternak had had a severe heart attack and must have known that his life would soon end. My visit was in January 1960; he died in May of that year.

Despite the pressures brought against him by the Soviet

authorities and the conflicts that tore at his personal life, there was an aura of triumph about Pasternak; through his art he had made the plight of his people known to the world. Yet as the first writer since the twenties to act clearly in defiance of the authorities, he was paying a high price for his stand. He was forced to give up his Nobel Prize. His house was under police surveillance. As we walked out of range of listening devices, he told me in detail about how he was being hounded.

I will never forget being with him. "Pasternak resembles both an Arab and his horse," the poet Marina Tsvetayeva once wrote. He was very handsome, with a strong profile and white hair against swarthy skin. His speech sounded like verse. To walk with him in the woods or to converse with him across the desk in his study was like living out one of his poems. I had never met anyone who could convey his love of life in conversation as forcefully, through his every word and movement and pause.

By the end of January 1960, even before I left Moscow, I knew it would no longer be enough for me to strive to become a good painter, or to ponder whether or not figurative art had a future. Speaking in his austere study decorated with picture postcards evocative of the religious scenes in *Doctor Zhivago,* Pasternak entrusted me with a mission consistent with my family's legacy: to join in the Russian intelligentsia's cause against a repressive government. "Someone with your background must tell the truth about us," he told me. "Remember that one of the goals of the Terror was to make us forget what truth is — truth is especially elusive in a dictatorial world. Of course, you'll also have to be careful about how you speak of us, since we live in a police state. But if you listen to your inner voice, you will be able to negotiate the difficulties. You mustn't say anything about the intimidations to which I am subjected; that would only intensify them and prevent your return among us. But do speak about my new play, and about the joy that the reception of my novel has given me."

Like Boris Pasternak, my younger Russian friends were counting on my reporting about them in ways that would not compromise them in the eyes of the authorities. Yet the Terror had ended; there were struggles at the top and, in the early sixties, a trend toward more tolerance. Least of all did these artists want *not* to be spoken about. For those dissenting, being known in the West was beginning to be viewed as a safety net. Notoriety could confer a measure of immunity. It was the opposite of what had happened in the Stalinist years, when only anonymity could help people survive.

But there were no clear-cut rules; an error in judgment might be dangerous for those I was trying to help. At the time I still had a choice: I could simply write out parts of my conversations with Pasternak for *The Paris Review* and return to a life of painting. Flying back to the West, high above the Baltic, I was in anguish. Countless miles were stretching ever further between my Russian friends and me.

∽ 2 ∾

The Thaw

M Y RETURN TO NEW YORK was joyous. It was the
era of night-long literary parties, and those given
in George Plimpton's apartment on Seventy-sec-
ond Street were especially festive. He and Humes were sat-
isfied with the story of my visits with Pasternak, although
it did not conform to the format of the "Writers at Work"
series. I had brought back other interviews as well — with
Ehrenburg and Sholokhov, Yevtushenko and Voznesensky.
At the suggestion of Robert Loomis, a young editor at
Random House, I set about to write a book about my Russian encounters. My husband's help and that of Robert
Loomis and his wife, Gloria Loomis, were crucial: I had
never before written anything directly in English. In *Voices
in the Snow,* which was published in 1963, I was able to
write about those among my Soviet acquaintances who
had wanted to be known in the West. I had to listen to that
voice within evoked by Pasternak, to keep closely informed, through newspapers and friends, about the mer-
curial political developments in the USSR. This was easier
now, since more Westerners than ever were traveling to
Russia. While *Voices in the Snow* was coming out, a brief
cultural spring was taking place in the USSR. Khrushchev

had decided that, to insure his political survival, Soviet intellectual life had to be liberalized. But it was too late; in 1964 he lost to the Party conservatives, and a period of repression began in the Soviet Union.

As a reaction perhaps to the lack of interest of the previous years, and thanks to the popularity of *Doctor Zhivago,* everything Russian was becoming fashionable in New York in the mid-sixties. Americans wanted to know what was happening in Moscow, and their curiosity was matched by that of Russian intellectuals toward their Western counterparts. In Moscow my book about the Russians received the highest literary award in the USSR: *Voices* circulated in the Soviet Union in samizdat, the Soviet answer to fifty years of censorship — a spontaneous, illegal dissemination of manuscripts in typescript.

Although I never gave up painting, *Voices in the Snow* led to literary assignments that made it possible for me to return to Moscow four more times — in 1962, 1964–65, and twice in 1967. I traveled on tourist visas and stayed free of governmental involvement. In the course of my visits, I became acquainted with many young artists — the poets Joseph Brodsky, Bella Akhmadulina, and Bulat Okudzhava; the painter Eric Bulatov; the sculptor Ernst Neizvestny and a young mathematician, Alexander Zinoviev, who went on to write *The Gaping Heights,* a modernistic novel inspired by the intellectual ferment in Ernst Neizvestny's studio in the sixties; and Vassily Aksyonov, the future author of *The Burn,* another panoramic novel about Moscow in that era.

For a time it looked as if Stalinist officials might be swept away and a new era would begin for Russian culture; indeed, my older friends like Chukovsky and the painters and writers of my own age believed that release from censorship and intimidations was imminent. In the spring of 1962, during long twilight walks along the quays of the Moscow River, the poet Andrey Voznesensky assured me that freedom was coming to Russia. As the sky turned pink and evening descended, he would recite his poems, which dealt with these hopes more or less explicitly, and poems by Pasternak dating back to 1917.

But Voznesensky's hopes were premature, as Pasternak's had been during that short-lived summer of 1917, before the Bolshevik coup d'état, which he described in *Safe Conduct:* "The simple people opened their souls and conversed about what is most important, about the meaning of life and how our only conceivable and worthy existence should be lived out. An infectious common exaltation erased the boundaries between people and nature. In that memorable summer of 1917, in the interlude between two revolutionary deadlines, it appeared as if roads and trees and stars were joining in the people's assemblies." But this mood was not to last — not in 1917, and not in 1962.

Inspired by my friends in Moscow, I undertook a second project — an anthology of contemporary Russian poetry in translation. In the Soviet Union at that time poetry played a central political role. Poems written during one of the greatest ages of Russian poetry, the 1920s and '30s, were coming to light for the first time. They were appeals for freedom — artistic freedom, personal freedom, civic freedom. Tsvetayeva and Mandelstam were discovered by the general reading public in the Soviet Union, causing a sensation. Mandelstam wrote:

The arguments of freedom shall now die,
The Roman Senate testifies to this . . .

The same faith was proclaimed in the verse of the younger poets who read at public gatherings where attendance of six or seven thousand was not unusual. Without other means of pressure against the government, they were expressing their anger through their poems, which often remained unpublished in their country.

It was during the heady spring of 1962 that I first met

Nadezhda Yakovlevna Mandelstam, Osip Mandelstam's widow. She was then working on her *Hope Against Hope,* one of the great books to come out of Russia at that time. Nadezhda Yakovlevna proved a steadfast supporter of my anthology, *Poets on Street Corners.* An English scholar with an excellent knowledge of American contemporary poetry, she shared my preference for "imitations" of poems over literal translations. Nadezhda Mandelstam was a friend in yet another important way: she gave me a sense of worth as I assumed more fully my role as a literary intermediary. "Dear Olenka, with your self-doubts and your desire to help, you are nothing but an old Russian intellectual — self-doubt is an intellectual's fundamental attribute," she told me. "I look at you with nostalgia; you are so very old-fashioned. There are few people like that left in the country — their parents were the first to be killed after the Revolution."

To be regarded by Nadezhda Mandelstam as "an old Russian intellectual" was the highest praise I could imagine. But then my friend would pull out a cigarette and look at me and sigh. "I think you are becoming too involved in our affairs. We Soviets are ruthless, the conditions we've lived under have made us that way — surely we are not to be blamed. I worry for you, you make yourself vulnerable! Why don't you write that book about your childhood you mentioned the other day, or do more painting? What you do is valuable, but it is also risky in all sorts of ways." Yet Nadezhda Mandelstam herself used me as a courier. She gave me messages for the editors in Paris of her husband's work and asked me to help her find a publisher for her own work. My husband was very effective in that matter.

In those years she was full of gaiety, despite her tragic life marked by her husband's death in 1938 in an unknown Siberian camp and by her harsh existence for years afterward. She had boundless curiosity and was always ready for new adventures. Bundled in a heavy woolen coat, a knitted cap, and a long gray muffler, she took me all over Moscow to look at the small Orthodox churches her husband had especially liked. She was the first to introduce me to Georgian cooking, inviting me for dinner at the Aragvi, a fine Georgian restaurant. She made wild plans to take me to Georgia — to Kahetia, where she had traveled with Mandelstam. She led me to the studios of Moscow painters whom she admired — she had studied with the famous constructivist Vladimir Tatlin, who had once been in love with her. She introduced me to the theater designer and painter Alexander Tishler. Whenever Anna Akhmatova was in town, Nadezhda Mandelstam brought us together.

It was Nadezhda Mandelstam who gave me the only glimpse of the Russian province that I ever had — under Soviet regulations my stays in the USSR were confined to Moscow and Leningrad and their suburbs. On New Year's Eve of 1964–65, she invited me to visit overnight with her at the home of mutual friends in Tarusa, the Ottens. Tarusa, about a hundred kilometers from Moscow, is a sleepy town on the bank of the Oka River where Tsvetayeva had spent summers as a child. It was closed to foreign tourists.

As she was wrapping my head in her long gray muffler in preparation for the train ride to Tarusa, during which I would have to blend in with the other travelers and not open my mouth, Nadezhda Mandelstam said with a laugh, "Now we'll make you *look* like a real old Russian intellectual!" We celebrated the New Year in the company of close friends. The next day we walked for hours in the snow. With its very wide streets bordered by wooden houses behind carved fences, Tarusa looks like a setting out of a nineteenth-century Russian novel.

Nadezhda Mandelstam took me to meet Polya, a peasant woman who had taken her in during her homeless wanderings after her husband's arrest. I remember Polya's smooth, round face and her house with the wide vestibule to one side, the enormous tiled stove in one corner of the main room. Polya's speech was caressing, as if an ancient lyrical Russia were speaking through her. To me she said, "Here you come from faraway France and you speak like one of us! I never believed that all the people who left during the Revolution were traitors. Had your parents stayed home they would have been killed like Osip Emilevich and so many others. But I am certain that one day you'll all come back to live with us, and you will be happy here."

Our hosts, the Ottens, who were translators from the German, gave me messages for the playwright Friedrich Dürrenmatt — I was going home by way of Switzerland, where my parents were living. At dinner we had a heated argument about the respective merits of Russian and German Romantic poetry. It was a lovely gathering. I could imagine I was home at last in my family's Russia. I began to believe that Voznesensky's bright dreams would come true.

But by the time of my next visits to Moscow, in the spring and again in the fall of 1967, the atmosphere had become ominous. Khrushchev's Thaw, named after a bestseller by Ilya Ehrenburg, was ending. Soviet liberals, the dissidents, were intimidated and threatened with arrest. The messages I was asked to memorize were frantic pleas for well-known Western literary figures — Dürrenmatt, Böll, Sartre, Steinbeck, Cheever, Updike — to intervene with the Soviet authorities. These pleas often didn't help, but I passed them on anyway; I had not forgotten Pasternak's injunction that I participate in the cause of Russian freedom. Implied from the beginning was an acceptance of failure. Nor did I in my more lucid moments have any illusions about possible pitfalls. I could not help thinking of the Russian folktale about the rabbit who mediates between the wolf and the fox.

∾ 3 ∾

Alexander Solzhenitsyn's Mission

WHEN I ARRIVED in Moscow in March of 1967, it was still quite wintry, but spring could be felt in the air. Already one could enjoy the long twilight walks that to this day provide Muscovites with a diversion from their uneasy daily lives. At that time intimidations of the intelligentsia, which affected many of my friends, were multiplying. The apartments of people suspected of contact with the West were said to be bugged. Private conversations could be had only out of doors.

That spring I left my hotel on foot almost every afternoon, going unnoticed to the studio of the sculptor Ernst Neizvestny on Vassilevsky Lane off Stretyenka. He is the subject of a study by John Berger, *Art and Revolution* — in the second half of the sixties in a rundown loft in a working-class section of Moscow, he presided over an informal salon while he drew or sculpted for hours on end, entertaining his guests with his witty, erudite, and somewhat conspiratorial conversation. Ernst had recently discovered the writings of Mikhail Bakhtin and was making illustrations for an edition of *Crime and Punishment*. His knowledge of art, philosophy, and literature was encyclopedic, and so were his insights into the arcane world of

Soviet politics. His art, expressionistic and massive, was admired by certain highly placed functionaries with whom he sometimes partied at night. In the daytime a small group of independent-minded young men came in and out of his studio, nonconformists with a Marxist background, some of whom have since become preeminent in various ways. Alexander Zinoviev went into exile in Germany, where he published *The Gaping Heights,* based on the encounters that once took place on Vassilevsky Lane. Yuri Karyakin, who had spent time in Dubček's Prague, is now an influential pro-democratic politician in Moscow. Another frequent visitor was the soft-spoken, brilliant philosopher Marab Mamardachvili, who died tragically in 1990.

In Ernst's studio, in 1967, the talk, more often than not, was about the dissident writer Alexander Solzhenitsyn, a former *zek* (labor camp inmate) whose novel *The Cancer Ward,* with its transparent denunciations of Stalinism, was beginning to circulate in Moscow in samizdat. Solzhenitsyn had become famous in the Soviet Union five years before, in 1962, because of his *One Day in the Life of Ivan Denisovich,* a novella about a Russian peasant's fate in a camp. Its publication was authorized by Khrushchev on the prompting of Alexander Tvardovsky, the talented elderly poet of peasant background who was serving then as the editor-in-chief of the journal *Novii Mir.* It was Lev Kopelev, an enthusiastic supporter of Solzhenitsyn's, who had given Tvardovsky this heartrending story about one man's day in the Stalinist gulag.

Alexander Solzhenitsyn was known personally to some of Ernst's visitors, but, in my presence at least, no one said so. The writer was under growing attacks by the government, and it could have been compromising both for him and for his acquaintances. Though trustworthy in their eyes, I was a foreign journalist. What they did not know was that my parents had met Solzhenitsyn in the early sixties and that he had entrusted to them, for safekeeping, the microfilm of a long, many-faceted novel about the lives of Russian intellectuals in a special scientific institute staffed with prisoners. The novel contained a devastating portrait of Stalin. I had read parts of it in Switzerland the previous year and was convinced, as were my parents, that it could not be made known, much less published, without the gravest consequences to its author.

However, other works of his which were available to Muscovites in samizdat were discussed openly and with passion in Ernst's studio. The emergence of Solzhenitsyn's fiction was the most important event in Russian letters since the nonpublication of *Doctor Zhivago* in the Soviet Union. Among Ernst's friends, *One Day* was admired especially for its driving narrative, reminiscent of the ancient Russian *skaz,* a folkloric storytelling mode.

Everyone there was as impressed by the author's fearless personality as by his books. In progressive Moscow circles there had been lingering hopes that *The Cancer Ward* would be serialized in *Novii Mir,* but the Soviet hard-liners were winning out. Tvardovsky was about to lose his job; contacts with the West were curtailed. If only Solzhenitsyn could become known there, the young men said. Here was an authentic spokesman for Stalin's victims, who deserved to be heard worldwide. His writing would help the cause of the persecuted Soviet intellectuals, making their plight better known in the West.

I listened in fascination. What was being said suggested that Solzhenitsyn, a man who in his writings time and again identified himself with former Soviet officers betrayed by Stalin, might one day decide to challenge the Soviet authorities with his books, much as Pasternak had done in 1958. One thing seemed certain in view of the events that had surrounded the publication of *Doctor Zhivago:* with *The Cancer Ward* now easily available in Moscow, and therefore likely to be smuggled out and published abroad, the KGB would be closely following the author's activities and those of his friends and relatives.

Born during the Revolution, Alexander Solzhenitsyn grew up in the southeastern plain of Russia in Rostov on the Don. His father, an officer in the First World War, was killed accidentally before Alexander was born. His mother, well educated and a believer, had supported herself and her son as a typist. The young man, gifted in mathematics and physics, was given what was known at that time as a Stalin Scholarship to the local university. Interested in literature no less than in the sciences, just before World War II he enrolled in a correspondence course at the Moscow Institute of History, Philosophy, and Literature. He graduated in mathematics from the University of Rostov on the Don a few days before Hitler invaded Russia in June 1941. Drafted soon afterward, Alexander Solzhenitsyn reached the rank of captain in the Soviet artillery and received the Order of the Red Star for bravery.

While engaged in battle in Eastern Prussia just before the war ended, he was arrested for having written an irreverent letter about Stalin which had been intercepted by the Soviet military KGB. Taken to the Lubyanka in Moscow, he was sentenced to eight years of forced labor followed by exile. It was at that time that he lost his faith in Marxism-Leninism. After Stalin's death Solzhenitsyn was released from camp to a life of "eternal exile" in Central Asia, where to support himself he taught mathematics.

Eventually he was allowed to join his wife, a chemist in the provincial town of Ryazan, some three hundred miles out of Moscow. There at first he continued to teach high school mathematics. After the dazzling but short-lived success of *One Day,* he was invited to meet Khrushchev at a Kremlin reception. He was even put up for a Lenin Prize, which the Writers' Union prevented him from receiving. Soviet ideologues together with the KGB began persecuting him. After Khrushchev's fall the anti-Stalinist *One Day* was perceived as a threat to the regime, creating a precedent for further denunciations of Stalin. Nonetheless, supported in part by his wife, Solzhenitsyn now wrote full-time, occasionally visiting Moscow and staying with Chukovsky, whose reputation as Russia's most cherished children's author provided his visitor with a measure of protection from KGB interference.

The facts that emerged in Ernst's studio were confirmed by what Chukovsky told me when I called on him in Peredelkino. He spoke about the author of *One Day* in reticent yet tantalizing terms, not without declaring each time beforehand, "Now, Olenka, mind you, it would be extremely dangerous for you to meet Alexander Isaevich. Dangerous for you and also for him. Fortunately, he is far away in Ryazan, working on a new novel. He is a talented, prodigiously prolific writer. In all my life I have never seen anything like it. Whenever he stays here I marvel at his working habits. I consider myself disciplined, but compared to him I am a schoolboy."

But shortly before I left Moscow that spring of 1967, mutual friends introduced me to Alexander Solzhenitsyn. Within a couple of days I was to meet him, as if by accident, at several gatherings. Just before I left the USSR, he offered to walk me back to my hotel, through parts of old Moscow which were then being torn down to make way for what is now Kalinin Prospect. He had a commanding, almost military presence, but he was also charming in a somewhat deliberate way. The friends who introduced us were all, without exception, under his spell. Solzhenitsyn must have learned in camp how to put his charm to use: he had the gift of making whomever he was with feel unique — that is, put in his path by a benevolent Providence determined to help save Russia from her Communist masters. Even in that year he was surrounded by enthusiastic helpers. Evidently each felt linked to the writer by a secret trust.

As for me, in the dark of night, in an eerie setting of rubble that only a few hours before had been an ancient Moscow house, with the dust still hanging in the air, Solzhenitsyn asked me to be his representative for the publication in the United States of one of his books. It was not *The Cancer Ward* — that, he told me, he had just given in secret to a visiting Yugoslav journalist.

"This one is a big book — my life," he said. I realized at once that he was referring to the novel brought out of the Soviet Union in the pockets of my father's trenchcoat in 1965 — *The First Circle*.

That year, while my parents had stayed in Moscow in connection with my father's literary affairs, Solzhenitsyn came to know them quite well, mainly through the philologist Lev Kopelev, the early promoter of *One Day*, who had been a campmate of Solzhenitsyn's. My parents appeared worthy of Solzhenitsyn's trust. The precious microfilms of *The First Circle* would be kept in the safety of their apartment in Geneva. Ostensibly the microfilms were there for long-term safekeeping, to be released only in the event of the author's death.

"Of course," said Solzhenitsyn as we walked on through the dark streets, "it will all have to be done in the greatest secrecy. You can imagine what would happen to me if you were found out."

Since we had just become acquainted, the mission I was being charged with was clearly a reflection of Solzhenitsyn's high regard for my parents. His confidence may also have been confirmed by three individuals whom he would have consulted independently from one another. Kornei Ivanovich Chukovsky might have vouched for my respectability. Kopelev and his wife, Raisa, a scholar of American literature, knew about the friendships with writers and publishers which Henry and I had in the United States. It would be Kopelev, unaware of my secret compact with Solzhenitsyn, who on my subsequent visit to Moscow insisted that I take an active role in promoting the author of *One Day* for a Nobel Prize. (Kopelev, a generous, expansive man, is portrayed as Rubin in *The First Circle*.)

Finally there was Natalia Stoliarova, an intimate friend of my family with a revolutionary background similar to my mother's. Born in pre-Revolutionary emigration, she was arrested in 1935 upon her arrival in the Soviet Union and spent more than two decades in the Soviet Gulag. Stoliarova was now working as Ilya Ehrenburg's secretary and had frequent contact with Western visitors in Moscow. It was she who had first introduced my parents to Alexander Isaevich, who at the time had expressed admiration for my father's book about his childhood. Stoliarova would prove to be an invaluable intermediary between my family and myself and Solzhenitsyn: I knew her to be a passionate admirer of the author of *One Day* — as a writer, as a man, as a former *zek* who had not forgotten his fellow prisoners still detained in Soviet camps.

Back in Connecticut, where we then lived, I consulted at great length with Henry. He was convinced that Solzhenitsyn's request presented us with a moral responsibility that was impossible to turn down. In his opinion, only a tightly organized, large-scale Western-style publication — the "explosion" the author had requested — would have a chance of gaining for him the sort of international reputation that might keep him out of prison. We sought counsel from a very few well-informed, trustworthy friends, notably Harrison Salisbury of the *New York Times*.

During a trip to the USSR in the fall of 1967, I confirmed in person to Solzhenitsyn my acceptance of his mission. I became Solzhenitsyn's secretly authorized representative in the West for all matters regarding *The First Circle,* under a trusteeship established in Moscow and valid under New York law.

A year later, in September 1968, the publication of *The First Circle* in the Americas and Europe — coinciding with that of *The Cancer Ward* — made Solzhenitsyn famous throughout the world. Henry's guidance in publishing strategies and his work with me as editor and translator had contributed to this success, and Solzhenitsyn soon afterward entrusted us with the publication of *The Gulag Archipelago*. The previous June, on Trinity Sunday, my brother, Alexander, at great personal risk, had brought the microfilms of the entire work out of Moscow. In his 1975 memoir, *The Calf and the Oak*, Solzhenitsyn would praise my brother's feat as "the miracle of the Trinity."

Back in January 1968, nine months before Harper & Row's publication of *The First Circle*, Solzhenitsyn instructed us, through my brother, to inform the publisher of the existence of *The Gulag Archipelago* and of our authority to control its eventual publication according to its author's directives. *The Gulag Archipelago* would have to be published within two or three years at most. In the meantime repression was reaching a new intensity in Moscow. Alexander Solzhenitsyn and Andrey Sakharov were making history battling the Soviet authorities through open appeals to Western public opinion.

To our intense disappointment Solzhenitsyn never sent us the agreed-upon signal to bring out *The Gulag Archipelago* in English, though on his orders everything was arranged for its prompt release by Harper & Row. The translation of the first volume was ready. By 1972 Harrison Salisbury was urging me to allow its publication without Solzhenitsyn's signal; at that time, after a series of dramatic confrontations with the authorities, the author appeared to be on the verge of arrest. However, I could not in conscience do so. With the continued collaboration of our co-translator, Thomas Whitney, Henry and I pushed ahead with the translation of the second volume.

At first Solzhenitsyn was elated by the publication — highly publicized, carefully orchestrated with many foreign firms yet with no apparent authorization from him — that *The First Circle* had been given by Harper & Row: it may have helped protect him from the KGB's blows and contributed to his nomination for the Nobel Prize. However, for him political and personal pressures were mounting. He had divorced his first wife, accusing her of complicity with the KGB, and had fallen in love with a younger woman, with whom he would have three sons.

In 1970 he received the Nobel Prize and resounding international acclaim. Some Western critics greeted him as an heir to Tolstoy and Dostoyevsky. The historical significance of his books was recognized in the most diverse quarters. By telling the truth about its penal system, Solzhenitsyn helped destroy the Soviet system; only Andrey Sakharov and Mikhail Gorbachev, each in his own way, would do as much to undermine it. Solzhenitsyn had reaffirmed the power of a writer to change the course of history. Lev Kopelev's dream of glory for the author of *One Day* had been fulfilled.

Little by little, however, a different individual was emerging in place of the intense yet charming novelist I had met at Natalia Stoliarova's and at the Kopelevs' in 1967. Solzhenitsyn was now embracing Russian Orthodoxy in earnest and was becoming a stern moralist. His extraordinary accomplishments lent weight to his public utterances on politics, religion, education, and the future of the world threatened by Communism, yet his anti-liberal slant surprised many of his new admirers. Solzhenitsyn was becoming imperious in his relations with others. As his trustee I had made contractual commitments in his name which he now seemed determined to undo. It was perplexing and indeed frightening in view of the vulnerability of my family and friends within the USSR, and that of his own circle of supporters.

First, innocuously enough, he focused his displeasure on the translation of *The Gulag Archipelago* — this in a note that in a lighter moment we nicknamed "Feet of Clay." The note arrived in October 1972 via Dr. Heeb, a Swiss lawyer whom Solzhenitsyn had hired to look after his published interests in the West. He was now famous enough to engage a foreign representative openly and go unpunished by the Soviet authorities, at least for a time. In the note Solzhenitsyn wrote that he was especially sensitive to English translations and that he was not pleased with "any of the big translations." It was not a question of author's sensibility: "on [translation] the whole solidity of my legs depends, and I cannot give in to *anyone* out of good feelings."

But by February 1973, paradoxically, Solzhenitsyn was demanding that we continue precisely in the role in which we had most disappointed him — as translators. His long letter was in response to my decision to relinquish all my responsibilities as his trustee in favor of Dr. Heeb. The first volume of *The Gulag Archipelago* was ready to go to press at Harper & Row, but now Solzhenitsyn was unwilling to deal with the publisher on the terms he himself had approved. In our family this communication became known as the "Into the Fire" letter. He announced that the fate of *Gulag* must be completely special. The translators would not be chosen by the publishing houses but in most cases by him personally. The translators would do their work and then, when the job neared completion, *they* would recommend appropriate publishing houses [my emphasis]. However, he went on, most publishing houses would cringe at the unusual conditions he would impose, including an extremely small profit margin. "[*Gulag*] will not become a commercial commodity, will not be sold at demented Western prices ($10! This is sixty rubles. This cannot be conceived by our compatriots!)." With obvious satisfaction he predicted that Harper & Row in particular would not like his new conditions.

Then came the astonishing request (in view of his harsh criticisms of the collaborative translation we were carrying forward with Tom Whitney — the same method that had produced the widely praised American edition of *The First Circle*) that I retract my decision to disengage: "I will be sincerely happy if you keep for yourself the right [*sic*] of translation." If, however, my decision were to be irreversible, then, he concluded, "I see one way of terminating the affair, just for all and offensive to no one: FIRE!"

Evidently, despite our anguished warnings through various messengers, Solzhenitsyn and his lawyer did not comprehend how dangerous it might be for the Solzhenitsyns to disregard Harper & Row's rights to *The First Circle* and to *The Gulag Archipelago*. Harper & Row was a commercial concern, with responsibilities to its stockholders. If necessary to protect its rights, Harper & Row might be forced to make public what its editors took to be the bona fide legal authority they had received from us to publish the two books. After all, the publishing house had acquired them by paying out faithfully the author's earnings to the bank account established for his benefit.

But to us the most disturbing part of this letter was the word "FIRE" (*ogon*). When we read it we were amazed. Why burn anything? Mikhail Bulgakov, the author of *The Master and Margarita*, once remarked that "manuscripts do not burn." We wondered how this instruction could have been written by the man who in *The Gulag Archipelago* is shown sorrowing as ash is falling around him on the roof of the Lubyanka — all that is left of manuscripts that the KGB is burning day and night in the great wave of post–World War II arrests.

We did not realize it when we first received the letter, but in fact it contained the seeds of a calculated attempt to discredit Henry and me. In the spring of 1975, some months after he was forcibly exiled from the Soviet Union, Solzhenitsyn included the following footnote in the first Russian edition of *The Calf and the Oak*, a lengthy autobiographical work:

> Earlier, following immediately after the Russian edition [in 1973], the American edition was to appear. I had done

everything for it, but two or three dry, mercenary people of Western education turned everything to ashes . . . The American edition will be late by a half year, will not support me by pulling me across the chasm — and for this reason I think there was the denouement [expulsion]. Yet it would have been, it could have been — conceivably the leaders giving in, if by New Year of the year 1974, all of America was really reading the book, but now in the Kremlin they only know how to weave tales to the effect that it celebrated the Hitlerites . . .

Evidently Solzhenitsyn felt uncomfortable with the fact that, perhaps to ensure his new family's safety, he had not released the explosive *Gulag Archipelago* in English until exile had caught up with him. Or was the delay an attempt to try to deprive Harper & Row of its rights to the books? Was that why he was now blaming the delay on us, mercenary Westerners? To people with a Soviet education, it is well known that "mercenary people of Western education" may be vilified and forgotten once they are no longer useful. That was one of Lenin's precepts.

When *The Calf and the Oak* was finally published in the United States, the nameless mercenaries were named. Solzhenitsyn maintained that Henry and I had prevented him from being heard in the West in time, thereby causing him to be exiled from the Soviet Union. We had also prevented the Soviet leaders from acting on his recommendation, spelled out in the 1973 *Letter to the Soviet Leaders,* to replace their Marxist ideology with Russian Orthodoxy without necessarily giving up their posts. Even though we did not live in the Soviet Union, Henry and I felt we were caught up in the kind of political maneuvering that Soviet officials used to entrap overzealous underlings who showed signs of gaining too much authority.

There were other twists to Solzhenitsyn's vendetta against our family. Soviet kitsch. He and his young wife arrived at my parents' in Geneva with an oversized box of chocolates to show their appreciation for all that my parents had done for them. And indeed, beyond their activities as advisors and intermediaries, my mother and father had over the years sent many packages to the Solzhenitsyns — stationery, a tape recorder, baby food for the newborns, medicines for the adults, colored pencils for a stepson. That day, along with his thanks, Solzhenitsyn brought a somewhat muffled confirmation of his displeasure with our performance in his service. My father, who greatly admired Alexander Isaevich for his courage and his literary skills, was too stunned at first to fully comprehend his strategy. He failed to understand Solzhenitsyn's tactic of bringing our participation in his affairs into the open so as to denigrate it publicly, at considerable risk to those left behind in the Soviet Union. Eventually my father wrote him a letter defending our honor, but on the day this letter reached Solzhenitsyn in Zurich, my father died of sudden heart failure. My mother received a letter of condolence from Solzhenitsyn. It explained why he had not revealed my villainy to my parents when they had last met: "I understood that it would have been painful for you to learn the disagreeable truth, evident to all in America who have had anything to do with this affair."

My mother died shortly afterward. She, who had been so brave as a girl in the Lubyanka and as a young woman under the German Occupation, spent the last months of her life in a state of depression. She felt that Solzhenitsyn's behavior toward us had been typically Soviet: the attempt to create a breach within our family, the innuendoes, then the groundless public denunciations. In her mind the ruthless Bolsheviks had once again overwhelmed the naïve SRs. She died believing that after six decades of Communism there was no hope for Russia.

In the late seventies I recorded whatever could then be told of our six-year involvement. *Solzhenitsyn and the Secret Circle* — recently serialized in the Moscow literary journal *Voprosy Literatury* — is about the group of friends in and outside of Russia who helped Alexander Isaevich to be published abroad. As I wrote this book I was looking for a key to Solzhenitsyn's aggressiveness toward those who had tried to help him over the years. On that subject in 1978 George Kennan wrote to me in a letter that to some degree helped mitigate the sadness I felt at that time:

> What you ran across, in your effort to be of help to Solzhenitsyn, was something that has impressed itself on me in many ways over the years and has affected my thinking about Russia quite strongly: and this is the extraordinary lack of tolerance and common charity in the Russian political mentality, not only, unfortunately, in the Bolshevik, or radical-socialist mentality, but pretty much across the boards; with it, the capacity for a total, heartless rejection of anyone who does not share one's own orientation and outlook; and with it, finally, a tendency to be as unfeeling in one's attitude towards the individual man as one is solicitous (or claims to be) for the fate of man in the mass . . . In the case of Solzhenitsyn this is compounded, surely, and understandably so, by the coarsening and primitivizing of the Russian character produced by sixty years of Soviet rule.

Henry and I survived our involvement with the author of *The Gulag Archipelago*. We moved away from the house in Connecticut where we had worked on his manuscripts and conducted his affairs, settling in San Francisco. There, upon learning that Alexander Isaevich intended to publish fresh disparagements of our activities on his behalf, we filed a lawsuit against him in order to ward off further attacks. (The First Amendment shielded Solzhenitsyn from liability for his published denunciation, but to date our suit has achieved its purpose.) I gave up any thought of ever going back to Russia, and indeed for two decades was officially unwelcome there.

∾ 4 ∾

Return to Russia

I N THE LATE EIGHTIES the miracle occurred. Mikhail Gorbachev took power in the USSR, and in a matter of months he challenged the hitherto inviolable Communist Party and introduced an unprecedented measure of freedom throughout the country. Political prisoners were released, and there was a partial lifting of censorship. In the beginning the reform movement appeared to be the work of one inspired leader calling upon the energies of those of his own generation who, since the death of Stalin in 1953, had believed in the possibility of "Communism with a human face," but soon, under the rallying slogans of glasnost (openness; literally, giving voice to what was hidden) and perestroika (reconstruction), it became increasingly clear that what was happening in the USSR would be one of the most far-reaching political events of the century.

Among the Soviets of Gorbachev's generation and anti-Stalinist views was my friend Zoya Boguslavskaya, who is married to Andrey Voznesensky. On a visit to San Francisco she joined with the Soviet consul general in encouraging me to apply for a visa to the USSR. I did so, and soon afterward a visa was delivered to the consulate, along with the invitation to attend the ceremonies marking Anna Akhmatova's centenary.

I set forth for Russia by way of Paris; but there in my native city, as the day of my departure neared, I suddenly felt reluctant to go on. Too much time had passed since my last visit to Russia. So many friends and relatives still alive in my mind had died — Nadezhda Mandelstam, Kornei Chukovsky, my Muscovite uncle Volodia and aunt Ariadne. And with those living, would I be able to reestablish contact severed by a separation of more than two decades?

Nor was I looking forward to resuming my role as a literary intermediary or as a journalist specializing in Russian affairs. In 1975, at a speech given at Harvard's commencement, a recently emigrated Solzhenitsyn had violently attacked the Western press for its immorality although, only a very few months before, that press had made possible his safe exile. Fighting the Soviet regime, Solzhenitsyn had adopted the enemy's tactics. A Russian citizen to this day, he detests journalists and pluralists equally. "Pluralists," in his terminology, are those who believe that the best of Western democratic traditions, plurality of opinions and tolerance, have a place in the modern world.

But a free press and political plurality were gaining ground in the Eastern countries. By 1989, Hungary, Poland, East Germany, and Czechoslovakia were breaking away from the Soviet orbit. Unexpectedly and irresistibly, freedom of speech was asserting itself in Eastern Europe and in the USSR. Many Russians were traveling to the West. Relatives were at last allowed to visit back and forth. Intermediaries of every kind were appearing.

In Paris in the spring of 1989 I learned that a swift, little noticed coup within the Politburo had consolidated Gorbachev's power in the Kremlin. Parisians were preparing to celebrate the anniversary of their Great Revolution, while in the Soviet Union glasnost was taking root. Nabokov and Solzhenitsyn were about to be published there. How to implement perestroika, a far-reaching economic and psychological restructuring, was to be discussed at the first democratically oriented parliament convening in Moscow that May. It seemed that the third Russian revolution — after those of 1905 and 1917 — was proceeding, and so far it remained bloodless.

Nonetheless, for a few days in May on my way to Moscow I wished I could escape the demands of my Russian background. In Paris I stayed with old friends. As a student I lived with them, and they have taken me in many times over the years. Being French and therefore thorough skeptics, they have long considered my Russian loyalty excessive, perhaps oversentimental — my double loyalty, to the ill-fated, idealistic socialists on my mother's side, and on my father's side to Leonid Andreyev, who after the October coup d'état had grieved for Russia until his death. However, when I told them of my decision to cancel my trip to Moscow they did not take me seriously. The ignominious years of stagnation had ended; the Writers' Union, which had treated me as an enemy — in 1968, in response to *Poets on Street Corners,* they bestowed on me what Chukovsky had called my "second National Book Award," a lengthy condemnation on the pages of *Literaturnaya Gazeta* by the notorious critic Pertzov — was inviting me to celebrate the great Anna Akhmatova, one of Stalin's long-suffering victims. How could I decline? Ridiculous, my friends said, and went off to shop for gifts for my relatives in Russia.

I was swayed the next day by a telephone conversation with my husband in San Francisco. "I know how much you want to see your cousin Aliosha and his children," he said. "That alone should be reason enough to go."

On a beautiful early morning my friends drove me to the airport at Roissy. The countryside to the north of Paris, often misty even in the good season, was on that day an

Impressionist painter's dream. The woods of Chantilly, pale blue in the distance, were an invitation to a day-long picnic. Though I had not yet left France, the aroma of airport café au lait and croissants filled me with nostalgia.

The Air France flight to Moscow provided the last taste of luxury that I would have for a long time. As I savored the freshly brewed coffee, an atavistic sense of dread was rising in me, which I had not experienced since my last trip to the Soviet Union. Shadows of long-dead Socialist Revolutionary relatives who had spent their lives in Siberia for challenging the tzar's authority were invading my imagination. I was also thinking of my late uncle Daniel Andreyev, who in 1947 had been imprisoned for reading parts of a novel to a small group of friends and spent ten years in prison. Dozens of people were arrested in connection with his case.

I recalled other flights between the West and Moscow which I had been on. The homebound ones as the plane travels west with the sun were always the happy ones, endless restful afternoons when time is suspended. One of the westward journeys I remembered best was not my own but Solzhenitsyn's, described in his book *The Calf and the Oak*. Solzhenitsyn gives the reader a graphic account of his feelings as he is put on a plane five days after his arrest in 1974 and realizes with a burst of joy that he is being flown not East to Siberia but to the West, to freedom.

But I was traveling eastward ever so swiftly. We were losing altitude, flying over a pastoral landscape of forests and lakes. A gigantic rose-colored city could be seen sprawling on the horizon. This was the heart of Russia, Moscow, after twenty-two years. I would soon meet my cousin Aliosha, whom I had not seen since the spring day of 1967, when prior to my departure from Moscow I was searched at Cheremetyevo, the airport where we were now landing. Saying goodbye to my cousin then, knowing we might not meet for a long time, I nonetheless could not share with him the secret I was taking home with me that day — Solzhenitsyn's request to publish *The First Circle* in the West. Now we would be able to say anything we wanted to each other.

At the passport verification booth inside the Cheremetyevo terminal, a man in khaki sitting high up in front of a tilted, mirrored partition studied at length my passport with its detachable San Francisco–issued visa. Then he looked at me steadily for perhaps a minute. He was young and blue-eyed, his military cap edged in emerald green, a KGB uniform. Wearily he placed his open hand over my passport and said solemnly, loudly, "Problem." After vanishing into the black recesses of his booth he reappeared at my side within seconds. He was very tall. "Problem. Big problem," he repeated. Without looking at me he led me to a waiting room within sight of the passport control booth. He made me sit down on a black leather couch under a single spotlight. Carrying off my passport, he walked away with a clipped military step as the last passengers on the flight from Paris filed past.

I was alone in the waiting room in the center of what looked like a modernistic stage set. Around me dark gray walls, set at odd angles, were marked by four or five doors, all closed. I felt enormous relief. I would be put on the next flight back to Paris. I was being spared the demands of a Russian visit. Judging by the KGB man's performance I was expected to be distressed, but what I felt was bordering on elation.

After a while the doors around me began to open one after another. Men — all young and tall — stepped out of them in turn, crossing the room diagonally. They passed my passport from hand to hand in silence. With their empty, frowning faces, their muscular shoulders and narrow waists, their black leather belts and boots and the ubiquitous green-edged hat, they looked like Bertolt Brecht's version of policemen. By my watch forty-five minutes had elapsed when the young man with the blue eyes came up to me and handed me my passport. "No problem," he said regretfully, then turned on his heels and disappeared. All the doors around the room were now shut.

It was up to me to find my suitcases behind a pillar and drag them past the empty passport control booths. My cousin Aliosha was on the other side, looking healthy and cheerful and, but for a full head of silver in place of his blond hair, apparently unchanged since I had last seen him in 1967. A beautiful young woman stood next to him. With her high cheekbones she bore an uncanny resemblance to my aunt Ariadne, Aliosha's mother, who had died in Moscow fifteen years before. "This is my daughter, Anya," Aliosha said between bear hugs. "She was born a year after your last visit here. Just now you were detained for forty-five minutes. That's not too bad — about two minutes for every year you were kept away. You mustn't worry. Nowadays the KGB has to entertain itself as best it can."

~ 5 ~

Aliosha

OUTSIDE, THE LATE AFTERNOON SUNSHINE was brilliant and the city I had glimpsed from above full of summer greenery. Our taxi sped into town along wide avenues bordered by red brick apartment houses interrupted by huge squares of unmowed grass. Though Aliosha's hair was silver, I knew at once that indeed he had not changed since our childhood on the Ile d'Oléron, his equanimitous, cheerful self intact despite the passage of time. In 1957, at the beginning of Khrushchev's Thaw, Aliosha's parents took him to live in Moscow, where he studied at Moscow University and became a distinguished mathematician. I had not seen him for over two decades, yet we were speaking to each other as if we had never been separated. On the other hand, Aliosha's daughter sitting next to him intimidated me: her resemblance to her grandmother, my aunt Ariadne, was disconcerting. Here was a very young woman who looked like a reincarnation of my favorite aunt as she had been when I was a child. But Anya at twenty could have been my daughter.

As soon as I heard Anya speak I lost my shyness. Born and raised in Moscow, she nonetheless has in her voice the familiar old-fashioned music of my émigré family. She also

has Ariadne's slightly reticent smile, her angular yet graceful movements. Our roles fell into place. I was my aunt
Ariadne in relation to Anya, and she the niece I had once
been. As we neared the cluster of buildings on Lomonosov
Prospect near Moscow University where Aliosha lives, I
sensed that I had an interesting new relative in Moscow.

Carrying my big suitcases with ease through Italianate
portals leading to a highrise built in the fifties, Aliosha explained that he had my Moscow schedule worked out for
me, at least for the first part of my stay. "After that the
Akhmatova scholars will be claiming you. But in the meantime, if you wish, Anya can be your guide. The city has
changed enormously since your last visit." Though he
translates Russian poetry into English and, I suspect,
sometimes writes poems of his own, my cousin is a mathematician foremost. Under his casual appearance — he
wears well-worn sports clothes and is usually laden with
bags bulging with books and tennis rackets — Aliosha is
extremely well organized.

"Right now, you'll want to do what all of us Muscovites
are doing," he said. "Since late May we stay home and
watch television. From morning till night every day the
People's Deputies' assemblies are televised in full from the
Kremlin." Aliosha went on to describe to me the first open
political debate in Russia since the Constituent Assembly
was disbanded by the Bolsheviks. "They make one think
of what 1917 must have been," he continued. "Do you
remember the 'memorable summer,' as Pasternak calls it
in *Safe Conduct?* But these changes might turn out to be
more than an interlude. We could be witnessing the beginning of democracy in the USSR."

As we squeezed the bags and ourselves into a rickety
elevator, I was struck by how rundown what had once
been a comfortable apartment house for the scientific elite
had become. Panes were missing from the glass entrance
door, walls around us were peeling, the elevator seemed

perilously out of breath. But Aliosha was oblivious to my reaction. "Now, about your weekends — that's when the deputies take a break and the luckier among us retire to our dachas." He told me that for the last two years Anya had been working as a weekend volunteer in Peredelkino, helping Lydia Korneevna Chukovskaya and her daughter, Liusha, run what they hoped would soon become officially the Kornei Chukovsky Museum. "Pasternak's house is also being turned into a public museum. Tomorrow, Saturday, you may want to go see the Chukovskys with Anya."

Aliosha had arranged for me to stay in what had been his parents' apartment, number 13 at 144 Leninsky Prospect. Anya's brother Dima was now sharing the flat with a young man named Oleg, a doctor and classmate of Dima's from medical school. But first I would go to Peredelkino, Aliosha told me. "Peredelkino will make you feel at home again among us. Many of your friends live there nowadays, notably Bulat Okudzhava, one of my heroes, the finest balladeer in our language, an artist of absolute integrity. And wonderful Bella Akhmadulina, who has not forgotten you — I ran into her at a poetry reading recently."

Anya would take me to Peredelkino the next morning. A second-year psychology student, she was dashing off to a review class at the university. As we got out of the elevator, she disappeared with a hug and a toss of her blond hair, running down the stairs with a lighthearted clacking of heels.

I spent my first evening in Russia in Aliosha's kitchen. His second wife, Lena, is a computer scientist and, under difficult circumstances, a magnificent homemaker. Born into a family of well-known mathematicians, soignée and slender, she is one of the Russian women whose combination of efficiency and femininity fills one with awe. Lena served us a supper of meatballs and fruit pies, a sumptuous meal in Moscow nowadays, while through the kitchen window we watched an orange twilight turn violet. Drinking tea we talked late into the night: in that season, at Moscow's northern latitude, the days are endless.

I listened transfixed as Aliosha described his encounters with KGB operatives throughout the Brezhnev years. He had succeeded in keeping them at bay by stubbornly refusing to sign any sort of release after the encounters they periodically forced on him. He told of his conflicts at the university, where he had chosen to resign from his teaching post in the early seventies: he had written letters protesting Solzhenitsyn's banishment, and before that had opposed the anti-Semitic practices inaugurated in 1968 in the Moscow University Department of Mathematics. For some twelve years he had worked as an editor of a popular scientific journal. Now, at almost fifty, he was a professor of mathematics again, a researcher in the field of topology, and a volunteer tennis coach, and was involved also in math education for gifted adolescents. He was full of new plans, including a visit to the United States later that summer. He would come see us in Nantucket, he said. This would be his first trip West in almost thirty years. His father, like mine, had worked for the United Nations in New York after the war. Aliosha had graduated from New York University just before his parents took him to live in Moscow in the beginning of the Khrushchev era, in 1957, when it looked as if Khrushchev's reforms would take hold.

Now Aliosha and Lena were asking me about my years as the trustee of *The First Circle* and *The Gulag Archipelago* in the West. Despite my various efforts to send them copies of my book *Solzhenitsyn and the Secret Circle* through acquaintances traveling to the Soviet Union, it had never reached them. As I answered their questions I felt I was back in Moscow in 1967, when I first met Solzhenitsyn. Even Aliosha's kitchen on Lomonosov Prospect, with its small cement balcony and the double windows wide open to the trees below, was reminiscent of the apartment, also belonging to a scientist, where I had met Solzhenitsyn on my last visit to Moscow.

"I've heard only the vaguest rumors about this story," Aliosha said. "Now *The Gulag Archipelago* is about to come out in the USSR, and I hear that Solzhenitsyn will soon be invited to come back to live here."

Lena explained that in the Soviet Union Solzhenitsyn was now worshiped as a great hero. "However, many of his admirers belong to so-called nationalistic circles, the people who yearn for a return to the distant past and who are actively pressing for Jews to leave the country. Along with its positive effects, glasnost is releasing some ugly impulses, rooted in that past," said Lena, who is part Jewish.

I wanted to hear more about these new nationalists.

Lena told me that one of Solzhenitsyn's best-known supporters in Moscow was Igor Shafarevich, a mathematician who had been a prominent dissenter. Shafarevich contributed to a collection of essays, *Under the Rubble,* assembled by Solzhenitsyn just before he was exiled, most of which dealt with a forthcoming rebirth of the USSR under the leadership of the Orthodox Church. Since then Shafarevich had written *Russophobia,* which maintains that the Russian Revolution was a Jewish plot to destroy the Russian people. Jews are referred to in the book as "the small nation," a term which in certain circles became an accepted euphemism.

I had read *Russophobia,* which had not yet come out in the Soviet Union but had already created a sensation in the West. Some of Shafarevich's ideas are derived from Hitler's ideologist, Alfred Rosenberg.

Aliosha reminded us that Solzhenitsyn lives in Vermont and could not be held responsible for what was happening in Moscow. "We don't know that Solzhenitsyn shares Shafarevich's ideas," he said. "I want to believe that an era of national reconciliation is at hand. Solzhenitsyn would be the first to welcome it, I'm sure. *The Gulag Archipelago* was decisive in stemming the tide of lies about this country." When he was preparing to resign from the university, Aliosha had been sustained by Solzhenitsyn's essay "Not by Lies," which had appeared in *Under the Rubble*. It had helped him resist officialdom's immoral, illegal pressures.

Before going to bed we read some poetry aloud. Trilingual in English, French, and Russian, Aliosha is very fond of Joseph Brodsky's works. He wanted to compare his verse in English and in Russian, but since I was getting sleepy I asked him instead to recite Pasternak's "Hamlet," the poem which had haunted me on that day in late fall when I couldn't tell him about my secret agreement with Solzhenitsyn. The last line of the poem reads, "To live a life is not to cross a field."

I was put to bed in a small study overflowing with books and papers. Skis were stacked in a corner; above my head like a Marcel Duchamp construction a bicycle hung from the ceiling. Through the uncurtained window, beyond clusters of fragrant midsummer trees, I could see the lighted towers of Moscow University; behind them, the rising moon. That evening in Moscow, where *The Gulag Archipelago* was about to be published, I felt exhilarated. I put out of my mind what Lena had said about the new Russian nationalists. Aliosha had to be right that Russia was on the eve of a national reconciliation. The time for forgiveness had come, and for freedom of speech, and with it, eventually, freedom of the press and democratic reforms — the intelligentsia's dream since the Decembrists' uprising in 1825. The Soviet phase of Russian history was ending and a new era was beginning for Russia and for the world.

~ 6 ~

To Peredelkino

B Y NINE O'CLOCK the next day Anya and I were on our way to Peredelkino. Anya looked rested and fresh in a white shirt and slacks, and she was full of energy. Again the day was hot and sunny. The subway was mobbed with Muscovites headed for the country for the weekend — students, workers, bespectacled intellectuals, soldiers in uniform, many with Asiatic faces. I hung on to Anya as the tightly packed escalator rushed us at breakneck speed into the bowels of the earth. We changed trains in a vast, vaulted marble station; everyone in sight was hurrying off somewhere with the anxious air of people who are perpetually late.

We emerged into the open air before the Kiev Station. Near the entrance elderly women were selling big disheveled white peonies and minuscule bunches of radishes and dill. Throngs of peddlers were offering beer and *pirozhkis*. Queues of shoppers snaked along the sidewalks and into the street. "There is nothing to buy in Peredelkino," said Anya. She suggested we pick up supplies for the Chukovskys at the station, and flowers for Pasternak's grave. We bought fruit, cheese, vegetables, and lovely multicolored tulips, which we chose with care.

It turned out that Anya knew whole poems by Pasternak by heart, including one of my favorites, about the train to Peredelkino. As we walked toward the railway tracks she recited:

There, as in church, I humbly watch
those I revere: old peasant women,
workers and simple artisans,
young students, people from the countryside

Fixed in every sort of posture,
sitting in groups, in quiet knots,
the children and the young are still,
reading, engrossed like wound-up toys.

As we waited in the sunshine in an ever thickening crowd, I noticed that the concrete platform on which we were standing was literally crumbling under our feet. The rusty train that was pulling up had surely not been painted since my last visit to the USSR. Moscow, a modern urban center in the sixties, now looked like the capital of a populous Third World country. The crowd carried us into the train, shoving us toward the rows of wooden seats, everyone laden with bundles, with children in tow. Pasternak's studious travelers were nowhere to be seen on that midmorning train to Peredelkino.

But thirty minutes later, as we were nearing our destination, our coach was half empty and the passengers sitting next to us suddenly appeared to be out of Pasternak's poem, reading their books and newspapers "like wound-up toys." To my left a young boy of about fourteen was immersed in *Hadzhi Murat,* Tolstoy's novella about Russia's conquest of the Caucasus in the nineteenth century. Pasternak was the first to tell me about that story. Even before we reached Peredelkino, his world was drawing us in.

In Peredelkino, seen from the elevated railway platform, what had once been the open countryside now looked like a resort of scattered small cottages. I had never seen Russia in summertime, and here it was, complete with dachas, flowering meadows, and pine groves. Here was the short-cut to the writers' settlement, a path overgrown with wild-flowers such as one would find in New England in May, and the brook that each year told the poet when spring would come. On a hillock to the right I could make out the cemetery where Pasternak is buried.

And here was the freshly tilled, open field stretching be-tween the writers' settlement and the cemetery, still mirac-ulously undeveloped. Along the road peasant women in red kerchiefs and rubber boots were tending their vegeta-ble gardens, calling out to one another. From the distance I could catch only a glimpse of Pasternak's house through the trees. I wanted to linger, but Anya had to be at the Chukovsky house at once to conduct the first of several daily museum tours.

∽ 7 ∾
Kornei Ivanovich Chukovsky

A S I STOOD before the green gate of Kornei Ivanovich's dacha I thought of my last visit to him, in
1967. It was hard to believe that he would not step
forward to greet us with outstretched arms and thunder-
ous exclamations of welcome. That morning everything
surrounding the two-storied cottage was bursting with life.
Inside the garden a small group of tourists, looking like
students on a holiday, was waiting to be taken through the
house. One young woman held a small girl in a bright blue
pinafore by the hand. Another, in walking shorts with
a rucksack slung across her back, presented Anya with
a bunch of daisies "for Lydia Korneevna." An elderly
woman who might have been a schoolteacher was leaning
on a cane. "For fifty years I've wanted to come here," she
said to no one in particular.

As Anya ushered the visitors in, pausing in the vestibule
to provide everyone with canvas overshoes designed to
protect the old parquet floors, I noticed that the wooden
house had aged. The distinctive ultramarine wallpaper in
the dining room was full of cracks, the rugs were thread-
bare, the doors no longer closed tightly. Yet the house was
still standing, still alive with people. Staying in the back-

ground I followed Anya's tour. With illuminating detail, but in few words, she led the group from room to room describing Chukovsky's role in the survival of Russian culture.

Chukovsky had been a representative of that segment of society which had weathered the Soviet years without emigrating, never betraying the humanistic traditions that had been the ideal of the Russian intelligentsia. His erudition, his love of children, his relationships with other writers — Andreyev, Gorky, Pasternak, and later Solzhenitsyn, whom he received in his house while Solzhenitsyn was hounded by the KGB in the early seventies — these were the aspects of his life that fascinated Anya's audience.

Chukovsky was a self-made man. Born out of wedlock to a woman who worked as a servant, he supported his mother at a young age. He became a superb journalist and traveled to England to study the English language. In the teens and twenties he was regarded as one of Russia's most authoritative literary critics. Victorian English literature was one of his great loves; later on, another of his loves, that of children, saw him through the Stalinist years, although his career as a critic had come to a standstill. His books of poems for young people, which every Russian child knows by heart to this day, were so popular that to have arrested him would have caused a sensation throughout the USSR.

Thus for many years Chukovsky lived in seclusion in Peredelkino, as did Pasternak, whom Stalin also left alone, most probably because of his reputation in European literary circles in the thirties. In 1958 Chukovsky was the first to congratulate Pasternak when he was awarded the Nobel Prize. There are photographs of him at the Pasternaks' table raising his glass to the poet, celebrating the event with champagne. After Chukovsky's death in 1969, his daughter, Lydia Korneevna, carried on her father's legacy, going further than he to become one of Russia's most determined and celebrated literary dissenters. Now in her eighties, a scholar who is also an elegant novelist (her novella *Sofya Petrovna* was recently made into a film in Russia), she is recognized as an incarnation of intellectual probity, a link between the world of Pasternak and Chukovsky and today's world, Anya's world — and in fact, despite their differences in age, Anya and Lydia Korneevna are close friends.

The tour moved on, but I stayed back in Chukovsky's study. Sunlight was streaming into a room where nothing had been changed since I was there two decades before — such was Lydia Korneevna's decision. The red and green plaid blanket on the daybed, the books on the shelves, Kornei Ivanovich's portrait by Mayakovsky, the photographs on the desk — every object had been left in its exact place after Chukovsky's death, including pictures of my parents and me, and a copy of Henry's novel *The Contract*. In Chukovsky's study on that spring day I knew Aliosha had been right: returning to Peredelkino would make it easier for me to come to terms with the past — with the death of a whole generation and with what had happened to me as a result of my involvement with Solzhenitsyn.

As he gazed at me now with a mischievous smile, the very young man drawn by Mayakovsky, I settled on the daybed covered with his plaid blanket, recalling the evenings spent here. Visiting with Chukovsky in his study had been like having an all-knowing teacher.

Tall, athletic, with a booming voice and warm heart, Chukovsky had had an all-embracing personality. Pasternak's "Lieutenant Schmidt," written while the poet was still possessed by revolutionary fervor; the Brownings' poetry; Salinger's *Catcher in the Rye;* my uncle Daniel's visionary poems, which were then considered seditious in the USSR — there was no literary subject that left Chukovsky indifferent. He considered it his responsibility to share his knowledge and his convictions with the younger generation, and he did this in a forceful way, making no allowances for ignorance or sloppy thinking. Like Pasternak, like my grandfather before him, he belonged to that strand in Russian culture which balanced love for Russia with reverence for the splendors of Western culture. Andreyev's passion for Goya, Pasternak's admiration for Goethe and Shakespeare, Chukovsky's for the Brownings — these were the European loves that had formed these writers.

Chukovsky, who had helped bring Solzhenitsyn into my life, had long before that made it possible for me to meet Pasternak. In both cases he had not fully condoned meetings, which could have been dangerous for these writers, yet he deliberately created situations that made meetings inevitable. His prudence made some Muscovites say that Chukovsky was afraid. He was, with good reason, and this made his countless brave efforts in helping the persecuted all the more admirable. I had recorded my last visits to him in the fall of 1967 in *Solzhenitsyn and the Secret Circle:*

Not without regrets I decided to limit my encounters to people who were sufficiently well established not to have too much to fear from their association with me should my connection with Solzhenitsyn ever come to light. I would spend most of my time with my favorite older friends, Nadezhda Mandelstam and, especially, Kornei Ivanovich Chukovsky. They were the people whom I might indeed not see again in this world, those from whom I had most to learn both about the past and my own place in the present.

Tall, snowy-haired, vigorous, his face ruddy and full after a "good summer's work," as he put it, Chukovsky received me that September with particular warmth, as if he too sensed that this autumn's encounters might be our last. As on my earlier visits, he soon turned the conversation to Andreyev, whom he had loved and had admired for his talent, considering himself his protégé. This time too he played the game he had played with me ever since my first visit. Each time he would try to pay me back a hundred rubles he said Andreyev had lent him in his impecunious youth. I would refuse. Chukovsky would persist, distracting me with wonderful anecdotes about my grandfather — how he had once lain down between railroad tracks and let a train pass over him, how he had received guests in his wooden mansion in Finland, where my father had grown up, how after my grandmother's death the elegant ladies of Petersburg had literally lined up to meet him and try to marry him — while all the time trying to tuck a hundred-ruble banknote into my pocket.

Over tea with black bread and butter he told me about Andreyev's and Gorky's stand against anti-Semitism in an era of government-promoted pogroms. And about Andreyev's love for my grandmother, known as Lady Shura, a delicate woman of great inner strength who had helped my grandfather overcome his addictive drinking: "She died in childbirth — when your uncle Daniel was born," Chukovsky said. "Her death so young was a tragedy for Russian literature."

After his afternoon nap, a ritual he regarded as essential to his continued literary proficiency, Chukovsky took me for a walk along the narrow lanes of Peredelkino, still summerlike and fragrant in the late September sun. He told me about the dissident movement, lowering his booming voice as we strolled under the firs along the lanes. Ardently he talked about the dissenters he knew and admired most — Andrey Sakharov, the Litvinov family. To one who had kept silent, at least in public, all through the Stalin years, the boldness of these independent voices was a revelation and an inspiration. I gathered from what he said that now he was helping others besides Alexander Solzhenitsyn.

When he mentioned Solzhenitsyn's name there was nothing in his voice to tell me whether he knew of my meetings with the writer the previous spring. All I could be certain of was that his own assistance to Solzhenitsyn and other dissenters, while secret, had given him a new taste for life. He held his handsome head high and his movements, always energetic, had a new dramatic assertiveness. Once the soul of prudence, he now voiced loudly his disgust with the KGB and the turn Soviet politics was taking, giving emphasis to his feelings by waving his arms as we walked and sometimes clapping his fist loudly into the wide open palm of his hand.

Better than anyone else in Russia, Chukovsky knew how to create a sense of life's continuity for one brought up in the limbo of emigration. One afternoon he had had a surprise for me, one that joined past and present in a way I would never forget. He had called me out into the garden, where a drab gray truck, like a closed delivery van, was parked under the trees. Two young men stood by the truck. With the authority of a theatrical director, Chukovsky set them in motion. One opened the back of the truck and I saw that it was filled with electronic recording equipment. It was a sound truck from a Moscow TV station, which was making a filmed interview with my host. Chukovsky climbed inside. Both young men disappeared after him. Soon Chukovsky summoned me into the crowded interior and handed me a pair of earphones. I put them on and heard a lot of crackling, some coughing and wheezing noises, then a male voice, strangely enthusiastic, slightly breathless. It resembled my brother's voice. It was youthful, aware of its own effect, a bit tentative because of this. I realized that the man speaking was my grandfather. He was addressing an anti-Tzarist political rally more than half a century ago; he would have been about my age then, or younger. When the recording ended I took off the earphones with wonder. Chukovsky was nodding in delight.

"This is the live Andreyev — Andreyev's live voice," he said.

Now, in Peredelkino again in 1989, I thought back to that day in 1967 when I heard Andreyev's live voice for the first time. What would the "live Andreyev," who loved Russia passionately, have thought of my participation in Solzhenitsyn's mission? Of its outcome? Might the fact that it had to be covert cause him to disapprove? Would he have felt it worthy to fight Bolshevism through literature? Despite Chukovsky's friendship and the sound of Andreyev's voice, I remember feeling very lonely that day.

Several years before that, in 1960, Chukovsky had deliberately made it easy for me to meet Boris Pasternak by showing me how to find his house while ostensibly discouraging me with vigorous waving of arms and stamping of feet from ever trying to call on him. In 1967, he had praised Alexander Solzhenitsyn while at the same time cautioning me about "this man who is possessed" *(oderzhimiy)*, for all his restrained, even affable exterior. He was the first to suggest to me that Solzhenitsyn's years in camp had made him into a very complex, steely human being. A hard-working writer himself, Chukovsky appreciated Solzhenitsyn's ability to concentrate, the speed with which he wrote. The speed especially he found phenomenal.

Once during my last visit to him, in 1967, Chukovsky had said, out of the blue, "You, with your literary friendships in the West, you ought to alert international opinion to Alexander Isaevich's situation. Russia's most promising writer hounded by riffraff in Ryazan where he lives, and even here whenever he visits me! It's dreadful! Do you realize that the man is nearly destitute? And fiercely proud — won't accept a thing from anyone." Then with hardly a pause he added, "Funds must be raised. Money to help him. Why don't you do something about it when you get back to the United States?"

When I had inquired how funds could reach Solzhenitsyn if he refused all material aid, Chukovsky had waved this question away. Somehow funds had to be raised and a way found to make them acceptable to Solzhenitsyn. He would take it upon himself to induce him. But then he had seemed to change his mind. "Now that I think of it,

Olenka, it's not at all a good idea for you to concern yourself with Solzhenitsyn's affairs," he told me. "You shouldn't compromise yourself and your family. The more I think about it, the more I think you should remain a free observer. Let those of us who live here take this sort of responsibility."

I had been perplexed. Was Chukovsky retracting his suggestion about aiding Solzhenitsyn, or was he referring to my secret engagement with him and warning me to abandon it? I couldn't tell. Then, like a prestidigitator, he drew living pictures of my grandfather's house in Finland, the guests coming in the immense entrance hall, the fireplaces, the white bearskin rugs, Andreyev appearing on the stairs in a black velvet jacket, lost in sorrow, grieving for Lady Shura and, Chukovsky told me, for Russia, whose future he saw as dark and frightening. Chukovsky's own words of warning worked deeper than these images. In a low voice he had quoted Alexander Blok:

Children, if you could only know
Of the cold and fear of future days.

Now, sitting alone in Chukovsky's study, the fresh smell of the woods coming in through the open window, the pine trees outside rustling, I wanted to think that the days of "cold and fear" were over.

∾ 8 ᖾ

Chukovsky's Granddaughter

OWNSTAIRS IN THE TINY KITCHEN once ruled
by a silent housekeeper from the countryside and
now the domain of the museum volunteers, Anya
was putting together a luncheon of cottage cheese and
salad. Three of us — Anya, Liusha Chukovskaya, and I —
ate at the round table in the ultramarine dining room, still
presided over by Chukovsky's wife, looking down de-
tachedly at the guests out of her turn-of-the-century pastel
portrait. The daisies presented to Lydia Korneevna
brightened the table, but she herself would not be here. She
had been held up in Moscow, putting the last touches on
her monumental study of Anna Akhmatova, which was
being published later that year in honor of the poet's centenary.

At lunch, Liusha, Lydia Korneevna's daughter, who
looks after her grandfather's legacy, explained that although there was a small sign tacked on the Chukovsky
house classifying it as a museum, it had not yet been allocated the government funds necessary for it to function.
Yet the building and grounds had to be maintained, manuscripts preserved, museum tours conducted: the financial
situation was becoming an emergency. Happily, soon

afterward the Soros Foundation became a sponsor of the museum, ensuring, at least for a while, its survival.

There was no lack of exciting subjects for the three of us to discuss on that day — the future of the museum; the publication of *Doctor Zhivago* in the USSR; the resurrection of my uncle Daniel's poetic works; Solzhenitsyn's decision not to return to Russia until his every book was available everywhere in the USSR — "a remote prospect," said Liusha regretfully. Acquainted with him since the days when Solzhenitsyn lived at the Chukovskys', she is a champion of his interests in the USSR. My own difficulties with him, which I felt compelled to share with her in some detail, she attributed to "a misunderstanding caused by Solzhenitsyn's unbending nature — the price of his greatness."

"The country is in the throes of an enormous book hunger," Liusha said. "Today a black market for books is flourishing. It is unrealistic of Alexander Isaevich to make the availability of his books here a condition for his return."

Liusha, who is my age, had hardly changed since I had last seen her. Her dry manner, her deliberate lack of sentimentality, which I remembered from the past, were still evident. But whenever she addressed Anya, whose deliberate matter-of-factness matched hers, she became quite affectionate. I remember thinking that Liusha's restraint, in such contrast with Chukovsky's geniality, was most probably a legacy from Anna Akhmatova. Akhmatova abhorred displays of emotion — and through her mother's intimacy with the poet, Liusha had grown up in her aura.

Anya, the child of divorced parents, had found a new home in the Chukovsky household, which in today's Russia is an island of stability, while Liusha, the childless heir to a formidable literary legacy, responded with appreciation to Anya's goodwill. At that time, besides the salvaging of her grandfather's house, Liusha had the publication of his lifelong diary on her mind. That was the only work Chukovsky intended for himself alone and kept locked in his desk drawer. Its first volume was to be published soon, a small part of the twenty-nine notebooks that span almost seventy years.

Some months later, when it was being published at last, Liusha explained to me that originally she wanted the diary, whose first volume includes entries up to 1929, to extend to 1934. It was to end with Chukovsky standing over Kirov's coffin, a turning point for the epoch and for Chukovsky — the assassination of Sergei Kirov, the popular Party chief from Leningrad, disguised as an automobile accident, had signaled Stalin's ascendancy to absolute power. But the paper shortage necessitated excluding the last 150 pages of the first book, although its index runs for dozens of pages, many entries being people who were executed or perished in camps and others who emigrated.

"For seventy years names were proscribed or tarnished with insulting labels," said Liusha. "I won't be telling you anything new when I say that we still have no literary history, that it is yet to be written. After 1934, when every written word could be used as evidence against someone, people stopped writing letters and keeping diaries. Self-censorship outdid formal censorship. Kornei Chukovsky became a severe censor of his own writing; he also lost the precision and vividness of his earlier descriptions."

Nonetheless, Liusha felt offended when one writer recently said of her grandfather's generation, "What's the good of publishing them? Theirs was the literature of the Third Reich." "Too many people I loved and respected belong to that generation," Liusha said. "Kornei Ivanovich was one of them. Chekhov was his favorite writer. Chukovsky set great store by Chekhov's theory of 'little deeds,' which used to be ridiculed in Stalin's time. Every day he helped someone get care at a hospital, obtain a residence permit, get published.

"We mustn't generalize about the survivors of that horrible time," Liusha continued. "Maxim Gorky, Vladimir Mayakovsky, Alexei Tolstoy were canonized, they became masks created by propaganda. Whatever in their literary work suited the political needs of the day was promoted, while everything else was stifled. To some extent this was true also of Chukovsky. Officially he was a benevolent old man, a friend to all children, Grandpa Kornei. But Chukovsky began as a brash and controversial critic whose reviews were regarded as highly subjective. Today Chukovsky the critic is forgotten. I hope the publication of the *Diary* will help change this."

After lunch, before the museum tours resumed, Anya and I sat for a while on the Chukovskys' porch, now leaning perilously to one side. "The public isn't allowed here, it is in danger of collapsing," Anya said, "but if we sit very quietly we'll be all right." And she brought out two straight chairs from the dining room and set them out in the shade. We sat facing the pine trees, which now tower above the dacha. An aromatic midday had settled upon the woods edged with tall grass and Queen Anne's lace. There was no place in the world I would rather have been at that moment.

"In Peredelkino in the summer Pasternak always seems nearby," said Anya. "He must have loved this place very much. Lydia Korneevna speaks about him often." Anya asked me to describe what I remembered best about Pasternak.

"I can't separate my memories of Pasternak from his early verse," I said. "There was such energy in his every phrase, such unexpected twists." I recited a stanza from an early poem written during the "memorable summer" of 1917:

Split your soul like wood. Let today froth to your mouth.
It's the world's noontide. Have you no eyes for it?

Look, conception bubbles from the bleached fallows;
fir cones, woodpeckers, clouds, pine needles, heat.

(Translated by Robert Lowell with OAC)

At four o'clock the Chukovsky museum was closed to the public, but visitors kept appearing at the gate. Anya and Liusha urged them to come back the following weekend. Standing there, however, they looked so disappointed, so meek, so imploring, that Anya offered to conduct one more, abbreviated tour. By the time we set forth for the cemetery the air was cool. Shadows around us were lengthening while we gathered a few wild grasses and daisies to complement our bouquet of tulips. First we walked up to the church on the hill above the cemetery. Lilacs billowed over the stone walls that partially enclose it, filling the air with their smell. Apple trees were in bloom. To me it all looked improbable, a golden dream of a long-lost Russia.

∾ 9 ∽

Tulips for Pasternak

A SERVICE WAS TAKING PLACE inside the small Church of the Transfiguration, which for seventy-two years was the seat of Moscow's patriarch, the highest prelate within the Russian Orthodox hierarchy. Before that for centuries the Dormition in the Kremlin held this function, but after the Revolution that venerable cathedral, Russia's most illustrious, became a museum while the patriarch was exiled to Peredelkino. In the fall of 1990, in the first religious procession to unfold in Moscow since 1917, the patriarch was to return to the Kremlin in triumph: the Dormition and its sister, the Cathedral of the Ascension, were being reopened to Russian Orthodox services. Not long afterward, the Orthodox Church would be claiming as its property most of the ecclesiastical treasures of Russia.

That afternoon inside the darkened Peredelkino church a choir was singing softly as the faithful shuffled toward the gilded holy gates before the altar. Candles glittered. This was the eve of the Feast of the Ascension, and the atmosphere inside the church was solemn, yet a guarded feeling no longer prevailed in churches. Many among the worshipers were Anya's age or younger. The elderly women had lost their hunted look. Gone were the hostile *babushkas* who used to make churchgoing in the Soviet Union painful.

Once outside, we walked down to Pasternak's grave next to the three tall pine trees that make it easy to find in the maze of tombs and shrubs covering the hillside. A white stone relief of the poet in profile now marks it. Nearby his two wives' small tombstones stand, and that of his brother, Alexander Leonidovich, whom I had met at the Pasternaks' in 1960. An architect, he is the author of a lovely memoir, *A Vanished Present.*

Armfuls of flowers were scattered over Pasternak's grave, and more were brought while we stood there. Anya divided our bouquet before putting it down, keeping half of it for Chukovsky, who is buried just below Pasternak. On that day the Peredelkino cemetery was almost as crowded as the church. Families on a spring afternoon outing were tending their relatives' graves, weeding, planting seedlings, bringing up buckets of water from the brook at the foot of the hill where children played in the shallow water.

On our way back to the Chukovskys' I asked Anya whether we could stop by Pasternak's house. "Let's not," she said. "You might be disappointed. The house is being renovated right now and it doesn't look like itself." She explained that not long ago Pasternak's family came close to being thrown out of it by the Writers' Union — the house had been assigned as a summer residence to Chingiz Aitmatov, one of its more influential members. When people protested, it was decided that it would become a museum, but by then the house had been gutted. Now it was all white and empty inside, with a cement walkway cutting through the garden. It was to be restored by the following winter, in time for a Pasternak centenary celebration. But it was his grave, not his house, which had become a shrine, like Pushkin's grave in Pskov. "Next week for the anniversary of his death hundreds of people will gather in the cemetery and read his poetry aloud late into the night," Anya said. "I'm planning to be here with a group of friends. We'll bring some blankets."

I remembered a letter my father wrote me in the fall of 1960. Later, in San Francisco, I reread his letter. My father was describing his trip to Pasternak's home a few months after the poet's death in 1960, when Peredelkino was still a tiny village and Pasternak's house was occupied by his widow, Zinaida Nicolaevna:

A great deal has changed in Russia since 1917, but certain traits of the Russian people have remained. As contradictory as ever, they coexist in one person in unfathomable fashion: hospitality and rudeness, melancholy and gaiety, kindness and harshness. Certain habits too are unchanged, in particular a passion for travel. One need only walk into any railroad station to see a commotion familiar since my early childhood: sheepskins, coats, uniforms, suitcases bound with cord, food baskets, the air blue with smoke, and an endless, nameless crowd striving to get somewhere but in the meantime patiently awaiting their train.

Through the drafty waiting room of the Kiev Terminal Pasternak passed nearly every day, dashing over the icy quay. In *Winter Expanse* he describes those war years when suburban trains ran right to the front which was closing in on Moscow, when it seemed that one additional effort by the German army was enough for the USSR to lose the war. Pasternak remained among the diminishing number of those who believed in a Russian victory against all odds. It is in the course of those years that he truly discovered his country and fell in love with Russia passionately.

I buy a ticket for Peredelkino, the train is crowded. From the window the Moscow University building can be seen, and also the belt of newly erected apartment houses eight or ten stories high which have altered forever the sil-

houette of Moscow as we knew it: "Our cities find new
faces sooner than the heart."

Little by little the landscape changes, wooded hills stand
at the horizon. Beyond the window, a grove of small pine
trees, sown some fifteen years ago right after the war. The
trees, the height of a standing man, spread to the horizon
in neat rank and file. A forest of tall evergreens is now
coming up right to the railroad track, it covers a steep hill,
wooden houses flicker between the reddish tree trunks. We
are in Peredelkino.

I reach the cemetery by walking along the railroad
tracks, away from the rustic railroad station. Along the
gleaming tracks up on the hill there is a switchman's shack
guarded by a chained brown dog — and beyond it the
Peredelkino cemetery.

A protective wall encircles Western cemeteries, but Russian graves are usually placed in complete disorder, while
each individual tomb is enclosed by a small wooden fence
as if to say: "If there can be no privacy in life, let there be
some at least in the hereafter." Most graves are marked by
crosses but sometimes one sees a red obelisk on the tomb
of an unbeliever. On a little elevation facing south, beneath
branches boldly spread out, a fence painted green encloses
a large rectangle of earth — Pasternak's grave. It is covered
with freshly cut autumn flowers, their slight smell acrid.
Every day visitors bring them from Moscow.

I must tell you about Boris Leonidovich's funeral last
spring as I heard about it from Kornei Ivanovich. On a
sunny spring day his open casket was brought here, carried
on outstretched arms. On the eve of Pasternak's funeral,
leaflets began appearing on Moscow walls, telling when
the ceremony was to take place and how to get to Peredelkino. They were torn off but more leaflets kept reappear-
ing, particularly in the neighborhood of the Kiev Station.

No Soviet writers of note were there, except for Kon-
stantin Paustovsky. Mme. Ehrenburg attended in the absence of her husband, who was in Stockholm. The funeral
service had sent a car to take the coffin to the cemetery,
but Pasternak's family and friends disregarded it. The

pianist Svetoslav Richter played a Beethoven funeral march on the poet's piano as the body was carried out of the house in a profusion of spring flowers, in a heavy smell of lilac, high above the heads of the crowd, as was due him. The great majority of the men of letters then residing in the rest home did not attend the funeral. During the procession I overheard a local *baba* grumbling: "They (the writers from the Union who have their dachas in Peredelkino) have not bothered to honor him . . . The cowards, we will not bother to go to their funerals when their time comes."

After Pasternak's blossom-laden coffin was lowered into the grave, young men from the crowd started to read his verse — they began with "Hamlet" from *Doctor Zhivago,* which was taken up in unison by the whole assembly. Young poets took turns reading Pasternak's poems and their own dedicated to him, others made speeches. When a gaunt and poorly dressed man began a dull, religious-minded speech, the single official representative tried to stop him. A young man in workman's clothes pushed the representative aside, shouting: "Leave the speaker alone, this is not the Writers' Union here, you cannot stop us." The poetry reading lasted for hours, late into a warm May night.

When I call on Zinaida Nicolaevna, we settle in the room where the grand piano stands. "Boris Leonidovich was lying in this room during the last days of his sickness," she says. "The physician whom he especially trusted stayed in the house. Everything was done to lessen his suffering. Two nurses relieved each other at his side. The piano was moved out while he lay in this room, but now we had it put back because it always stood there."

Through the window facing the couch I see a maple losing its last leaves. When Pasternak last looked through this window it was May, the maple leaves had just begun to unfurl: spring comes late in Moscow. I go upstairs to his study following the wooden staircase. Without him at the desk, the emptiness of the room is overpowering. On the desk lie some pencils, a fountain pen, a pocket watch, a small round hand mirror. Beside the window a bookshelf, Shakespeare in English, *Doctor Zhivago* in foreign editions, not many books in all. On a little table in a corner I see Pasternak's death mask under glass. A few black eyebrows are caught in the white plaster. The face is unchangingly masculine, magnificent.

∾ 10 ∾

Pasternak: A Russian Poet

L ATE AT NIGHT on our way back to Moscow in an empty train, I told Anya a story I heard from Pasternak in 1960. I had not forgotten it, though at the time I did not transcribe it for fear of compromising the poet. It was about his friend Marina Tsvetayeva. During my visits to Peredelkino, Pasternak often spoke about Tsvetayeva, whom I had known in my childhood — in Paris, she was a close friend of my family. Because his story, told in a lowered voice, was about the Terror, it took on threatening, Shakespearean overtones. It was a variation on the story of St. Peter's betrayal. By then the poet's Christian beliefs had found their expression in *The Poems of Doctor Zhivago,* which he himself preferred to his earlier writings; today, in a time of religious reawakening, this is by far his most popular collection in Russia.

Pasternak's tale about Tsvetayeva touched on that persistent Russian myth, the notion that for a Russian writer to live in exile is not only spiritually debilitating but also somehow sinful, even when exile is inevitable. This same myth had made Tolstoy and Dostoyevsky angry with Turgenev — for proving it wrong; Turgenev savored the sweetness of French life while retaining his unassailable Russian character.

As I sat across from him at his writing desk in the January twilight, Pasternak recounted that in Paris in 1935, while he was experiencing a shattering inner break with revolutionary ideals, Tsvetayeva, an émigré since 1922, asked him about the wisdom of her moving back to the Soviet Union. Tsvetayeva's husband, Serge Efron, and her daughter, Ariadne, were pressing for the family's return, prompted, in Pasternak's words, "partly by homesickness and sympathy for Communism and the Soviet Union, and partly by the notion that Marina Tsvetayeva could never be happy in Paris, that she would perish, living in a vacuum without readers." It is said that Tsvetayeva's husband went to meet Pasternak at the railway station, imploring him not to discourage Tsvetayeva from returning home.

Though he was aware that the Great Purges were under way, Pasternak was noncommittal with his friend. When Tsvetayeva came back to Moscow in 1938, at the height of the Terror, he was unable to look after her. Alone, abandoned by all her Soviet acquaintances, her husband and daughter arrested, Tsvetayeva committed suicide on August 31, 1941. Pasternak could not forgive himself his evasion, which he attributed to the state of despair that had deprived him of sound judgment during that fateful writers' congress in 1935.

Before that Pasternak and Tsvetayeva had corresponded for decades. Pasternak had in his possession more than one hundred letters from Tsvetayeva. The story of how he lost these during the war, giving them for safekeeping to a friend who commuted to her job and who one day forgot them on a train, was in his own eyes the ultimate metaphor for his failure to save Marina Tsvetayeva's life. As he spoke, Pasternak was exorcising his guilt at a time when it was still dangerous to mention the events of the previous decades. His grief was overwhelming — as was his belief that, regardless of persecution, living outside Russia was, for him, unacceptable.

Raising his voice as he talked to me, Pasternak said that

he had been in earnest in the famous letter to Khrushchev extracted from him: "I am linked to Russia by my birth, life and work. I cannot imagine my fate separated from and outside Russia . . . A departure beyond the borders of my country would be for me the equivalent of death, and I therefore request [you] not to take this extreme measure against me." Only now, in the nineties, are Russians beginning to see emigrating as a legitimate choice.

Boris Pasternak was born in 1890 in Moscow, the eldest son of Leonid Pasternak, a successful post-Impressionist painter, and Rosa Kaufman, a concert pianist. He grew up in an artistic, warmhearted milieu. Leonid Pasternak was a follower of Leo Tolstoy. Anton Rubinstein, Alexander Scriabin, Rainer Maria Rilke, and Emile Verhaeren were friends of this accomplished Jewish family, a family that was in many ways representative of the Moscow intelligentsia at the turn of the century.

As a child Pasternak wanted to become a composer; Scriabin was his idol. However, on an impulse, at the age of about twenty he gave up music and went to study philosophy at Marburg with Professor Herman Cohen, a famous neo-Kantian. An unhappy love affair caused him to plunge head-on into poetry, and philosophy became a secondary concern for him. "I think a little philosophy should be added to life and art by way of seasoning, but to make it one's specialty seems to me as strange as eating nothing but horseradish," Lara says in *Doctor Zhivago*.

In the twenties Pasternak was recognized in Europe as one of Russia's leading poets. During the years of repression when his work was seldom published, he earned his living with translations. His renderings of the Georgian poets and of Shakespeare, Goethe, and Schiller are among the finest in Russian. He also wrote two remarkable autobiographies, in 1931 and 1957. The first, *Safe Conduct*, is a masterpiece of its genre, ranking with Tolstoy's *Child-*

hood and Adolescence and Mandelstam's *The Noise of Time*. The second one, *I Remember*, written more simply, is no less moving.

In 1935 Pasternak was literally forced to go to Paris to attend an international writers' congress sponsored by the Communist Party. Aware of the widening Stalinist purges and the oncoming war, he was suffering from insomnia and depression. He made a brief speech at the congress, which gave him a standing ovation.

> Poetry will always be too simple to serve as a subject matter for discussion at public assemblies; it will remain the organic function of a happy human being, overflowing with all the felicity of language that thrills in a candid and generous heart; and the greater the number of happy men, the easier it will be to become an artist.

Few among those who acclaimed him, including André Malraux and Roman Rolland, realized that he was on the verge of emotional collapse and that the Soviet Union was plunging into yet another wave of terror. Thereafter Pasternak lived in seclusion in his country house in Peredelkino. Miraculously he escaped Stalinist persecutions, despite — or perhaps because of — his Tolstoyan heritage, which committed him to truthfulness at all times, both as a writer and as a man. Pasternak's candor was extremely rare in those years. Recently published transcripts of writers' meetings in which he participated show he was extraordinarily outspoken. His fearlessness may have protected him: "Let this cloud-dweller be," Stalin allegedly said of him.

After the war the publication of *Doctor Zhivago* outside the Soviet Union unleashed a violent reaction in official Soviet circles; Pasternak was expelled from the Writers' Union and ostracized. Meanwhile, his international fame grew steadily. Posthumously he received a measure of rehabilitation in the Soviet Union. His *Selected Poems* were published there in 1965 in the prestigious Poets' Library founded by Gorky. This volume, with a preface by Andrey Sinyavsky, written shortly before his arrest, includes most of the poems from *Doctor Zhivago,* regarded nowadays as one of the finest achievements in Russian poetry.

In 1989 *Doctor Zhivago* came out at last in the Soviet Union. That year, on a spring evening near a bookstore on Gorky Street — now Tverskaya — Anya and I saw a crowd of two or three hundred people standing in line. Walking with Anya around the city I knew that her impulse, like that of every Muscovite, would be to get in line even before she knew what was available at the end of the queue: such is the state of the Soviet economy that people are in permanent search of everything they need to survive. In this case, however, Anya stepped out of the queue right away. The crowd was waiting for a shipment of *Doctor Zhivago,* not due to arrive until the following morning. "I read the book years ago," Anya said. "I have it in my library in a samizdat edition. It is good that all Russians can read it now." Anya seldom acknowledged that anything positive could be happening in the Soviet Union.

In 1958 it had taken extraordinary imagination and courage to send *Doctor Zhivago* into the world, and Russian readers remember this. Pasternak's cult continues to grow even as glasnost showers its sumptuous, long forbidden literary gifts upon them, revealing Berdyaev and Nabokov, Remizov and Sinyavsky to them. In the winter of 1990 the Writers' Union celebrated Pasternak's centenary in Peredelkino. Andrey Voznesensky, who had helped organize the event, wrote in *Moscow News,* Russia's most liberal newspaper at that time: "For millions the poet has become a symbol of intellectual incorruptibility."

As for Pasternak's artistic legacy, at a time of radical reappraisals it is difficult to ascertain who his heirs might be. Joseph Brodsky, a poet of extraordinary intellectual and linguistic gifts, might be considered, but Pasternak's view of the world was much broader and more compassionate than Brodsky's. In the words of one critic, Pasternak was able in his poetry "to turn the sky upside down." But on the other hand, Brodsky's dignified attitude and willingness to let glasnost prove itself are admirable, coming as they do from a writer who suffered terrible humiliations at the hands of the Soviet state.

Some ten years after the publication of *Doctor Zhivago,* as Khrushchev's Thaw was ending, Solzhenitsyn released his books denouncing Stalinism, and for a time his name became a household word in the West. His thoughts about the publication of *Doctor Zhivago,* recorded in his lengthy memoir *The Calf and the Oak,* are revealing of his sense of his own accomplishments:

> In 1958, I, a teacher in Ryazan — how I envied Pasternak: here is someone who will succeed in the fate I had conceived! *He* will be the one to fulfill it — he'll go at once [to Stockholm, to receive the Nobel Prize — *Translator's note*] and he will make a speech, and publish his other works, those he could not risk publishing while he lived here! Clearly his trip would take longer than three days. Clearly he would not be allowed back, but he would have changed the whole world in the meantime, and changed us — and then he would return, in triumph.
>
> Frankly speaking, after my camp experience, I was incapable of imagining that Pasternak might elect another course of action, have another aim. I measured him by my own aims, my own measure and I writhed in shame for him and for myself: how could one be frightened of newspapers' remonstrances, how could one weaken before the threat of exile . . .

This passage might well be seen also as Solzhenitsyn's blueprint for his eventual return to Russia, should the political situation ever be ripe — "in triumph."

In 1954 the Polish poet Czeslaw Milosz, a Communist diplomat who had defected to the West and later also became a Nobel Prize laureate, declared that a statue of Pasternak would stand one day in Moscow. Knowing Russian, he was able to measure the breadth of Pasternak's poetic genius. For those who do not know the language, that genius must remain a matter of faith. No monument to Pasternak stands in Moscow yet, but another of Milosz's judgments was prophetic: "To do his Hamlet deed, Pasternak had to write a big novel. By that deed he created a new myth of the writer, and we may conjecture that it will endure in Russian literature like other, already mythical events: Pushkin's duel, Gogol's struggles with the devil, Tolstoy's escape from Yasnaya Polyana." Indeed, Pasternak is now a legendary figure in Russia. He himself described his predicament in his "Hamlet," which has become one of the most famous poems in the Russian language. Its last line, a folk saying, is emblematic not only of Pasternak's life but also of that of every Russian who lived through the grim Soviet years:

The sequence of scenes was well thought out;
the last bow is in the cards, or the stars —
but I am alone, and there is none . . .
All's drowned in the sperm and spittle of the Pharisee —

To live a life is not to cross a field.

(Translated by Robert Lowell with OAC)

Early in his career, in *Safe Conduct*, Pasternak had said, as if taking the measure of what lay ahead: "The more self-contained the individuality from which life derives, the more collective is its story in the most literal sense." From the beginning, without ever losing his sense of honor, he was seeking the universal as it is expressed through the unique, be it in art or in life. Russia's dark times turned him into an archetypal figure, the incarnation of the writer challenging a merciless state. It is both the terror and the glory of Russian literature that it exacts high deeds from its artists.

TWO

1989

∾ II ∾

Sakharov's Hopes

I SPENT THE DAYS following my visit to Peredelkino at Aliosha's. Apartment 13 at 144 Leninsky Prospect, where I was to stay for part of my Moscow visit, was not yet ready for my arrival. A three-day party had been held there to celebrate the departure for Paris of one of my niece Anya's school friends. A trip to France was an unprecedented event for my niece's contemporaries. The party had been splendid, Anya's brother, Dima, reported on the telephone, but the room I was to occupy was still full of sleeping celebrants. It would take a little time to get everything back in place to make it possible for an important guest, an aunt from America, to move in.

Once again the weather was beautiful. My cousin Aliosha offered to take me on my first Moscow walk. "It's Sunday, let's go to the Kremlin," he said. "It's closed to the public during the week because of the parliamentary meetings, and yet you won't have truly come home to Moscow until you make a pilgrimage there." I was pleased; I remembered Aliosha as a fine guide to Moscow. On our walk I also wanted to share with him my impressions of Peredelkino.

Many years before, my cousin and I had strolled through Moscow in winter. I remembered the Kremlin as the heart of a northern city, silent and white and secretive. But that afternoon in the midsummer light it looked resplendent. As we came to the drawbridge that leads to the gate at Trinity Tower, we had a view, from below, of Ivan the Great's belltower, its freshly gilded cupolas shining. The brick ramparts with the whimsical towers enclosing the fortress were set off by the early summer foliage. Red and emerald green against a turquoise sky, the Kremlin looked almost Venetian from a distance.

For me on that first Moscow walk in 1989 the sound of Russian was like lovely music. I had not expected that Russian spoken on the streets and in the subway would be so moving. It was as if the whole city were filled with friends and acquaintances — in my everyday life in the West it is only they who speak Russian. The language made me feel at home in a new Russia where people spoke their minds. When I had been there last, Muscovites had kept silent in public places: the KGB was everywhere. But now they were all speaking at once, loudly — about everyday matters, about Gorbachev, about Yeltsin and Sakharov. The sound of their own voices was buoying their spirits — no one was asking yet how perestroika, the forthcoming restructuring of Soviet society, might be implemented.

Inside the Kremlin the feverish atmosphere of the city vanished. In the impeccably tended public gardens, mothers were pushing baby carriages while children played and lovers held hands. There were foreign tourists everywhere, recognizable by their bright clothes, their cameras, their relentless picture-taking. A border of tiny red begonias did little to cheer the incongruous black statue of a sitting Lenin, who surveyed the scene from the edge of the cobblestoned Cathedral Square at the center of the Kremlin. "Who knows, perhaps he soon will be gone," Aliosha said cheerfully. "In the meantime, isn't it nice that the Palace of Congresses, which should never have been built here in the first place, is at least put to good use?" He pointed to a modern structure where the new Soviet parliament was holding its daily meetings.

We crossed Cathedral Square, surrounded by Russia's holiest churches. We came first to the Dormition, the most holy of them all, whose exterior is elegant and yet austere. It was modeled after an earlier cathedral of the same name in the town of Vladimir. Aliosha explained that the grand princes of Muscovy were eager to stress their kinship to that city's monarch, Vladimir Monomah, an ancestor who lent legitimacy to their claim over Moscow. Crowned by five golden domes, the stone Dormition is smooth and pale gray on the outside. Inside it is dazzling. Its golden spaciousness and its treasures are those of an authentic shrine: it was built in the fifteenth century when the Russian Orthodox faith was in full flowering.

Some of the great Orthodox relics are housed in the Dormition: the twelfth-century icon of St. George, the curly-headed incarnation of the ideal warrior; the celebrated dark Savior of the Fiery Eye; and the holy guardian of the Russian State, the Virgin of Vladimir. "The princes of Muscovy needed all the holy relics they could assemble," Aliosha said. "We mustn't forget that it was as the Tartars' tax collectors that they had come to rule over the other princes of Central Russia."

It was in the celestial-looking Dormition that we came upon an odd, vaguely menacing tentlike object carved of dark wood touched with gold and red paint. "Ivan the Terrible's throne," said Aliosha. "Here is a symbol of the power the Kremlin commands — in Ivan the Terrible's days, and in Lenin's and Stalin's, and in Gorbachev's as well. Ivan the Terrible, who laid the foundations for a Russian empire, is buried right here, and Stalin and Lenin just below on Red Square. Today the Kremlin still wants to hold together the huge, discordant empire, but it won't succeed for long."

I remembered that in the sixties Aliosha had predicted that the high birthrate in the outlying republics would eventually create a challenge to Soviet rule. This was happening now.

"It's only a question of time — it will be an explosion," Aliosha said. "It may be that the government will try to implement Solzhenitsyn's recommendation and call on the Orthodox Church to help keep the Soviet Union together: in Russia the church has been in the service of the state from the very beginning. And now in this atheistic country we still have no separation of state and church — not yet, although a law on freedom of religion is being considered. Its passage would be one of Gorbachev's greatest accomplishments. It would at last allow Jews and Catholics and the ever growing Protestant communities scattered all over to worship without threat of reprisals. But surely the Orthodox Church can't stop the spread of Muslim sentiment in Central Asia, nor force the Lithuanians and Estonians to love us, their occupiers. I hope that the Church will stay out of the upcoming political upheaval."

Stepping out into the sun-drenched square, we walked to its edge and looked down upon Red Square. From where we stood we could see St. Basil and Lenin's tomb. "St. Basil is my favorite Moscow church," Aliosha said. "Unlike the Dormition, it has always been a neighborhood church, reaching out to the people across the city's main square. As he was fleeing Moscow in 1812, Napoleon's last order was to blow it up. The order was not carried out. The church is still here, still reaching out. It was its spirit that drove the Tartars out of Russia, and the French, and later the Germans."

"Wasn't St. Basil built by Italians?" I asked. In answer he recited Mandelstam's early lines, addressed to Marina Tsvetayeva:

The five-headed churches of Moscow,
With their Italian-Russian souls,
Are like Aurora's apparition,
But with a Russian name and wrapped in furs.

"Though some of its churches were built by Italian masters, the Italianate beauty of the Kremlin is deceptive," Aliosha said. "At the time of their building Russia had barely been touched by the Renaissance. The Kremlin is a stronghold of Russian autocracy, and Russian autocracy is what killed Mandelstam. He feared the Kremlin."

"What about Pasternak?" I asked. "He lived nearby, yet as far as I can remember he never wrote about the Kremlin."

"Yes, he did," said Aliosha. "He too was in awe of it:

The Kremlin, grandiose, all about
The past, a visionary divination,
Rushes forth, smashing
Into the year nineteen-nineteen.

At twilight the belltower
Of ringing copper tries to break
Into my window, as if fearing
That the year might slip by unrecorded.

"But for all his emotionalism," Aliosha went on, "Pasternak wasn't sentimental; he never looked upon cupolas and towers as privileged expressions of Russianness. Pasternak's inspiration came from Pushkin and Tolstoy, from Russia's free spirits."

We were standing at the edge of Red Square, near the Hotel National, where Aliosha's mother and mine had lived under arrest at the beginning of the Red Terror. Shortly before she died my mother wrote down everything she remembered of her years in Russia during the Revolution, and in the mid-seventies Ardis published her memoir, *Cold Spring in Russia*. In my luggage I had a copy of it for Aliosha, not having dared send it by mail. I mentioned the book to my cousin now. "The picture it gives of the Bolsheviks as they took power is chilling," I said. "The memoir became an anti-Soviet book just by being truthful."

"Only freedom of speech can turn this country around," said Aliosha. "That was what Khrushchev failed to understand. If only he had allowed Soviet citizens to speak out, his experiment in liberalizing the USSR might have succeeded. We would be spared some of the difficult political choices we will have to make sooner or later. And the economic corruption that has spread enormously since the sixties."

We strolled across Red Square to St. Basil. The painted stone cluster of tulips and pine cones was turning bright pink in the late afternoon light. St. Basil was the creation of Russian architects who with obvious delight were learning the intricacies of perspective: Aliosha dismissed the legend that after it was built Ivan the Terrible had its creators blinded so they could never build another church like it. "Russian history is bad enough without gory fabrications," he said.

I remembered that Ivan had built St. Basil to commemorate his victory over the Tartars, who had held the country in bondage for almost three hundred years. Ivan, a mad, bloodthirsty ruler with a streak of artistic genius, won his victory over the Tartars the day of the Virgin's Holy Intercession — St. Basil was originally dedicated to her, before being renamed for a neighborhood saint. On the day of the decisive battle the Virgin was said to have spread a robe of rain clouds across the sky as a blessing to the Russians. Ivan saw his kingdom as blessed; Muscovy would be the Third Rome, destined to lead Christendom as Byzantium and Rome had.

As if reading my thoughts, Aliosha frowned in a way that I remembered from childhood. "I'm very much afraid," he said, "that the messianic dream hasn't quite died here. Some people are still nostalgic for it. Their notion of the so-called Russian Idea, expressed by religious philosophers at the turn of the century, is perverted — an excuse for Russian chauvinism. Like it or not, you'll soon be hearing about this new version of Russianness. Your aunt Alla is an enthusiast."

As we neared St. Basil my cousin added wistfully, "Who knows, dark as Russian history has been, perhaps St. Basil's promise of national fulfillment will still come true. Over the next few days, as you watch the People's Deputies' assemblies on TV, you'll see that with Sakharov at their head, the Soviet Union has a great many independent-minded citizens."

When we returned to Aliosha's apartment I looked for my mother's memoir hidden under some clothing at the bottom of one of my suitcases. As I pulled the book out a yellowed newspaper clipping fell from it. I didn't realize it had been there when I packed; had I known, I would have removed it, in case of an airport police search. In 1989 the Socialist Revolutionaries' destruction by the Bolsheviks was not yet acknowledged by Soviet historians.

Lena and Aliosha were fascinated when at teatime we read aloud from that yellowed paper — a very long letter to Lenin from Victor Chernov, Aliosha's maternal grandfather and mine. It had been written in 1919, when Chernov was living in the underground somewhere in Moscow, hiding from the Cheka, while Lenin was settling in as the supreme leader in the Kremlin. Chernov could not forgive Lenin the destruction of the Constituent Assembly — a fateful event that opened the way for tyranny — or the creation of the Cheka, which still haunts Russia today, under the name KGB.

The letter had been reprinted by an émigré newspaper in Paris sometime in the twenties. It opens:

Dear Sir:
    O, yes, you are not a thief in the vulgar sense of this word. You wouldn't take someone else's purse. But if it were a matter of stealing a man's trust — and in this case of the people's trust — you would go to any extreme of cunning, of deception and maneuvering. You would not falsify a check, but there is no political step that you wouldn't take were it needed for the success of your plans

[the disbanding of the Constituent Assembly in January 1918]. It is said that in personal life you are fond of children and pets, but now with one stroke of the pen you are spilling blood, endless blood, anyone's blood, with total cold-heartedness, with a wooden indifference worthy of the most hardened criminal . . . You are a profoundly amoral man. You have overstepped all boundaries of human decency . . .

"If only Chernov could be watching the Kremlin meetings with us now," said Aliosha. "He would be amazed as to how huge the rivers of blood proved to be, but he also would realize that perhaps at last the nightmare is ending. For the first time in seventy years there is a promise of freedom in this country."

"You can't imagine what it meant to us when Andrey Sakharov spoke out for the first time, in 1967 or 1968," Lena said. "That was when dissent was born, just about the time you were here last." Sakharov had written a letter to Brezhnev in defense of four arrested dissenters, people he called *volnomyslyashchie,* those who think freely. These included Alexander Ginzburg and Yuri Galanskov, who had recorded the proceedings of the Sinyavsky-Daniel trial and circulated the transcripts. At that time Sakharov put the number of political prisoners in the Soviet Union at about 1,700,000.

As I sat with Lena and Aliosha drinking tea, we talked about Sakharov and then about Solzhenitsyn. I began to understand what it was that made Sakharov, the father of the Soviet H-bomb, one of the century's great scientific geniuses, so effective in his new role as the informal leader of the parliamentary opposition to Communist officialdom. His were moderate, sensible views, closer in spirit, say, to Turgenev or Chekhov than to Tolstoy or Dostoyevsky. For decades my cousin and his wife had lived in an oppressive atmosphere sometimes verging on outright madness. How else to describe the circumstances of Solzhenitsyn's exile from the Soviet Union — the arrest, the plane journey to an unknown destination? Or Sakharov's treatment at the hands of the KGB? Yet Sakharov's quiet, wholehearted acceptance of the ideals of the Enlightenment filled Aliosha and Lena with enthusiasm and even hope.

For those like myself who did not know him personally, many admirable qualities emanate from Sakharov's writings, from his presence on television: simplicity, moral and intellectual rectitude, passion combined with tolerance. Lack of dogmatism, kindness toward all, equally. An unwavering optimism in the face of adversity. Russian patriotism without chauvinism. Sakharov himself once commented, "There was nothing chauvinistic about my family's attitude to Russian culture, and I do not recall a single derogatory remark about other nationalities — rather, the contrary."

Born in 1921, Andrey Sakharov, the son of a professor of physics, became the best incarnation and the eventual moral vindication of the Russian scientific intelligentsia of the first half of the century. Over the years this group has been unfairly belittled, in part because it was so modest, so self-deprecating. It was attacked by the philosophers of the Vehi movement, which urged a rebirth of national religious consciousness after the failure of the 1905 revolution, and more recently by Solzhenitsyn, who refers to some of its members as an assemblage of "smatterers." Before the Revolution, the refined, West-oriented Petersburg elite sometimes called it the "demi-intelligentsia." And indeed, because its members were scientists rather than men of letters, it is remembered mostly through portraits written by outsiders which verge on caricature, such as Chekhov's "eternal students" or Bzarov in Turgenev's *Fathers and Sons*. Yet in his monumental *Memoirs,* published in 1990, Sakharov describes this class of people more warmly: "In the late nineteenth century in Russia, there existed something of fundamental importance — a solid, middle-class, professional intelligentsia which possessed firm principles based on spiritual values. That milieu produced committed revolutionaries, poets, and engineers."

To some extent the spirit of this milieu survived the Revolution, which by and large its members considered inevitable, the result of the corruption and ineptness of the imperial ruling class. The intelligentsia's habits of frugality and endurance served it in good stead: some of its values — basic decency, an unobtrusive day-to-day religiosity — were easily converted into the more altruistic aspect of Communist morality. Although it was decimated by the great purges of the late thirties and again after the war, universal education replenished its ranks, often with talented, resourceful people of peasant or working-class origins. Scientific excellence is hard to fake, though some got away with it, like the notorious Lysenko, who, on Stalin's prompting, denied the existence of genetics. Today, members of the scientific community are usually supportive of the changes in Russia and its former empire. Before that, in the Brezhnev era, many of the dissenters came from their world. The public revelation, in 1956, of Stalin's crimes, combined with the cynicism and squalor of the years that followed Khrushchev's rule, caused the intelligentsia's gradual disaffection from the Soviet system.

Right after World War II, the young Sakharov, already one of Russia's most distinguished scientists, worked with total absorption on establishing nuclear parity between the Soviet Union and the United States. To the end — he died in December 1989 — he never quite rejected the political wisdom of this involvement, although he condemned it wholeheartedly on humanistic grounds. His conversion, from passionate researcher and uniquely effective servant of the Soviet state to an imaginative and yet always rational critic of it, makes his life story particularly inspiring to younger members of the scientific community like Aliosha and Lena. The notion of radical transformation is imbedded in the Russian sensibility: the lives of the saints, one of Russia's oldest religious-literary forms, often touch on such conversions. And it could be that only a leap of faith will ensure the survival of the battered Russian national consciousness.

Over the weeks of my visit Aliosha and Lena introduced me to close friends from their milieu. Some of them had been involved with Sakharov's Human Rights Movement, which led to his six-year exile in Gorky. Most of the scientists I met in Moscow, some of whom had been sent to the gulag because of their nonviolent political activities against the Soviet state, had backgrounds similar to Sakharov's. The majority believed that in the Kremlin a federated, American-inspired form of government might eventually be established. While admiring Solzhenitsyn for his courage and the literary distinction of his early books, they were unconvinced by his program of salvation for Russia, consisting of self-denial, stern religious obedience, control of some parts of the Russian empire, and a return to pre-Revolutionary moral and social values — in fact, to the patriarchal norms that ruled Russia before Peter the Great.

Sakharov too had been dismayed by Solzhenitsyn's political and social program when he learned of it through the 1973 *Letter to the Soviet Leaders,* and before that through personal encounters with the writer dating back to 1968. At that time Solzhenitsyn had solemnly told him, "Any convergence [with the West] is out of the question." For Sakharov, convergence with the West — what we see happening in the early nineties, however haphazardly — seemed the only hope for the survival of the planet, and he gained the moral authority to say so. Physically weakened but strengthened spiritually by the extreme suffering inflicted on him by the KGB during his exile to Gorky (now again Nizhni Novgorod), he saved the country's honor through his ordeal; he restored to the Russians their collective right to self-esteem.

On the other hand, Alexander Solzhenitsyn's studious

decades behind an electronically operated gate in Cavendish, Vermont — years marked by personal feuds and by innumerable ex cathedra declarations about the decadence of the West and the dangers of world communism — slowly sapped his earlier prestige, although his feat, the writing and publishing of *The Gulag Archipelago,* will not be forgotten. Ironically enough, in 1968, in an open controversy with Sakharov he had acrimoniously condemned the concept of emigration. Many within the Soviet scientific elite now see Solzhenitsyn as a utopian. Some remember his address to God in *The Calf and the Oak:* "The Higher Hand will correct me in many ways. But this does not cloud my breast. What gladdens me and strengthens me is that I do not invent and implement everything, that I am only a sword, well sharpened against an impure power, magically empowered to cut it up and disperse it."

The Higher Hand was kinder to Sakharov, keeping him forcibly in Russia and giving him a remarkable wife. Elena Bonner, an independent, strong-willed woman, is a formidable human rights activist in her own right. Earlier, her efforts joined with those of her brilliant, even-tempered husband to create an extraordinarily effective, visible team. She is one of those women who seem to have become stronger with adversity — as did Anna Akhmatova and Nadezhda Mandelstam before her. As for Sakharov and Bonner, with whom the KGB played endless repulsive games, they became symbols, the embodiments of the world's concern with the Soviet Union's wholesale violations of human rights. Committees all over the Western hemisphere worked on their behalf.

The fact that Elena Bonner is part Jewish further dramatized the Sakharovs' plight. As a Jew she was entitled to emigrate — her children elected to exert that right — while her Russian husband, a keeper of the Soviet Union's atomic secrets, was not. The Soviet authorities spread tales about the noble Russian man fallen prey to a Zionist Mata

Hari. Solzhenitsyn, critical of Elena Bonner, did not hesi-
tate to voice his censure. He accused Sakharov of waging
his fight against the Soviet authorities "in defense of those
close to him, of ideas not his own. Such was the inspiration
of Sakharov's efforts . . . specifically in support of the right
to emigrate, which seemed to take precedence over all
other problems."

Sakharov wrote in his *Memoirs* that the hostility toward
his wife struck him as "demonic," reminiscent of the notorious *Protocols of the Elders of Zion.* That forgery, ever
since the days of its fabrication in the 1920s, has disseminated the legend that Jews are trying to infiltrate and destroy non-Jewish nations. Mercifully, however, the descen-
dants of the scientific elite that nurtured Andrey Sakharov
are gaining a measure of political power. It is on their advice that, in a series of goodwill gestures toward the United
States, the Russian government is starting to dismantle the
enormous nuclear arsenal the Kremlin still controls. Some
members of the scientific intelligentsia occupy responsible
positions in the present government of Russia. As for Andrey Dmitrevich Sakharov, he is venerated as a national
hero by Russians of the most varied backgrounds.

∽ 12 ∾

Apartment 13

A LIOSHA AND LENA'S apartment is quite small. When I moved into apartment 13 at 144 Leninsky Prospect, which had been my uncle Volodia's place, I entered a world totally new to me, a world inhabited by Muscovites in their early twenties. There, in an apartment looking out onto a small birch grove, my nephew Dima was my host. I had last seen Dima in Moscow at my aunt Ariadne's, his grandmother. The Sossinskys' eldest grandchild, he had been a pretty five-year-old boy with huge dark eyes. Dima still had those huge eyes, but now he was tall and slim in blue jeans and a black sweater. He was a medical student, soon to receive his M.D. Unlike his sister, Anya, he didn't resemble anyone else in our immediate family, yet he had an intense interest in our family's history and an even more intense one in émigré literature.

Literature is Dima's consuming passion. He received me cordially — and with innumerable questions about the poets I had known over the years. Dima is a true Russian intellectual; his motto could be, in Brodsky's words, "If life doesn't respond to the standards suggested by literature, it's an unworthy life." It is this attitude that explains in good part the vitality of Russian culture despite up-

heaval and deprivation: for those with literary inclina-
tions, life is consistently interesting. Even in the darkest
years many Russian educators encouraged the study of national classics.

Dima had taken care of my uncle Volodia, Aliosha's father, until his death in 1987. His roommate, Oleg, also a
medical student, had helped Dima with the nursing, which
had been long and difficult. Now the two young men were
living in my uncle's apartment in a highrise on the periph-
ery of Moscow, close to the pediatric hospital where they
were working.

The arrival on Leninsky Prospect of the aunt from San
Francisco was not entirely auspicious. Aliosha brought me
there on a morning when Oleg and Dima had time off and
could be there to greet me, which they did most graciously.
The apartment was freshly scrubbed — no vestige left of
the three days of partying. Anya too was there, although
at that time she was sharing a small apartment in town
with a friend. As a greeting she had prepared a breakfast
that included things I especially like — cherries and soft-
boiled eggs and black bread.

However, as we were settling down to breakfast I
realized that my young hosts were casting expectant
looks toward my suitcases, which Aliosha had heroically
dragged into the hall. There was an awkward silence. Finally Dima asked in a low voice, "Where are the books?"
He spoke shyly but firmly.

"What books?" I asked, seized with dismay at the
steady gaze of his huge black eyes. "I did bring a few that
I left at your father's — my mother's memoir and a book I
wrote about Solzhenitsyn. I am afraid that what I have
here is mostly clothing. Mine and some for you and Anya,
blue jeans and sweaters. Oh, and I do have a paperback
copy of *The Golden Bowl* by Henry James."

The three young people looked grim. I had no one to
turn to for comfort — Aliosha had dashed off to the uni-

versity. We ate in silence in the sunny kitchen. Eventually Anya spoke up in her most direct manner. "It's all a terrible misunderstanding. We had hoped that, coming from Paris, you'd bring us some books. Some Nabokov perhaps, and some Remizov. And Poplavsky — you can't get him anywhere, not even on the black market with the best connections. I guess you couldn't know how much we in Moscow need books."

This sounded like an exaggeration, but I said nothing. In truth, I had found Aliosha's apartment so encumbered with books as to be claustrophobic, and here too in apartment 13 I saw books — Russian and foreign classics — everywhere I looked, on floors, on top of dressers, piled up on chairs. More books? I could only make my apologies. I had been away too long, had not known what Russians in the days of glasnost need — books! And more books!

Throughout his last illness my uncle Volodia, a poet and scholar with an ebullient and somewhat eccentric personality, had told Dima and Oleg about his youth as a White cavalry officer in the civil war and about our life in émigré Paris, where the writers Tsvetayeva, Remizov, and Poplavsky were close friends of our family. To the young Muscovites these stories seemed magical, especially those about bohemia on the banks of the Seine.

Even though I was a small child in the years my uncle spoke of, Dima and Oleg looked to me to confirm and expand on his tales. Had my uncle Volodia and my father, roommates before they married the Chernov sisters, lived solely on baguettes and tea in their small Left Bank hotel room, consuming so much tea in just three months that they managed to stop up a gutter pipe seven floors high with tea leaves? Did Volodia fight a duel to defend Tsvetayeva's literary honor when she was slighted by a monarchist critic? What kind of weapon had they used, how did it all end? And the poet Poplavsky — had he been in love with my mother, or was it with her twin sister, my aunt Natasha?

And had I ever heard the émigré poet Georgi Ivanov recite his poems? What was his style of delivery — was he a good public reader? Had he been a friend of Akhmatova's? Was his *Petersburg Nights,* about that city before the Revolution, full of outrageous inventions, as Akhmatova maintained, or was the memoir reliable? Oleg and Dima hoped it was true; the fanciful, risqué tales about young poets in Petersburg had charmed them.

My answers, based more on family lore than on remembered facts, were often vague, but this did not discourage Dima and Oleg. My visit to Peredelkino had rekindled my memories of the sixties, which in turn brought back memories of my childhood — Tsvetayeva reading Pasternak's *1905* aloud, her sharp profile and ringing voice that never seemed to tire; Boris Poplavsky arriving at our house from Paris on a Sunday morning, a volume of Nostradamus tied to the handlebars of his bicycle. At lunch Poplavsky had read aloud to us predictions about the coming of the Antichrist, and then his own nostalgic "Flags," my favorite to this day among his poems. Le Plessis, where we lived, was a pastoral suburb of Paris. Poplavsky was revealing to us not only the mysteries of the future, which soon proved all too true, but those of Paris as well, a tantalizing city where, in my judgment, I was taken much too seldom by my parents.

For Dima and Oleg I wanted to bring to life the Paris of my childhood, a city of flags and of broad avenues and parks and handsome, dangerous bandits known as *apaches.* I was five years old, I listened to "Flags" and dreamt of an *apache* in a *casquette* and striped tee shirt concealing a knife in his sleeve — I half hoped he might abduct me and take me to live in Paris with him. But then there were other reasons to want to go to Paris: Tsvetayeva lived there, and the Remizovs, my godparents, whose apartment was dark and full of toys and of ancient Russian embroideries pinned to the walls. There Alexey Mikhailovich Remizov read aloud his fairy tales to children who were offered chocolates out of a box lined with mauve satin. "A la Marquise de Sévigné" was inscribed on the lid, each chocolate embossed with the French writer's profile.

As we sat at the kitchen table and drank red Georgian wine a grateful patient had given Oleg, I tried to recapture the texture of my childhood for my new friends. I wanted to live up to my uncle's legacy. Uncle Volodia had been an expansive man, a self-appointed archivist who was also a fine storyteller. He had spent his life, shattered by war and exile, keeping a diary, trying to save books, photographs, manuscripts, and especially memories, fragments of a forbidden Russian past that would be resurrected when freedom was returned to Russia.

Preserving the past had been one of Volodia's avocations. As we spoke until two in the morning, I began to understand what my uncle's last years in apartment 13 had been like, his resonant, ever optimistic voice echoing in the forced silence of the Brezhnev years. Dima guessed my thoughts. "You are late by some three years," he said. "Grandfather believed to the end you'd come for a last visit. But then for him the important thing would be the fact that you are here with us now, that we can say whatever we want to each other and remember the past as it was, the good with the bad."

Dima explained that my uncle Volodia believed Russia would be free one day soon. "That's why many people in Moscow considered him crazy — that and the enthusiasm with which he told stories about Paris and lent his books out to friends and friends of friends. As a result, we have almost no library left in apartment 13." In the years before his death people would borrow his émigré editions and not return them. But, Dima assured me, that was all right with Volodia. Having spent so much of his life away from Russia, he wanted to share with people what was otherwise unavailable to them. His stories about the Paris of his youth helped dispel the lies told about the hopelessness of émigré life.

As Dima talked I remembered how my uncle had always shared everything he had. He had even managed to smuggle presents to us from a German prison camp during the war, to get them from Düsseldorf to our island in the Atlantic. Tiny boxes made out of tree bark, a necklace of small, polished river stones, a book about the artists of the Renaissance — the book that inspired me to become a painter.

I fell in love with apartment 13 and with its inhabitants. My uncle's spirit was alive there, well suited to the new times. The place was unkempt and no meals were prepared at regular hours, yet I felt at ease, day after day. Anya came and went, and so did Oleg's and Dima's girlfriends, graceful nymphs who seemed the embodiments of aloof femininity. In Anya's opinion they all lacked personality. I never got to know any of them well — they were very shy.

Dima and Oleg worked twelve-hour shifts at the hospital. On Sunday mornings they played tennis on a court near their apartment building. Their friends, trustworthy friends chosen over the years with an eye to the Brezhnev repression, during which people like my uncle and his family were of interest to the KGB, came to the apartment once or twice a week. That spring they often brought along some visiting foreigner, usually a student. Aliosha and I were flattered to be asked to join in.

On these occasions when extra chairs were brought into the kitchen, Anya served food bought at the free peasant market near the university, and, if luck would have it, some hard-to-get wine or vodka. Staying up till two in the morning was customary in apartment 13. I got used to it — in any case, I had no choice: the apartment's telephone was located in the room where I slept, and there were occasional night calls from the hospital. But in truth the endless May twilights made staying awake in the evenings easy.

In the daytime I cooked whatever provisions their patients gave the young doctors — a huge hunk of beef, a sack of potatoes or onions. Or enough cherries to make jam, although, as I remember, they were consumed fresh in just one day. At the price-controlled market near us, a malodorous, hangar-like store, one could always find eggs, milk, and bread. Once in a while I went to the hard currency store in the Hotel Tourist nearby for delicacies and liquor. Despite Dima's supplications, I tried to get out of buying him cigarettes, which were getting scarce on the open market. Somewhat reluctantly Dima forgave me.

The birch grove near 144 Leninsky Prospect was full of wildflowers. When Dima had time off he and I sometimes went there for strolls. I enjoyed his company; he was thoughtful and kind and made one think of a young man of another time, perhaps the 1860s. He would have been Bazarov's counterpart, a medical doctor with a romantic's rather than a positivist's sensibility. He, like Bazarov, was devoted to his patients, and they adored him, as Oleg was quick to point out. Dima, on the other hand, recognized Oleg's medical seniority and nicknamed him "Doctor."

Dima reminisced about Volodia, whom for years he had brought to this grove for daily outings. I'd gather a small bouquet while telling Dima what I remembered about Tsvetayeva and about some of the American poets I had known, Robert Lowell and Robert Penn Warren. There were peonies for sale at the entrance to the terminal of the Southwestern metro line linking our neighborhood to the center of town. We were never without bouquets in apartment 13 — no guest would arrive without a peony or a bunch of roses bought for an exorbitant price in a flower shop in town.

I wanted that spring to last for a long time, and it did, until I had to leave for Akhmatova's festivities in Leningrad in mid-June. Except for one spectacular thunderstorm, when the sky behind our birch grove turned dark purple and a great rain washed our neighborhood thoroughly, the weather in Moscow remained magnificent.

∾ 13 ∾

A Memorable Spring

I SPENT MY DAYS that spring watching television in apartment 13. An extraordinary ceremony was unfolding in the Kremlin, a ceremony linked to the fate of my entire family — to Leonid Andreyev and to his younger son, the poet Daniel, my uncle; to my father and to my uncle Volodia, and to the three little girls who had been locked up in the Hotel National in 1919. The proceedings were decisive for the future of Russia. My sense of disbelief was mounting. Here was a momentous and seemingly irreversible process — the long drawn-out public denunciation of the Communist Party after seventy-two years of its holding absolute power in the Soviet Union. The Party had driven my family out of Russia, killed dozens of friends and relatives, destroyed the ecology of a continent, annihilated people by the million, and for more than forty years enslaved Eastern Europe. But now these crimes were being revealed, perhaps inadvertently, the result of maneuverings by one man, a Communist himself.

Gorbachev was unopposed by his fellow Communists, who seemed too stunned or too divided to stop him. The parliamentary process enacted on the screen was so novel for the Soviet Union that viewers were bewildered, although many of the comments I overheard in public places were remarkably perceptive. The question remains as to whether Gorbachev was aware of the consequences of the process he had initiated. Shortly before Andrey Sakharov's death he said that Gorbachev had never ceased to be an enigma to him. The political proceedings Gorbachev was masterminding felt like a happening in the sense given to that term in New York in the late fifties, a theatrical event devised to be played out as an improvisation. But then, stage-managed as they are, the most spontaneous-looking happenings are often the result of complex manipulations.

Deftly, Gorbachev was undermining a colossal bureaucratic machine so corrupt and so entrenched that it seemed incapable of grasping the danger it faced. Nor were my young friends in apartment 13 fully aware of the scope of the events at hand. To them it all seemed too little too late, a parody of what was needed — some total, radical transformation of their lives. They had no opportunity to demonstrate it publicly, yet their discontent was not unlike that of students in the West in the late 1960s. Nothing would do short of an instantaneous "normalization" of their existence. *Normalno* — or, rather, *ne normalno* — is a word often used today by exasperated citizens calling out for that minimum of normalcy — of good sense and comfort missing from daily life.

Even as a veteran observer of the Watergate and Iran-*contra* hearings I was in awe. Television was demonstrating once again its power to unmask scoundrels. In open view of the Soviet nation, which was allowed not to work for two full weeks so as to follow the proceedings, what the Communist Party had done to the country was revealed in all its enormity. About two thousand deputies, elected earlier that year, were participating in the debate through a system deliberately favoring the Party — at least two-thirds of them were rank-and-file Communists. The remaining third were not, and these included liberals from

every Soviet republic. Andrey Sakharov was their acknowledged political and spiritual leader, the leader of the
Opposition. Gorbachev was constantly on stage, directing.

As a rule each deputy was given equal television time
regardless of his affiliation. All that the non-Communist
deputies needed to do during the time allocated to them
was to report truthfully about their constituencies — the
dying villages of Central Russia, the polluted cities of the
Ukraine, the neglected Eskimo tribes of the far north, the
Georgians recently massacred by the KGB. The all-too-fa-
miliar, self-congratulating drone of the unrepenting Communists, although they were in the majority, only dramatized and amplified a lamentation never before heard in the
Soviet Union, except perhaps on the stage of the Bolshoi
Theater in *Boris Godunov*. More often than not, the Opposition deputies expressed themselves in the muted tones
of those who have never had an opportunity to voice their
views freely. Merging together, however, their speeches
were a list of grievances without end, the howling of a
wounded animal. Hearing them, one wanted to weep for
the Russian people and for the nationalities incorporated
into their empire over the centuries.

That May I seldom went out of apartment 13 in the
daytime. Once in a while Aliosha would drop by to sit next
to me in what had been my uncle's room, to converse and
watch television. He was no less bemused than I, no less
hopeful. Together we saw two of the most dramatic confrontations of that time, though we were unwilling to believe they were a sign of things to come. In the first confrontation, an exasperated Gorbachev, who early on had
demonstrated his intolerance of separatist sentiments
within the Soviet Union, rudely interrupted Sakharov,
whose speech was going over the five minutes allocated to
him. The subject was the unexplained killings of civilians
in Tbilisi that April. One night special KGB troops armed
with shovels had assaulted a peaceful pro-Georgian vigil in

the center of Tbilisi, murdering two dozen people. Now Sakharov, speaking for the Opposition, wanted to know who had ordered the attack.

The other episode was no less upsetting. On cue, Sakharov was booed by the Communist deputies for having allegedly slandered, in the Western press, the actions of the Soviet military in Afghanistan. Aliosha and I were alarmed: it was clear that Gorbachev's tolerance of Sakharov's democratic agenda was wearing thin. It was shocking to see an exhausted man who was the embodiment of Russian honor publicly humiliated by well-fed, cynical politicians who had held him and the whole country in bondage for such a long time, bringing it to a state of ruination whose scope was too huge to be fully comprehended. Aliosha said, "They will make themselves felt yet, these pigs."

Like the kitchen, the airy bedroom in which the black-and-white television stood overlooked the leafy birch grove, which gave apartment 13 a feeling of the Russian countryside. Throughout the day, settled on my uncle's bed, I took short breaks from watching television and tried to phone those of my Moscow friends who I knew were still alive. I reached a few; to speak to them was lovely and somehow otherworldly. Theirs were voices I had not expected to hear again.

For the most part, however, Muscovites had had their telephone numbers changed over the years, and it took time and Anya's help to find them. But I did see several friends loom before me on the TV screen. Middle-aged now and graying, they still looked like themselves, and I had the impulse to call out to them. I was elated because my contemporaries, who could have given so much to their country had it not been for Brezhnev's ice age, could again be active. They had not been a lost generation after all; their talents would be of service to Russia. And they were making converts on the spot. Andrey Sakharov reported afterward that as the parliamentary debate proceeded, deputies elected through Party connections were joining the Opposition and making democratic ideals their own.

Over the days I saw Yevgeny Yevtushenko and Yuri Karyakin, a friend from Ernst's studio in the sixties who had helped me locate some little-known Dostoyevsky landmarks in Moscow (my husband and I were translating *The Idiot* at that time). And here was Vyacheslav Vsevolodovich Ivanov, known as Koma, a friend of my whole family's, a dissident whom I had last seen on the evening before my departure from Moscow in 1967 at a gathering attended also by Solzhenitsyn. Koma is the son of the well-known Soviet novelist Vsevolod Ivanov. In Peredelkino, where Koma lived as a child, Pasternak had singled him out and befriended him, inspiring him to become a poet as well as one of Russia's leading linguists. At that time Koma, a Soviet deputy, was trying to create for the USSR an equivalent of the American Library of Congress. He now teaches in California for half the school year. I have the privilege of continuing, together with Henry, a friendship that began in the sixties with an affinity between Koma and my father as poets.

During my weeks in apartment 13, my closeness with Anya grew. Almost every evening after school she came to see us. Whenever Dima or Oleg were there we improvised a simple dinner; Anya put the food together and I washed the dishes afterward. We sat by the open window in the kitchen and talked for hours on end. I quickly discovered that my young friends became impatient whenever I touched on the social problems in the United States today. To them my remarks sounded like old-fashioned Soviet anti-American propaganda, but sometimes I persisted — my hosts professed to hate every form of deception. Moreover, Anya and Oleg, each separately, were dreaming of going one day to the West for postgraduate studies.

Some evenings Anya would take the four of us to the

theater. She had a friend named Ella who knew many suc-cessful actors and actresses in Moscow and was able to procure tickets for the most sought-after shows in town — for a theatrical adaptation of Bulgakov's *The Master and Margarita,* for Trifonov's *The House on the Quay* at the Taganka Theater, and for Bulgakov's *The Fateful Eggs,* which an experimental group was presenting as a work in progress. There were two Andreyev plays staged in Mos-cow at that time, *The Thought* and *Darkness,* but we did not go to see them. I regret that now; I have still to see an Andreyev play performed in Russian — I have attended only Western productions of my grandfather's works, whose staging was discouraged during the Khrushchev era.

But though Andreyev was popular in Moscow that spring, he left the inhabitants of apartment 13 cool. "We do like Andreyev, but for us he is a little obvious," Oleg said. It was Mikhail Bulgakov my young friends adored. They knew long passages of his books by heart. Sometimes they would impersonate one or another of Bulgakov's he-roes, especially Woland, the Prince of Darkness, and his retinue of entertaining lesser demons. Indeed, Bulgakov is tremendously popular in Russia. We were all in agreement: Bulgakov is the great Russian prose writer of the twentieth century, equaled only by Nabokov, whom readers in the former Soviet Union are now discovering. Dima and Oleg were unequivocal: I would be welcome in apartment 13 soon again, no later than the following spring, but I was not to come back without copies of Nabokov's novels in English, a language they were both studying.

That year my stay in Moscow, with its coincidences and touches of whimsy, felt at times as if it were conceived by Nabokov or Bulgakov, both of whom were inspired by that most visionary of all Russian classics, Nikolai Gogol. One memorable encounter was with Alexander Askoldov, a Soviet filmmaker, the author of a celebrated Soviet film, *Commissar,* whom I had met during his visit to San Francisco at the beginning of glasnost. It so happened that shortly after Stalin's death, it was Askoldov who had helped Bulgakov's widow, Elena Sergeevna, preserve her husband's manuscripts by hiding them under the Askoldovs' bed. The manuscripts remained there for several years.

Askoldov's tales about Elena Sergeevna gave a sense of her intelligence and of her imperious feminine charm. She had served as an inspiration for Margarita in *The Master and Margarita,* Bulgakov's masterpiece, which chronicles in phantasmagoric terms life in Moscow in the late twenties. Like Nadezhda Mandelstam, whom Askoldov also knew in the forties and fifties, Elena Sergeevna had been a quintessential Russian literary widow, saving her husband's legacy in the face of police searches and attempts at intimidation. Thanks to her the novel survived and, in a somewhat abbreviated version, was published in Moscow during the Khrushchev Thaw. It was recognized at once as the greatest modernistic novel of Russia. Compared to it, *Doctor Zhivago,* unconventional though it is, is a very traditional Russian work of fiction.

Mikhail Bulgakov, born in 1891, one year after Pasternak, was a medical doctor, as was Yuri Zhivago, Pasternak's hero. In the twenties Bulgakov was one of the Soviet Union's most admired playwrights. One of his plays, about the collapse of the White movement, even caught Stalin's fancy for a time. But eventually he was mercilessly hounded and wrote his last, greatest work, *The Master and Margarita,* in secret, living in extreme poverty in a cellar apartment that is now one of Moscow's unofficial shrines. The publication of his novel in 1965 marked the beginning of Bulgakov's literary glory in Russia. Today, the Master, an embodiment of the self-contained artist of genius; his beautiful, willful muse, Margarita; Woland the Devil; and the hapless poet Bezdomny are as alive for Russian readers as Anna Karenina or Natasha Rostova.

Right after my arrival in Moscow, when I was still staying at Aliosha's, there was an unexpected breathless telephone call from Tom Luddy, a San Francisco friend who was congratulating me on my return to Moscow. Along with Zoya Boguslavskaya, Tom, a film producer, had encouraged my return to the Soviet Union. It was he who had first brought to the attention of the Soviet consul general in San Francisco the fact that the Soviet authorities under glasnost were keeping Leonid Andreyev's granddaughter out of Russia.

Before that, during the years I was not allowed into the Soviet Union, Luddy had made a point of bringing me together with those Soviet artists who were occasionally allowed to visit in the United States — the film directors Askoldov and Abuladze, two glasnost activists, and, shortly before his death, the talented Yuri Trifonov, whose play *The House on the Quay* I would see with Anya, Dima, and Oleg. Now Luddy, who had just arrived in Moscow, was inviting me to a banquet at the Filmmakers' Union Club. He was in the city on business and wished to celebrate with some of his friends from the Union who had been the first to fight for the lifting of censorship in the arts. Among those I knew, Alexander Askoldov would be there.

Tom's party turned out to be a lively and slightly improbable affair. The Filmmakers' Union Club, like its literary counterpart, the notorious Writers' Union Club on Vorovskaya Street, closely resembles the club immortalized in *The Master and Margarita,* where abundance reigns in the middle of a deprived city. The novel recreates the end of the New Economic Policy, the NEP, introduced by Lenin after years of terror. Free enterprise was officially encouraged for a time, but it all ended in a merciless witchhunt against "black marketeers" and "profiteers," many of whom happened to be Jewish.

At the Filmmakers' Union Club, vodka, Georgian wine, sturgeon, *shashlik,* beef Stroganoff, and even caviar were brought out relentlessly to an exuberant crowd of Soviet artists and foreign guests much too euphoric to know what was really happening in the city in the meantime. One of the themes of *The Master and Margarita* is the mischievous yet deadly takeover of Moscow by satanic forces — the beginning of Stalin's reign, barely noticeable at first. But on that spring evening in the late eighties, I wanted to believe that Tom Luddy's dinner was a sign of things to come. The balmy night illuminated by a huge moon, the meeting of American and Russian intellectuals, the discussions of joint Soviet-American movie projects, my drinking champagne sitting next to my newly found niece, Anya, whom Tom had asked me to bring to the party — all of this was dreamlike.

My only regret was that Askoldov and his wife, Svetlana, had not been able to come at the last moment. However, a few days later Askoldov called to invite me to dinner, once again at the Filmmakers' Union Club. Svetlana was out of town, and he felt unequal to cooking supper at home — the shelves of his neighborhood stores were empty.

My young friends in apartment 13 had just seen Askoldov's *Commissar* and were pleased that my first Moscow outing on my own would be with this legendary film director regarded in their circle as an incarnation of artistic probity. A number of my friends from the sixties did not meet their standards of integrity either as artists or as political activists. My knowing Askoldov redeemed me somewhat in their eyes.

ᏘᏘ 14 ᏘᏘ

Alexander Askoldov

THE FILM *Commissar,* enhanced by a score by Russia's foremost composer, Alfred Schnitke, who combined Russian and Jewish folk melodies, was completed in 1967, at the very end of Khrushchev's Thaw. The only film made by Askoldov to date, it tells the story of a determined Red Army commissar, Vavilova, during the Russian civil war. Vavilova, who has become pregnant by accident, is assigned quarters with the family of a Jewish handyman, the Magazaniks, in a Ukrainian town recently conquered by the Reds. After giving birth, the commissar, who is in charge of political indoctrination in her cavalry regiment, rejoins it, leaving her infant behind, one more child for the large Jewish family to care for.

Set in a mythic-looking, war-devastated town, the film combines a realistic narrative with powerful, surrealistic sequences. Some are battle scenes: using cavalry formations, they echo Vavilova's birth pangs. There is religious feasting celebrating the child's arrival, and scenes filled with terror which foretell pogroms at the hands of the advancing White armies and the holocaust in which the Magazaniks will eventually be annihilated. In his film Askoldov contrasts the Jewish reverence for life with the

Russians' determination to bring universal justice to the world at any cost. *Commissar* is about violence, what violence does to the human psyche. One of its more anguishing episodes suggests that despite their parents' horrified reaction to their war games, Jewish children will eventually learn to be killers themselves. A *cri de coeur*, the film is also a work of art, a luminous black-and-white movie in the great tradition of the early Soviet cinema.

Commissar is based on a 1934 short story by the Russian Jewish writer Vasily Grossman, whose monumental *Time and Fate* — banned in 1960 for having been the first novel in the USSR to equate the excesses of communism with fascism — was being posthumously published in Moscow that year. Though Askoldov is not Jewish, his film is evocative of yet another Russian Jewish writer, Isaac Babel, better known in the West than Grossman. Askoldov has Babel's gift for evoking larger metaphysical themes through detail. He captures unerringly the assertive way a Red officer, played by the great actor-writer Vasily Sukshin, lights a cigarette while his orderly shows off a silver watch he has just stolen; he shows us a young woman's movements as she does the wash, bathes her children, and handles the tiny kerosene stove widely used in the early years of Soviet power.

It is Askoldov's recreation of the holocaust, the most powerful of the dream sequences in *Commissar,* which explains why his film, threatened with destruction at the hands of irate Soviet film officials, was released only through an accident of glasnost. Anti-Semitism, always strong in Russia, was for a long time officially forbidden by Soviet law. Nonetheless, after World War II it grew steadily, and by now it has become quite open, with the establishment of groups such as Pamyat. Traditional Slavic anti-Semitism has been fanned by diehard Communists and KGB operatives.

Back in the sixties, anti-Semitism was exacerbated by

envy as some Jews were allowed to leave the Soviet Union. Askoldov's theme, of universal, shared guilt for what had happened to the Jews in World War II, was being disavowed in the Soviet Union as he was finishing his film, yet he refused to cut it in any way. Had he accepted the authorities' decision to suppress *Commissar*, he could probably have made other films, as did most Soviet filmmakers after one or another of their works was forbidden. Instead, Askoldov, a stubborn believer in communist ideals, kept appealing his case to the authorities to the point of being bodily evicted from Goskino, Moscow's main film studio.

For many years Askoldov supported his wife and daughter by working as an assistant director in a small theater. He lost that job also — for alleged professional incompetence — as rumors began to circulate about the fact that a copy of *Commissar* had survived after all. Askoldov's unbending temperament, his readiness to speak out combined with a mystical belief in the sanctity of the Russian Revolution, had earned him the lasting enmity of the Soviet establishment. In *Commissar* he had allowed Jews to teach Russians a moral lesson, something that is hard for average Russians to bear.

During our first meeting in San Francisco, at the American première of *Commissar* in 1988, Askoldov told me that back home in 1967, unbeknownst to him, his wife stole film cans of his movie and hid them in a linen closet to save them from being burnt by enraged bureaucrats. As I listened I had a sense of déjà vu; I remembered Nadezhda Mandelstam telling me that during a police search in the thirties she had concealed the poems of her husband in the saucepan in which she usually made soup. Like the preservation of Mandelstam's poetry, that of Askoldov's film was a gift to Russian culture by yet another heroic wife.

The film was selected for screening at the San Francisco Film Festival in 1968, but Soviet troops invaded Czechoslovakia, the film disappeared, and its director was persecuted and forgotten. When glasnost came, a Conflict Commission was created at the Soviet Filmmakers' Union to review some 140 films which the authorities had shelved over the years. *Commissar* was the last to be released. Askoldov was considered too cantankerous to deal with, and, in any case, officially his film no longer existed.

Then in July 1987, the San Francisco delegation at the Moscow Film Festival, including Tom Luddy, who remembered Askoldov, became determined to get the film "freed from prison." The Filmmakers' Union was still reluctant, but after a tumultuous public confrontation, a hastily put together version of the print once hidden away by Svetlana Askoldov was screened after all. The director and those of his actors who were still alive were given a standing ovation at the conclusion of the festival. In early spring of 1988, the film was given a special homecoming in San Francisco, exactly twenty years after its scheduled screening there. *Commissar* became a success in film circles throughout the West. Today it travels all over the world as a symbol of Russian resistance against anti-Semitism, even as dark elements within the country are disseminating books like *Mein Kampf* and *The Protocols of the Elders of Zion*.

As we were becoming acquainted in 1988 in peaceable San Francisco — the *New York Times* had asked me to interview Askoldov — the director's intractability was reflected in everything he said. Askoldov was humorous, with a courtly manner, but the fact that his professional life had been curtailed for a generation filled him with a mixture of pride and sorrow. Tall and youthful-looking for his age — he was then fifty-seven — his receding hair still dark, he had the sorrowing eyes of Baptiste in *Children of Paradise*. In the course of a single conversation he could be in turn depressed and exhilarated.

Askoldov, who leads a modest existence in Moscow without a car or a dacha, found it hard to believe that he had at last been allowed to travel to California. "When things were bad," he said, "we had a family joke. My wife and I remembered that in 1968 an invitation to present *Commissar* in San Francisco had been issued. We would say, 'To San Francisco! To San Francisco! One day we and *Commissar* will go together to San Francisco!' We longed for your city the way Chekhov's three sisters longed for Moscow." But in fact Askoldov is a passionate Muscovite with roots in the Moscow theatrical intelligentsia.

I asked him about his childhood. "Moscow has always been very good to me," Askoldov said. "I was the son of a Red commissar, a high-ranking army engineer who was shot in 1937. My mother, his wife, who was younger, a physician, was sent off to a labor camp. I was left alone — I was five. I walked out of our house in Kiev before the policemen could catch me and take me to an orphanage. With the help of kind neighbors I made my way to my grandmother's in Moscow."

His grandmother lived with her sister on what was then the edge of the city near the Novodevechy monastery. They were working-class women who took excellent care of him until his mother was released. "I still love that part of Moscow. My best friend there was the night watchman of the old Novodevechy cemetery — someday I'd like to make a film about him." Eventually Askoldov graduated from the Moscow Philological Institute ("That is of course why I don't speak English today," he says), and he then went on to graduate school in filmmaking. *Commissar* was shot in a small town southeast of Kiev, Kamenetz-Podelsky, which he suggests should be made into an historical monument, "it is still so uniquely beautiful, so haunting."

"When I set out to film the holocaust sequences of *Commissar*, it proved hard to find enough Jews in that area decimated by World War II to enact the scene. But a few were gathered from the neighboring *kolkhoses*, and I started to group them in the arcaded space where, in the film, Jews are herded to be exterminated. That was when, very slowly, a deep howl rose from the assembling crowd. It turned out that it was exactly in that spot that the Nazis had executed all the Jews of Kamenetz-Podelsky. After that the making of *Commissar* became a holy mission."

It is one which Askoldov feels is with him to this day. He told me that in the winter of 1988, shortly before his trip to California, he had taken his film to the provincial town of Tula, to be shown at a toolmaking factory. "It was one of the most moving evenings of my life," he said. "These working-class people who lead isolated, hard lives understood my film and the need for it now. They wept and wanted to know more about what had been done to the Jews. Suddenly in certain layers of our society there is this new, unexpected trust of the artist."

At a time when I had little hope of being allowed into the Soviet Union again, I was sad to say goodbye to Askoldov and his wife, a professor of American literature in Moscow. "Glasnost might bring us together again, and yet it is a very fragile flower," Askoldov said. "It has to be nurtured and cared for like a small, delicate plant." But now *Commissar* was being shown all over Moscow, and I was on my way to have dinner with its director at the Film-makers' Union Club in the heart of Moscow.

∽ 15 ∽
A Conversation with Oleg

I DECIDED TO TAKE the subway to the Arbat district
at the center of old Moscow and walk from there to
the Filmmakers' Union Club. Dima showed me on a
map how to find it. On my previous expedition there I had
gone with Anya by taxi. The geography of Moscow, once
familiar to me, was now disconcerting — so much of the
city had been rebuilt in the last twenty years. Since Oleg
also was on his way into town, we set forth together. The
late afternoon was pleasantly warm. We avoided busy Leninsky Prospect, strolling instead between residential blocks
built in the sixties. Before that, the entire area had been
covered with a thick birch wood planted in the aftermath
of the devastations of World War II.

Along our path flowering shrubs were in bloom in the
neighborhood courtyards, and the air was filled with the
smell of hawthorn. Camomile and cornflowers brightened
the tall grass that grew freely where lawns would have
been seeded thirty years before. The balconies above us
were filled with flapping laundry, and children and pigeons
were competing for space in the small playgrounds laid out
along the way. It looked like a working-class suburb of
Paris — a bit less tidy, perhaps, but quite cheerful in the

good weather. I was savoring the taste of early summer and the prospect of seeing Alexander Askoldov again, now that fresh possibilities were opening up for Russian filmmakers. But Oleg, usually full of amusing chatter, was quiet that afternoon. He is one of these brilliant young physicians who take pride in the exercise of their profession, whose vitality is undaunted by daily contact with death — he is a specialist in children's blood diseases.

After a while I asked Oleg what made him so thoughtful. Had it been especially grim at the hospital — had one of his favorite small patients taken a turn for the worse? In addition to the usual cases of leukemia, the pediatric hospital near us had received a contingent of young children injured in the earthquake in Armenia. Their arrival in Moscow, extensively covered on television, had caused Oleg and Dima to work extra shifts at the hospital.

Oleg seemed to have been waiting for my question. He stopped in the middle of the path and stared down at me. He is tall and broad-shouldered, with a round, cheerful face, but now he was glum. "I am going to speak for all of us in apartment 13," he started sternly. "I expect you realize that we like you. In some ways we regard you as an older sister, everyone's older sister, rather than an aunt. Nonetheless, I must say that we are shocked by some of your opinions — the time has come to say it."

Oleg went on to tell me that while misconceptions were common among visiting Westerners, with my background they had expected better of me. They were appalled at my innocent belief that things would soon improve in the Soviet Union, at my admiration for Mikhail Gorbachev. "You must understand that what you see daily on the TV screen is one more carefully rehearsed performance by the Communist Party. It may be otherwise in some Eastern European countries, but here in the Soviet Union democracy has no future. For one thing, the Party will simply not allow it. Moreover, we are too poor to afford it. The gap

between the governed and the governing is too great ever
to be bridged."

Oleg said he and his friends were proud of Andrey Sakharov, they worshiped him; but they didn't believe his
ideas could ever take hold. "You should see our hospital,
where children dying of leukemia caused by ecological neglect are brought in from all over the country! The misery
of the Soviet people is huge — we're no better off than a
Third World country." He offered to take me on a tour of
his hospital, the main pediatric hospital of the Russian republic, which by Soviet standards was a very good one.
"You'll see for yourself under what conditions we take
care of our patients. We have no equipment, no drugs,
no linens." He reminded me that the ruling class had its
own special institutions, including hospitals, and insisted
it would never give up its privileges. Even if the power of
the elite was officially curtailed, he maintained, it would
retain its enormous wealth. "In today's Russia, money is
all you need anyway," he said.

"The Communists own everything here," Oleg continued, "the land, the factories, the newspapers, the publishing houses, the schools, the churches, the police, the courts
of law, the banks. The people have nothing in the world
but their meager salaries." Oleg listed recent environmen-
tal disasters, most probably irreversible, the lack of public
health in the countryside. "It offends us to be told by an
outsider to be patient — that all will be fine in the end. We
can accept idealistic delusions more easily in someone like
Dima's and Anya's father. He lives here, he has struggled
for thirty years, trying to improve things from the inside,
and anyway he is an incorrigible optimist."

But that I, coming from San Francisco and Paris, should
tell them about the social ills of the United States, they
found absurd. "Anya and Dima are too polite to say this,
but I know they think as I do. Especially Anya — Dima is
so taken up by his love of books that he has no time to be

angry." Oleg fell silent and looked down at me with an expression of profound disapproval.

I had known all along that my three young friends found me hopelessly naïve. Should they ever come to the United States, I wondered, would their thirst for all the things they didn't have, including the adequately equipped, "normal" hospital Oleg dreamed of, blind them to the injustices that have become acceptable in our society? As we started again toward the subway, I told Oleg I would very much like to visit his hospital. And I reminded him that today the predicaments of the Soviet Union and those of American society are interconnected, that the ecological problems especially must be considered as a whole. I told Oleg that I rejected the notion, advanced by Solzhenitsyn and others, that the Soviet people are too backward to aspire to an eventual democratic order. Historically, democracy slowly replaced tyranny and established itself in France and in other European countries. "You will find it hard to believe, but in my opinion the Soviet government has been successful in one area at least: the average citizen here is surprisingly well educated," I told him. "Better than his or her American counterpart."

"It is precisely such notions that we find so ridiculous," said Oleg somberly. "We hope you'll learn to look at things here as they are, and not start telling people abroad how well educated the Soviet masses are, and how democracy is winning here. How soon we'll all be working together for peace. I wonder what Alexander Askoldov might have to say about our future here. But then it may well be that he too is an idealist, like your cousin Aliosha. There are people like that in our parents' generation — sixties people. We, the children, try to see things as they are, even if they are distressing. I hope you don't mind my saying all this," added Oleg in a lighter tone.

We were coming out onto the open expanse where the Southwestern subway terminal is located — a vast, muddy plaza where electric trams and buses serving the whole huge neighborhood noisily converge, where crowds come together at all hours of the day and night for every kind of purpose — for commerce, for friendship, for sex. The sky was turning dark; a storm was gathering to the east. I understood Oleg's feelings and I was disheartened. I had to keep in mind that, for the young, Lenin's and Stalin's Terror is the stuff of legend. They remember only the stolid Brezhnev years, and only vaguely at that. They lack both the sense of relief and the hope that inspired my Russian contemporaries in the sixties. But then what would happen to Russia without the idealists — what if there were none among the younger generation?

Swarming around us were the traders, the pioneers of the promised land, the free marketeers. There were mustachioed young men selling electronic calculators and electric razors, and peasant women brandishing bouquets of fresh flowers and minute bunches of radishes and dill. An old man with a huge box of soap cakes was making his way among the throngs of people heading for the subway entrance. A family of gypsies had built an open fire in the middle of the plaza and were cooking *shashlik* on improvised skewers made of freshly cut privet twigs that still had green leaves at one end. A long line of customers was waiting for the grilled meat while another was winding around a makeshift wooden booth out of which a young, pink-cheeked Russian beauty in a low-cut blouse was selling *kvass,* the national drink made of fermented bread. As customers returned their glasses, she would swirl them for a second in a bucket of gray water and put them right back into use. The smoky smell of roasting meat was drifting down the subway stairs.

The ride into town was bumpy and crowded. Oleg got off at the Moscow University stop. I rode on, absorbed once again by the sound of Russian around me, by the faces of the riders and what it was they were reading with such intensity of purpose — I could make out *Crime and Punishment,* a science fiction novel, the last issue of *Ogonyek, Pravda,* and the ubiquitous *Sovietsky Sport* — that spring Muscovites were almost as fascinated with the widely reported Wimbledon championships in England as with the assemblies in the Kremlin.

There were such human riches here! I did not want to believe that most probably Oleg was right, that there was no long-term prospect in the Soviet Union for economic improvement or stability, that the liberals who had survived the Brezhnev years would not have the power to turn their impossible, lovable country around. With Sakharov at their head they would prevail: the alternatives were too ugly to contemplate.

The subway lurched into the open air, revealing a wide view of the Moscow River. Its narrow sand beaches were dotted with sunbathers. Across the way I could see Luzhniky Park, where political rallies now routinely convene. Aliosha had promised to take me there one day. "It's our Hyde Park," he had said. "Just as free. It's great fun; every sort of political group is making itself heard." But Aliosha was an optimist. Recalling Oleg's decidedly pessimistic turn of mind, I felt chastised as I made my way to the Filmmakers' Union Club on a dusty street corner not far from the Arbat subway station.

∾ 16 ∾

The Master and Margarita Revisited

I SPOTTED ASKOLDOV near the entrance to the club. He led me up at once to the fourth-floor dining room, where unexpectedly I saw familiar faces. It turned out that the writer Andrey Sinyavsky and his wife were in Moscow and had just arrived at the club, causing great excitement there — Sinyavsky's trial in Moscow at the end of the Khrushchev era had been a notorious, tragic episode in the crushing of intellectual freedom in the sixties.

As we stood in a mobbed hallway, Askoldov congratulated me on my return to Moscow. He hoped that our dinner that night would be a celebration. It was the beginning of a new era in my life: I could now travel freely between my two homelands, Russia and the United States. Askoldov, taller and more composed than anyone else around us, was as courteous as ever. Still, as we waited there I sensed that he, like Oleg, was tense that day. It took a long time for a blond female maitre d' to assign us a table, although Askoldov had made a reservation. The Sinyavskys' presence was heightening the always lively atmosphere of the club. Andrey Sinyavsky, after five harsh years in a Soviet labor camp, followed by fifteen years in exile in Paris, had come home — an ethnic Russian who has taken for himself the Jewish pseudonym Abram Tertz and is arguably the most interesting man of letters of his generation in Russia.

I had met Sinyavsky in the mid-seventies in Paris at the time of the publication in the West of his masterpiece about his labor camp years, *A Voice from the Choir.* Just then Solzhenitsyn, another recent arrival from the Soviet Union, was engaged in trying to discredit Sinyavsky, destroying his personal and artistic reputation and branding him a venal Russia-hater. In fact, Sinyavsky's virtuoso literary voice is deeply ironic, in the tradition of two Russian writers in the early part of the century, Vasily Rozanov and Alexey Remizov. Solzhenitsyn, unwilling to acknowledge this or perhaps unaware of it, elected to regard Sinyavsky's bitter, paradoxical indictments of the Soviet regime as attacks on Mother Russia.

Solzhenitsyn's hatred for Sinyavsky, rooted perhaps in some deep-seated feeling of rivalry, proved relentless. In the closed world of emigration before glasnost, it was especially wounding. Sinyavsky was powerless to defend himself. The attacks against him were taken up by lesser émigré writers eager to ingratiate themselves with a man who took the stance of a future political leader. Russian literary hacks can be masters at exploiting chauvinism disguised as love of Russia.

But times had changed and the Sinyavskys were visiting Moscow. Well-wishers walked across the room to greet them — I too went over briefly to congratulate them. Now someone was taking pictures; a video camera was purring away. It was wondrous and disconcerting. Sinyavsky looked lost. A small, graying man with a bushy beard, he is without a doubt the shyest, most unassuming literary celebrity I have ever met.

Our dinner got off to a difficult start. Askoldov had carefully ordered beforehand a sumptuous sturgeon dish that was to have been preceded by pickled herring and mushrooms — but the appetizers did not arrive until after dessert. Nonetheless, after a time we did settle down to dinner and a conversation. I asked Askoldov whether the success of *Commissar* had lifted the weight of disapproval which had settled upon him in Moscow some twenty years before.

"Well, not quite," Askoldov said. "I am still suspect in the eyes of the movie establishment, and *Commissar*'s subject matter is exasperating to some. Our country has failed to go through a period of open mourning for the victims of Stalin, and yet the years of terror were too long, the atrocities too monstrous and widespread, to be simply forgotten. They have corroded our soul. Unless we undergo some collective rite of repentance, our souls will continue to fester, yet I doubt whether our current leaders have the authority or the vision to exact such an act of contrition. To regain our honor, we Soviet citizens must wash in public, not our dirty linen, but our red flag stained by the abuses committed in the name of the Revolution."

Yes, I thought to myself, Oleg is right: Askoldov is a man of the sixties.

Commissar had taken Askoldov all over the globe to film festivals and ceremonial screenings. He told me that abroad and in the USSR as well, for a certain kind of public, his film had become a symbol of a Soviet Union capable of looking into its own soul and discovering that anti-Semitism is a very old and deadly Russian illness. "The time to recognize this is now, before it is too late, before all the Jews leave," he said. I asked the filmmaker about his professional prospects — whether they had improved since our last meeting. "I do have good news regarding a project I have dreamt of for many years," he said. "I may have West German backing for a film about the actor Salomon Mikhoels."

He explained that Mikhoels was the director of the famous Moscow Yiddish State Art Theater, a magnificent

man, erudite and kindly, a great actor, a man full of life —
in *Commissar,* the actor Roland Bykov's little dance upon
getting up in the morning is an homage to him. Even Stalin
was in awe of Mikhoels, who went to the United States in
1943 to raise money for the war effort — "money for
steel," it was called. He toured the United States playing
an unforgettable King Lear in Yiddish. Although interna-
tionally celebrated, after the war he was murdered on Stalin's orders while on a visit to Minsk in Byelorussia. He
was run over by a truck — a Lend Lease truck, an American Studebaker brought to Russia as part of the enormous
military assistance program he had helped generate. The
Moscow Jewish theater closed forever, and thus began Stalin's new wave of terror, which culminated in the so-called
Doctors' Plot. "I hope to be able to celebrate both a very
great artist and those people who helped win the war on
the Russian front," Askoldov added.

The club's dining room was growing more and more
crowded as we finished dinner. Dishes we no longer
wanted kept arriving. People I had known decades before
came up to our table to say hello. With an effort I would
recognize them; many looked as if they had been sprinkled
with snow. I found it hard to remember that I had changed
no less than they. The setting had remained the same, but
this was no longer the Moscow I had known. Suddenly I
felt very tired. "Yes, this is still the city of *The Master and
Margarita,*" Askoldov said, as if reading my mind. "Nor
am I sure that the Devil has left it altogether."

"Certainly he has," I said, hoping that my optimism
would not earn me yet another scolding that day, but Askoldov only smiled a weary smile.

We went out into the warm twilight. It was past ten
o'clock and the midsummer darkness had begun to settle
upon the city. For a moment Moscow felt very much as it
had twenty years before. The fading pearly light, the old
pink stucco houses were unchanged. I asked Askoldov to

walk me to the nearest subway stop. He looked horrified. "No, that's impossible. You can't go back alone to Leninsky Prospect on the subway at this hour." He set out to find me a taxi instead.

That spring I had taken taxis in Moscow on several occasions. I had discovered that city cabs, the kind with a meter inside and a green light outside signaling whether the cab is occupied, were now scarce, apparent victims of the emerging free market. Nowadays one had to stop a passing car — any car — whose driver might mercifully decide to take one wherever one needed to go. At that time such a ride cost just a little more than a metered one. The drivers were likely to be average Moscow car owners eager to make a little money on the side, or perhaps drivers using an official car in an unofficial manner. It was said that rich foreigners had been robbed in gypsy cabs, but that was only a rumor. In any case, I did not look like a rich foreigner in my plain navy blue polka dot dress.

But Askoldov, a man of principle, would not hear of my taking a gypsy cab. I suspect it was an affront to his sense of propriety. It was *ne normalno* for a visiting lady to ride in an automobile driven by an unlicensed driver. And of course it could be dangerous. We stood on a street corner; not a vehicle with a shining green light was in sight. Ordinary cars slowed down and signaled their willingness to take us on as passengers, but Askoldov waved them off. Though I tried not to show it, I was becoming annoyed. It would have been so easy to take the subway back to 144 Leninsky! All my life I had ridden subways and walked city streets at night, but this obstinate Muscovite would not let me have my way.

After we had stood for perhaps an hour on that street corner, a cab with a green light on finally stopped. Despite my protestations Askoldov paid the driver in advance and helped me in. I said goodbye to him as cordially as I could manage. At last I was on my way home after an evening worthy of Bulgakov — closing my eyes I saw the gypsies cooking *shashlik* on leafy skewers, and Sinyavsky's face, bewildered and yet full of happiness at being home again.

As we drove on, the city around us looked deserted and a bit forbidding — 144 Leninsky Prospect is a good twelve or fifteen kilometers from the center of town. And then all of a sudden I began to feel queasy — the sturgeon, maybe? As I tried to sit back and relax, the taxi was shaken by something resembling a loud coughing fit. The driver swore under his breath and pulled up to the curb. "It did it earlier today, perhaps I can fix it," he said in a dispirited voice, and got out of the car. Lifting the hood, he busied himself with the motor in the dark.

We were stranded along a particularly gloomy stretch of Leninsky Prospect, still a long way from the tall Hotel Tourist, which serves as a landmark for the turnoff at number 144. There was no telephone booth in sight, no lit doorway, only boarded-up stores stretching as far as one could see on both sides of the wide, empty roadway.

After what seemed an eternity, the driver spoke into my lowered window. "There's nothing I can do," he said, and got in the taxi and sat down at the wheel in silence. I too remained silent. I was stunned. What did one do under such circumstances in Moscow? I tried not to think about Askoldov because my thoughts about him were uncharitable. Now I was out of reach of the subway, and not up to a trek of perhaps ten kilometers.

As we sat there in desperation a small car pulled up behind us. A man got out of it and walked up to the driver's window of my taxi. In a gruff voice he demanded directions as to how to get out of the city — quickly. My driver explained that Leninsky leads straight out of town, and then as an afterthought he said, "It's right on your way, you must take this woman along. She's a tourist. She needs to get to the Hotel Tourist — that's only a couple of kilometers ahead along the Prospect." Before I knew it, the cab driver was easing me into the back of the small car and slamming the door shut. This was precisely the kind of situation from which Askoldov wished to protect me — riding in a car with two unknown, rough-looking men in the front seat — and lying next to me in the back seat, under an old blanket, an unidentified something. What could it possibly be? It did not stir. Only Bulgakov's Woland would have sent such a car for my rescue.

Much too fast the small car was tearing along Leninsky Prospect. I searched the dark sky to my right for the illuminated tower of the Hotel Tourist. Once in a while I looked sideways at that thing lying next to me under the blanket. I was trying hard not to imagine what it was. As for the Hotel Tourist tower, it remained invisible, erased from the Moscow skyline by Woland or one of his wicked friends out of *The Master and Margarita*.

Rudely, never turning around to face me, one or the other of the two men would ask me every couple of minutes, "Well, where in the hell is that hotel?" And I'd say, "It's not far, I'm sure of it." I realized that my voice, which to a Soviet ear is slightly accented, was adding to the discomfort of the two bushy-headed travelers so eager to get out of town. "The cab driver made an error," I tried to explain. "The Hotel Tourist is farther along the Prospect than he said." And then mercifully ahead of us on the horizon Woland had put back the black tower shining against the night sky. The car stopped abruptly; as soon as I jumped out, it took off at full speed and disappeared. I ran toward the highrise at 144 Leninsky, past the familiar, fragrant birch grove.

My two doctor friends were kind to me when I got to apartment 13. By then I was sick to my stomach. The doctors put me to bed, gave me pills, and made me medicinal tea, explaining that such discomforts as mine were common in the Soviet Union, usually caused by contaminated water. When I told them about my adventures and about that frightening unidentified object lying next to me in the back seat of the car, Oleg said, "Better not think about what that might have been. Only from now on please remember not to look at everything here through rosy glasses. For us in Moscow adventures like yours are perfectly usual, only they don't always end as well."

∽ 17 ∾

Daniel Andreyev

B EFORE THE WAR, before my family moved to the Ile
d'Oléron and I escaped Leonid Andreyev's brooding
presence, his younger son, Daniel, also made his presence felt in our small apartment in Le Plessis. No less enig-
matic than my grandfather, in his photograph my uncle
looked lighthearted, almost cheerful. He lived in Moscow,
and he and my father had been separated since childhood.
Despite this separation, which he considered catastrophic,
or perhaps because of it, my father felt a mystic connection
between himself and his younger brother.

My father regarded his inability to be with Daniel as a
personal failing. One of the reasons he wanted so much to
go back to Russia was to be reunited with him, and yet
time and again the Soviet authorities turned down his request for a Soviet passport and a visa. In 1906, when my
father was only three, Daniel's birth had caused the death
of his mother, Alexandra Mikhailovna, Leonid Andreyev's
first wife. Thinking of it now, I suppose that for my father
Daniel was the one remaining link with his mother, whose
absence had haunted his childhood.

Daniel was brought up by the Dobrovs, his mother's
family, while my father remained with his father and his

second wife. When he was only two, for all practical purposes Daniel had been adopted by his aunt and uncle Dobrov. *Dobry* means "good" in Russian, and the Dobrovs' name was well suited to the cultivated, liberal family that gave my uncle a normal childhood in Moscow, in the city where his mother had once lived. Daniel's upbringing had been in contrast with my father's tormented one in Finland, living with his brilliant but depressive father and a hostile stepmother. Daniel escaped: when he was a toddler his stepmother had attempted to drown him "accidentally." She had tied him to a sled and sent him down a frozen Finnish hillside into a water hole in the frozen river below. Daniel was saved at the last minute and taken away by his maternal grandmother. My father, the older child, remained behind.

In the thirties and forties, the Russians of Paris were completely cut off from those who had stayed in the Soviet Union. All we knew of my uncle was that Daniel earned his living as a graphic artist and that he had married a young Muscovite painter named Alla. To my father's despair the two or three postcards we received from Daniel during Stalin's interminable reign were, though loving, about one thing only: under no circumstance were we to come to Russia. Each time this was expressed obliquely. Once he wrote, "Vadim, I am looking forward to your return just as soon as Olga has graduated from the Sorbonne." I was still in high school at the time.

My uncle's postcards saved our lives. After the war my father's efforts to obtain Soviet citizenship succeeded. Only Daniel's warnings kept us in France. Few families who went back to Russia at that time survived. Upon their arrival they were arrested and sent to prison or to labor camps. Children were taken to orphanages, families destroyed. This had been the case with the Ugrimovs, close friends of ours.

In the photograph brought out of Moscow in secrecy by

Gorky's first wife, Yekaterina Pavlovna Peshkova, Daniel looked a great deal like my father, dark-eyed and elegant, with a strong, narrow face. I was enamored of my handsome uncle, yet my father could tell me little about him beyond the story of his last-minute rescue from the ice hole below my grandfather's house in Finland. Only once, through an anonymous, circuitous channel, did my father receive a present from his brother — a hunting knife made in Finland.

This knife, now in my possession, has a sturdy, straight steel blade and two circular insets of amber within its black bone handle which look like rings of blood. Coming as it did from another world, in place of a message, it would have had an emblematic meaning — but emblematic of what? We knew through Peshkova that my uncle was a pacifist, an admirer of Gandhi and Tolstoy. The Finnish knife could not carry a message of violence. The only object ever to reach us from Daniel, it was a riddle. Did it represent some power of a higher kind, like Excalibur? Unbeknownst to each other, in their separate lives Vadim and Daniel had both become Russian poets. Now, so many years later, I see the Finnish hunting knife as a symbol of the force of poetry in a world muffled by separations and fear.

In 1957, four years after Stalin died, my father was allowed to visit Russia. After more than forty years he had a reunion with Daniel which intensified his sense of kinship with his brother. Afterward my father recounted that when he opened the door to the room where the now mortally ill Daniel lay, he had the overpowering sensation of seeing himself across the room. The reunion of the two brother-poets was an important event for both, a triumph over the evil that had all but destroyed their country, isolating them from each other throughout their lifetimes.

Daniel's fate turned out to have been tragic beyond the wildest imaginings of those who had lived in the relative safety of emigration. His ordeals turned my uncle from a writer with a traditional Russian Orthodox sensibility into a poet-visionary in the tradition of William Blake or St. John of the Cross. World War II was the first trial for the pacifist Daniel, though he was allowed to serve in it primarily as an orderly, burying the dead and taking care of the wounded. He later said to my father, "Anyone who returns from war a normal man is thereby abnormal." The poems he wrote about the war, a subject that inspired his elders Akhmatova and Pasternak with some of their finest achievements, are solemn and stark. Here is a fragment about the lifting of the siege of Leningrad, in which Daniel participated. He had reached the expiring city by way of the ice road across Lake Ladoga:

Night winds! Dark mountain skies
Over the snowy grave of Leningrad,
You were our trial and our prize.

Today I treasure like a relic
What I remember of that night
When stubbornly I marched
Together with the Russian people
Somber then, covered to its eyes with steel.

From the soft hills of Moscow,
The steppes of Saratov
Where waves of rye shine in the summer,
From the northern taiga where ancient
Cedars howl deeply in the wind,

All races welded into one
For a bitter military deed
— One long live rope on the black ice.

Daniel had a nervous breakdown when he returned to Moscow. He had inherited his father's ambivalence about the morality of war; he was a pacifist, but he also believed in the survival of Russia. Though he loathed the Soviet

Olga Andreyev Carlisle

government, he wanted his country to win in World War
II. Leonid Andreyev, also a pacifist, had actively supported
Russia's fighting against the Germans in World War I. Yet
to this day his novella *The Red Laugh,* written in the aftermath of the Russo-Japanese war — and which Gorky had
dismissed as too abstract — stands as one of the most eloquent indictments of modern warfare in Russian literature.
When I visited Pasternak in 1960 he spoke with reverence
of *The Red Laugh:* "Subject and form come together with
a grandeur that transcends mere literature. It's a huge,
awesome work."

Daniel's next trial came in 1947, most probably a con-
sequence of the messages sent to him over the years by my
father through friends returning to the Soviet Union after
the war. These, intercepted, might well have served as a
pretext for his arrest. We do not know for sure. In any case
Daniel was already suspect; he was known to be working
on a novel about Moscow intellectuals after the Revolution. One evening he gave a reading out of *Voyagers of the
Night* to a group of friends, and one of them denounced
him to the authorities. The writer and everyone who attended the reading, about twenty people in all, were arrested, including Daniel's wife, Alla. They were accused of
taking part in a plot to kill Stalin masterminded from Paris
by my father.

The prisoners were interrogated and tortured for more
than a year. No one was shot; in a show of humanitarian
make-believe the death penalty was officially outlawed in
the Soviet Union after the war. Daniel was sentenced to
twenty-five years in prison and Alla to twenty-five years in
labor camp, while the circle of people implicated in the
imaginary plot against Stalin continued to grow. *Voyagers
of the Night* was lost forever to the KGB, which destroyed
the one existing copy of the novel.

Daniel's fate took a fantastic turn after his arrest. Incar-
cerated for almost ten years in the sinister prison in the

medieval town of Vladimir, my uncle escaped from it — by becoming a mystic poet. Because of his meek, almost saintly disposition, even his jailers helped him at times, allowing him to keep the scraps of paper on which he wrote his poems. One of these, composed earlier, in 1937, is now well known in Russia. It was prophetic of what would be Daniel's earthly as well as his spiritual road — there is no better way to explain how the Russian psyche survived decades of terror. Its last line is famous:

No one will find you on your soul's high sea.

After Stalin's death, Alla and Daniel were released — she in 1956, he in 1957. While still in prison my uncle suffered a heart attack. He had been made to walk up stairs right afterward — up the stone stairs of the Vladimir prison — and this had been his death warrant. In freedom he lived on for only a year and a half. Yet with his wife's help he was able to transcribe almost eight hundred pages of his works, whole cycles of poems as well as a monumental, elaborate philosophical treatise, a cosmology he called *The Rose of the World*. His *Iron Mystery,* inspired by the medieval European mystery plays, is a masterful polyphonic creation. It demonstrates Daniel's exceptional poetic versatility: this is a symbolist's conception of the universe, in which harmony is finally established after a series of cosmic upheavals.

My father met with Daniel twice, once in 1957 and once just before his death in 1959. By January 1960, when I went to Moscow for the first time, Danya, as he was known in our family, had died. But I formed a friendship with his widow, my aunt Alla, my senior by some fifteen years, who has taken on the preservation of my uncle's literary and philosophical legacy as her mission in life. In time she too became one of Russia's exemplary widows, women like Nadezhda Mandelstam, Elena Bulgakovna, and Elena Bonner — powerful personalities whose chosen

Olga Andreyev Carlisle

missions of preserving their husbands' legacies have endowed them with considerable power in their community.

My aunt's work on behalf of Daniel Andreyev's art, her fierce belief in his poetic genius, made up for an unpalatable fact. As she herself said in a newspaper interview recently, during her year-long interrogations interspersed with torments such as systematic denial of sleep, Alla was manipulated into making statements that were used to trap her and her co-defendants.

After Daniel's release in 1957, when Alla journeyed to Vladimir to pick up his belongings — they were too heavy for him to carry after his heart attack — the prison director delivered them to her in a bag that he did not open. In addition to a prisoner's meager possessions, Daniel's bag contained eleven notebooks, a sizable portion of my uncle's poetic and philosophical works. Alla has reason to believe that a benevolent power has elected her to be the guardian of her husband's oeuvre.

Forbidden in the Soviet Union until glasnost, Daniel's writings have turned him posthumously, in certain circles, into a revered literary figure. An aura of martyrdom is attached to his name. In the fifties and sixties his works' very existence had to be kept secret, yet from that time on, the tale of his suffering at the hands of the Soviet government and the few poems that did circulate in Moscow gave him a small but ardent following. His cosmology, esoteric and personal as it is, proved particularly seductive for Soviet readers yearning for religious mysteries after seventy years of enforced atheism.

In prison Daniel, a fine classical poet, became a visionary as well, who like Dante traveled back and forth through the circles of heaven and hell. Like Dante, Daniel felt he was guided on some of his journeys by a mentor in whose company he traversed realms of darkness as well as realms of enlightenment. Drawing on an encyclopedic knowledge of Russian literature and history, on the *Divine*

Comedy, and on the Hindu Veda, Daniel created his own breathtaking philosophical construction. For those like myself who lack a mystical turn of mind, it is one that is difficult to embrace, but in Russia right now mysticism, as well as pseudo-mysticism of one sort or another, is extremely fashionable. There Daniel Andreyev is a figure of legend. For intellectuals interested in radical psychological mutations, Daniel Andreyev the visionary is a master far more revolutionary than his celebrated father. By the time I reached the Soviet Union in 1989, Daniel was becoming a celebrity in a country where poetry was still supremely important to millions of readers, although inevitably the lifting of censorship was removing some of its former urgency as a medium of national consciousness.

But the metaphysical urgency still exists. In the last couple of years, both in Petersburg and in Moscow, poems written by young people are of great interest to readers. Some of these poems, set in traditional Russian poetic forms, are striking indeed, most probably created in altered states of consciousness. Modernism, with its forward thrust, its celebration of the future, is now outdated. Today, Russian poetry is in good part a means to recover the past. Any link with it seems precious: one young woman in Moscow, upon learning that I was a niece of Daniel Andreyev, came close to fainting. Pasternak, Mandelstam, Akhmatova continue to be read with passion because they reveal what happened decades ago as a result of the Revolution. As to the future, readers turn to cryptic texts such as those of Daniel Andreyev to try to divine it.

For our family, the first order of business back in the sixties was to make sure that Daniel's works would be preserved despite the vigilance of the KGB, more determined than ever to destroy free thinking and free art in the Soviet Union. Little by little, my parents, my brother, and I smuggled copies of Daniel's manuscripts out into the West. We admired Daniel's poems and we shared them with other lovers of Russian poetry. We pondered his visions, though some of them, mixing Russian history and Hinduism, baffled us — they are not unlike a version of Peter Brooks's *The Mahabharata,* composed by a Russian mystic. It seemed problematic to try to publish Daniel in the West; depending on the time of their creation, his works seemed either too classical or too obscure to be rendered successfully into another language, not to mention the fact that in those years their dissemination would have been dangerous for his widow.

In the late seventies my brother and I gave copies of Daniel's papers to the Russian Archive at the University of Leeds in England, to whom our parents had already donated their share of Leonid Andreyev's literary legacy. This archive, which includes my father's papers, was originally intended for the Pushkin House in Leningrad. Sending it beyond the Iron Curtain, however, would not have been wise during the Brezhnev era, when the lifting of censorship in the Soviet Union seemed an improbable dream. Eventually Alla endorsed our decision and even sent to the Russian archives at Leeds some of the originals of Daniel's prison writings. Little by little my uncle is beginning to be recognized in the West. In December 1992 the American Association of Teachers of Slavic and East European Languages is devoting a series of lectures to his works.

On my way to Moscow, I had a poetic encounter with my uncle Daniel during a stopover in Paris. In the company of a French friend interested in medieval art I had gone to Editeurs Réunis, a bookstore on Rue de la Montagne-Sainte-Geneviève which specializes in Russian books. The hotel where my father and my uncle Volodia lived just before they married the Chernov sisters is around the corner, but that day I was not looking for family lore. I wanted to buy the Russian text of one of Solzhenitsyn's volumes about the Russian Revolution, *August 1914,* while my companion leafed through stacks of albums about Russian medieval cities — Yaroslavl, Suzdal, Vladimir.

As we were leaving the store I noticed high on a shelf a brooding, beautiful man's face on the cover of a volume propped upright. I thought to myself, "How strange, a photograph of Baudelaire I have never seen." We stepped outside, but on an impulse I went back in. I wanted to look again at that man's face. Standing on tiptoe, I reached for the volume and looked closely at its cover. It was oddly familiar. When I opened the book I saw it was a selection of Daniel's poems in Russian published in Moscow some weeks before. Except for a slim pamphlet issued in Moscow in the sixties, it was Daniel's first book of poems to come out anywhere. On its cover was a photograph of him dating back to the late thirties which I had not seen before.

~ 18 ~

My Aunt Alla

THAT SPRING I SAW my aunt Alla in Moscow even before I met with her in person. One evening in apartment 13 we turned the television set on and there she was, quite unexpectedly, the star of *Fifth Wheel,* a popular program out of Leningrad. The weekly show, Dima said, seeks to acquaint the Russian public with long suppressed aspects of its history. It is usually taped against the backdrop of the city, with its waterway and bridges and sunsets. That day it focused on Alla telling Daniel's story and her reciting some of his poems afterward. As a stage presence, my aunt combined theatrical flair with respect for the inner music of her husband's poetry. The show matched the elegance of the portrait of Daniel I had seen in Paris. It was hard to believe that when I was last in the Soviet Union, his was a forbidden, forgotten poetic voice there.

Now in her seventies, Alla was still very good-looking. Her Nordic, Garbo-like face — she is of Estonian descent — was barely marked by a few fine wrinkles. On *Fifth Wheel* the verse and the reader seemed equally inspired, and Dima and Anya, home that evening, were as impressed as I. I was surprised to hear Dima say at the end of the show, "I am relieved that Alla Alexandrovna does not express her political convictions in public. Your uncle's poetry deserves to stand on its own merit."

I remembered then what Aliosha had said about Alla's being under the spell of some new version of the "Russian Idea." When I questioned Dima about my aunt's convictions, however, he was vague. "I have the impression that Alla Alexandrovna has some strange notions about what the future of this country should be. But it may be a false impression based on hearsay. Although we are acquainted, I haven't called on your aunt for a long time." Dima said no more about Alla's politics, and I did not press him. Seeing Alla on screen, hearing my uncle's verse read eloquently for an audience of millions — here was a vindication that I wanted to savor without second thoughts.

The next day I was able to reach my aunt on the telephone and congratulate her. Alla said that it was the first time that Daniel's verse had been presented to a national audience in the Soviet Union. A selection of it would soon be available, part of a series of once forbidden verse called *Phoenix*. It was an advance copy of that book which I had seen in Paris. Ever since the beginning of glasnost Alla had worked tirelessly to bring about this publication. Now she hoped to see *The Rose of the World* and *Iron Mystery* published as well. Over the phone Alla sounded friendly, and I accepted her invitation for dinner that evening, a Sunday. A friend from the French community in Moscow would be there as well, Alla said. She was certain I'd like her.

My niece Anya offered to walk me to Alla's. I had never been there before; for years Alla had lived in a communal apartment in the center of town, in rooms inherited from her parents. However, in the seventies, with a new husband now deceased, she was able to buy into a cooperative apartment house, located on an ancient square off Tverskaya close to the Kremlin on the Manege side, which was being built by a group of artists. Anya and I took a roundabout way. We walked along the old lanes of Moscow which had been home in the twenties and thirties to my uncle Daniel and to Mikhail Bulgakov — the crooked lanes of Moscow which I had especially liked to explore in the sixties.

As we walked I thought of my night outing with Solzhenitsyn in 1967, and his request to help him publish *The First Circle* in the West. I told Anya how this plea was made at the exact moment when we had come upon an old Moscow house, a favorite on my city wanderings, reduced to a heap of pink rubble for the sake of modernizing Moscow. I remembered having been struck by Solzhenitsyn's barely repressed annoyance at my dismay before this act of destruction. It was no business of mine to mourn Russian losses.

I tried to tell my niece what it had been like to visit Moscow in those years, viewed by many as an immensely privileged intruder, useful at times, but also potentially disruptive and even dangerous. But now someone like me could feel like a Russian with a different destiny, no longer a threat or a tool. The feeling of acceptance, so spontaneous around apartment 13, I now found wherever I went. In my experience the average Muscovite was eager to become acquainted with a Russian from abroad.

Though many more old Moscow houses have been razed since my walk with Solzhenitsyn, in that part of town wedged between Manege Square and Tverskaya, a few are preserved, stylish rococo townhouses of pale pink stucco or white stone. Here, Anya said, the poet Tyutchev had lived, and Pushkin had stayed nearby during a Moscow visit. The Hertzen family mansion is close by, where one of the world's first schools of creative writing, the Literary Institute founded by Gorky, was established. Before that, following the October coup d'état, it had served as a residence for writers left homeless by the turmoil, including Mandelstam and Chukovsky.

These old mansions, now used for the most part to house city services of one sort or another, are rundown, the outlines of their gardens all but erased, but they are still standing. Anya assured me that they are now protected by law. As we came up to my aunt's apartment house, which faces a newly restored eighteenth-century church, I felt a pang of regret. Built of yellow brick like a straight wall seven stories high, it was put there during the Brezhnev era in defiance of the esthetics of that venerable neighborhood. But then, how could one criticize Muscovites deprived of housing for decades for moving into beautifully located, functional dwellings when at last the opportunity presented itself? I had to be thankful that my elderly aunt now had a suitable home in the heart of Moscow. And clearly the view from her seventh-floor flat would be stunning.

Anya declined to come up to my aunt's. "Not today. I'm running late, I have tickets for the Bolshoi — a Prokofiev opera never before performed in the USSR," she said. "But do give Alla Alexandrovna my regards; I like the way she reads your uncle's poems. Perhaps I could visit her with you one day? I'd love to hear more of Daniel's verse." And she was gone, leaving me by the elevator in a dark, derelict-looking hallway. However, seconds later, as the door to my aunt's apartment opened, I was dazed by a burst of red sunlight. Out of my aunt's wide windows one could see a huge sun setting beyond the Kremlin, with the five gilded cupolas of the Dormition at the center of the cityscape. I had never before seen so much of the Kremlin at such close range.

I was as dazzled by the sight of my aunt as I was by the view out of her windows. Alla's youthfulness was astonishing; she had hardly changed at all in twenty-two years, though her hair was now silvery and cropped short. It is said that people subjected to lengthy fasting retain exceptional youthfulness if they survive, and this was evidently the case with Alla. To meet her again, a woman still in her prime who was the mistress of a home with a view of Kremlin cupolas and watchtowers, was something I had never dreamed would happen. I remember thinking that our reunion had a touch of *The Master and Margarita* to it. It seemed to me that just then, should Alla and I have stepped out onto her kitchen balcony open to the sky and to the churches of the Kremlin, we might both take flight, soaring above Moscow as Margarita did when she set out for the demonic ball at the end of the novel.

Alla settled me on a narrow yet comfortable couch by the oval table in her kitchen. She propped me up with pillows and served tea with an array of delectable Easter delicacies, although that holiday was long past. Outside, the Kremlin was now lit up against the pale evening sky, creating a prodigious backdrop for our tea party. Ever since our first meetings years before, Alla was always affectionate toward my entire family. Her caring was still evident: she inquired about my brother, my husband and our son, and my aunt Natasha, my mother's twin, who had visited Moscow in the sixties.

Yet I knew then that the Alla with whom I had just been reunited was a different woman from the one I had once known. There was an assertiveness, an imperious edge to her manner now which I could well understand, knowing as I did about her life and about what she had done to help bring about my uncle's spectacular moral and literary rehabilitation. My aunt was telling me that in the last couple of years she was invited all over the Soviet Union to give readings of her husband's poems. For these she had worked out a program similar to the one broadcast on *Fifth Wheel*, a mélange of reminiscences and verse intermingled with a few explanations — highly simplified, to be sure — of Daniel's philosophical ideas.

Wherever she went, Alla said, whether to Minsk or to Kiev or to the various newly established Moscow literary clubs, she was received in triumph. Her readings were mobbed by poetry lovers awaiting the now imminent publication of Daniel's books. The philosophical works, complex as they are, were no less in demand than the earlier, classical poems. She had been asked to perform the following Sunday in Abramtsevo at the Aksakov estate some thirty kilometers out of Moscow, in one of the shrines of Russian culture — would I come with her? Years before, she had taken my parents on a memorable pilgrimage there. The doorbell rang as Alla was reminiscing about my parents, who had helped her out in the early sixties, when my father's books were published in Moscow and he had some money available to him there. She mentioned how much it had meant to Danya to meet with his brother before his death. He too had felt a mystic connection between them all his life.

The newcomer who joined us at the table for a fresh round of hot black tea was a diminutive, dark-haired French woman of about fifty, well dressed and well spoken. She was introduced by my aunt as a recent friend who worked in the French Foreign Service in Moscow. For a while we chatted about Paris and the recent Gauguin show there and how it compared with the smaller one at the Museum of Fine Arts in Moscow.

I had ahead of me a long subway ride back to Leninsky Prospect, and soon I was ready to leave. As I got up to go, absent-mindedly, having forgotten Dima's reference to my aunt's politics and the earlier comment of Aliosha's, I asked her whether she, like the other Muscovites I knew, was watching the proceedings in the Kremlin.

After a brief silence, looking past me at the illuminated Kremlin outside, my aunt said in an intense voice, "As one who has lived in this country all my life, I know for certain that democracy is unsuited to Russia. What we have there day after day" — she pointed to the roof of the Palace of Congresses next to the cupolas of the Dormition — "is an assembly of clowns mocking Russia, working to destroy her."

Unexpectedly the French woman chimed in, "Yes, that is what those men are — an assembly of clowns."

"But don't you even trust Dr. Sakharov?" I asked, wishing I had remembered Aliosha's and Dima's warnings, yet certain that Sakharov's name would help establish between us some ground for agreement. I was wrong.

"Sakharov may well be the best of the lot," said my aunt, "but we mustn't forget that it was he who designed the Soviet H-bomb in the late forties. He was for Stalin. I have it on good authority that he is working right now on establishing more nuclear installations throughout the Soviet Union, reactors similar to the one that blew up in Chernobyl."

The dark-haired French woman spoke again. "I can only report on what I have seen with my own eyes, and I can assure you that, in France, it was Communist Party members who supported Sakharov after he ran into trouble here. I remember them marching in the streets, organizing noisy meetings in his defense. He was just another Communist caught up in a family quarrel among those who are trying to subvert religion and decency throughout the world."

Using the subway journey ahead of me as an excuse, I said goodbye to my aunt and her guest. Alla embraced me and renewed her invitation to come with her to Abramtsevo the following Sunday along with a small group of admirers of Daniel's poetry. I accepted. I was anxious to find out more about the new Alla and her friends.

∾ 19 ∾
Slavophiles Old and New

I N PEREDELKINO IN THE EARLY 1930S, at Maxim
Gorky's suggestion, the Soviet Writers' Union turned
what had once been the Samarin estate into a rest home
for its members. Yuri Samarin was one of the Slavophiles
who helped shape the sensibilities of the Russian intelligentsia in the early part of the last century. Samarin's
house is gone now, but the old park that surrounded it still
stands. Pasternak, a neighbor, loved its linden trees as he
loved the local church, the "house whose beauty was marvel once":

> Cold and dark behind the fence,
> A house whose beauty was marvel once
> stands. The park is old:
> Napoleon camped here.
> Samarin the Slavophile
> Lived here and died.

Pasternak was proud of the Slavophile legacy in Peredelkino. Though his own roots were Jewish and urban, in
the second half of his life especially he came to embrace
some of the Slavophile ideals. However, neither his love of
the Russian countryside nor his Russian Orthodox piety

ever caused him to repudiate the glories of Western culture. Like his friend Anna Akhmatova, a Dante scholar with, according to Mandelstam, "the purest Russian voice," he was a quintessential Russian intellectual, poised between native and Western cultures, drawing on both for his art. Such a harmonious view of the world is rare among Russians. More often than not they see themselves as belonging to one camp or another, either Westernizers or Slavophiles, ready to do battle for their beliefs.

When it was first formulated, Slavophilism was but one expression of the Romantic sentiment sweeping through Europe in the first part of the nineteenth century. The Slavophiles, who had as a rule the benefit of excellent, European-oriented educations, were in love with their country, seeking her ancient roots. Coming from the well-to-do gentry, unimpressed by the Germanic ways of the court at St. Petersburg, they encouraged their compatriots to study their medieval past and use it as a foundation for establishing Russian values suited both to their idiosyncratic homeland and to the new age.

The Slavophiles created a "Russian style" for their country, a fresh sensibility drawing on ancient Slavic folklore, on patriarchal customs, on the lyrical Russian landscape. They were militantly Christian. Because the Russian peasants had been treated harshly by monarchs of foreign origin for so long, the Slavophiles wished to heal and rehabilitate them as Russians proud of their culture. They were concerned about the infringements of the Ottoman Empire upon the Slavic nationalities in the Caucasus and the Balkans. They were idealists, and yet they made enormous, lasting contributions to Russian culture. There would be no Russian opera and little Russian nineteenth-century painting without Slavophile philanthropists.

The Slavophiles' intellectual adversaries, known as Westernizers, believed that Russia had much to learn from Europe, especially in matters of government and the arts.

That Westernizer par excellence, Peter the Great, had modernized the country forcibly, building for himself a capital with an administration and a military on the European model. He created an open schism between old and new, a schism perpetuated to some degree to this day by the cultural rivalry between Moscow and St. Petersburg.

Though they themselves were not members of the Slavophile community, both Dostoyevsky and Tolstoy, who deplored the effects of the Industrial Revolution on Russian society, were, each in his way, closer to the Slavophiles than to the Westernizers. One was shaped by his revulsion before nineteenth-century urban misery, the other by his concern about the disintegration of the countryside. Both writers deplored the godlessness and mercantilism which Western Europe had brought to the world. Each in his own way wanted to believe that the Russian national ethos carried within itself the seeds of a new spiritual and earthly kingdom — that Russia could one day become the incarnation on earth of the loftiest Christian ideals.

Paradoxically, that most Russian of Russian writers, the author of *A Sportsman's Sketches,* Ivan Turgenev, was often dismissed by his contemporaries as frivolous, a Westernizer, no doubt precisely because he had such penetrating insights into the conflicts between Western and indigenous values within the Russian psyche. Turgenev, a wealthy landowner from central Russia, spent many years in Europe. His works and the story of his life both offer convincing studies of the contradictory impulses that tore at Russian society in his day and still do in ours, caught as it has been between the urge to emulate the West and its yearning for a defunct, idealized Russia.

Currently, right-wing political figures often indulge in crude mimicking of Slavophile postures, celebrating Russians' morals and sensitivity as against Westerners' amorality and crudeness. Russian chauvinists, often linked to the KGB, masquerade as patriots, but upon investigation some turn out to be opportunists or zealots. Many among them are former Communist Party leaders. Their claim of kinship with the nineteenth-century Slavophiles is unfounded. The original Slavophiles were not political reactionaries; they believed in the necessity of swift liberal reforms for Russia.

But in 1989 such patriots were seldom in evidence in Moscow. The public mood was distinctly Westernizing. Russians rejoiced in their newly established contacts with the West. Only Dima kept telling me about the Pamyat Society, made up of "Soviet fascists." Its members wore either outlandish pre-Revolutionary costumes or paramilitary garb. They could sometimes be seen in groups at public gatherings where they made a spectacle of themselves, taunting demonstrators and shouting anti-Jewish slogans; I was not to go home without having a glimpse of them. Though they were oddly provocative, the authorities left them alone. But I did not pay much attention to Dima's report; I was delighting in the peaceable evenings in apartment 13 and my visits to Peredelkino in Anya's company.

I was full of lighthearted thoughts on the Sunday morning when I set off for Abramtsevo in the company of my aunt Alla and three of her young friends who were particularly fond of Daniel's poetry. The sun was shining and Pasternak's lines about Samarin's park in Peredelkino sang in my memory. Abramtsevo, like Peredelkino, was once a Slavophile stronghold: in the first half of the nineteenth century it was the summer retreat of a remarkable literary clan, the Aksakovs. The father, Sergey Timofeevich Aksakov (1791–1859), one of Russia's earliest and most accomplished realistic writers, was a generous, much-loved man, an acquaintance of Pushkin, and the author of several lovely, unhurried books about his family's past and the pleasures of life in the country. His two sons, Constantin and Ivan, were also writers and committed Slavophiles.

Sergey Timofeevich is especially important to the history of Russian letters because he was a close friend and supporter of Gogol, who visited frequently in Abramtsevo. When toward the end of his life the author of *Dead Souls* published his astonishing, despicable *Fragments of Letters to Friends,* advocating absolute subservience to church and tzar, this publication was experienced by Sergey Timofeevich as a personal tragedy. The Aksakov circle, which worshiped Gogol as the greatest Russian literary artist since Pushkin, was appalled by the book. So were many of Gogol's readers, led by the liberal critic Belinsky. Sergey Timofeevich criticized Gogol hotly and openly, but the friendship survived. Gogol continued to visit Abramtsevo until his death in 1852, leaving its inhabitants with a bouquet of charming memories of his kindness, his practical jokes, and his proficiency as a pasta cook.

Despite Gogol's religious obsession in his later years, the Slavophiles never ceased to claim him as their own. A stone of Black Sea granite brought by horse cart from the south by one of Aksakov's sons served as Gogol's tombstone. In the 1930s, discarded by the Soviet authorities, it would be placed by Bulgakov's widow on the grave of the author of *The Master and Margarita.* It is a strange whim of history that the two greatest Russian satirical geniuses should share the same tombstone.

But the Aksakovs' years in Abramtsevo were only the first of a double Slavophile legacy linked to that estate. In 1870, some twenty years after Sergey Timofeevich's death, the estate was purchased by a Moscow industrialist, one of the great art patrons of the age. Sava Mamontov was a railroad tycoon who in his youth had wanted to be a professional singer. With great exuberance he turned Abramtsevo into one of the most influential art centers in Russia. He was the first to organize and underwrite what would become *Russian* opera and *Russian* decorative arts — Mamontov loved Russianness with a passion. As a collector he favored Russian folk objects and the more talented Moscow painters of that period, notably Valentin Serov and Mikhail Vrubel. A backer of Stanislavsky and of the operatic and theatrical genius Fyodor Chaliapin, Mamontov, artistic himself, had a very complex, overbearing personality. He was a robber baron with secret revolutionary sympathies who had a gift for friendship and for bringing artists together.

The Russian theater arts, first launched by Mamontov in Moscow in 1885, achieved worldwide recognition twenty years later, with the triumph in Paris of Stravinsky's music and of Diaghilev's Ballets Russes. As for Mamontov, he was a Muscovite foremost, proud of his colorful, old-fashioned native city, though it was Italy that had first awakened his and his wife's passion for the arts. Mamontov and his peers Tretyakov, Morozov, and Schukin were second- or even third-generation Slavophiles, determined to turn Moscow — long overshadowed by imperial St. Petersburg — into the cultural heart of Russia. The families who had been the initiators and immediate beneficiaries of the Industrial Revolution in Russia were now intent on making up for the ravages industrialization was inflicting on the splendors of traditional Russia. And they acted on a grand scale: *mamont* means mammoth in Russian.

Henry James or perhaps Dickens could have done novelistic justice to Mamontov's Victorian grandeur and to his downfall; Turgenev, who had met him in Europe and later visited Abramtsevo, would have been too diffident to deal with such a spectacular story. Mamontov's bankruptcy, his trial and final years in Abramtsevo, where his artist friends stood by him until his death, have the mark of what Pasternak called the fabulous nineteen-hundreds, "those years that are now receding in our memory and yet loom in the mind like great mountains seen in the distance."

The list of those who lived and worked in the peace of

Abramtsevo under the tutelage first of the Aksakovs and then of the Mamontovs reads like a *Who's Who* of Russian nineteenth-century art. From the beginning of their tenure at Abramtsevo, Sava Mamontov and his wife, Elizaveta, lived up to the Aksakovs' accomplishments there. They were as compassionate toward the peasants who surrounded them and served them, as loving of their artist friends, as involved in good works as the Aksakovs had once been. After the Revolution, Mamontov turned his estate into a museum. In the 1960s it was closed for repairs; I remember being taken there by the painter Eric Bulatov one gray winter afternoon only to find it boarded up, buried in snow. Now I was as eager to see it at last as I was to hear Daniel's poems read. Like my first day in Peredelkino, this visit would be a Russian midsummer celebration. Once the Feast of St. John had been a great holiday in Russia, a celebration of the summer solstice, with rituals that went back to the pagan Slavs.

◆ 20 ◆

A Slavophile Shrine

W E RODE TO ABRAMTSEVO on an electric com-
muter train through woods and meadows so vi-
brant, so fresh that they would have turned the
staunchest Westernizer into a Russian romantic. It was in-
effably sweet — the tall grass and the apple trees in bloom,
the small wooden houses with their carved shutters. I
thought of "The Thief," one of my grandfather's short stories, which Henry and I had translated into English not
long before. It contains an evocation of the rapture of escaping the city by train in early summertime: "It was early
June; everything, all the way to the distant, unmoving
stretches of woodland, was young and strong and green.
The grass was green, everything was so wrapped up in itself, so deeply immersed in silent, creative meditation that
if the grass and the trees had been human, their faces
would have been turned to the earth . . ."

But our party of five was not in a contemplative mood.
There was a lively debate about Anna Akhmatova going
on between my aunt Alla, two bearded young men, and
Ludmila, a young woman in her mid-thirties whom Alla
had introduced as her goddaughter. She and my aunt were
evidently very close: Ludmila was living with her a good

part of the time, my aunt said. Small, intense, very quick, Ludmila made me uneasy from the start. I had the feeling that she was taking advantage of my aunt in ways that I could not fully grasp, but it was only an impression. Alla told me that Ludmila was an idealistic young woman enamored of my uncle's writings and determined to serve them in a Russia free of censorship.

As for the men in our party, in their early forties, wearing dark clothes and bushy beards, they looked solemn, somewhat ecclesiastical, like church elders who had stepped down from some ancient church fresco. They were assisting my aunt with her reading. One, with a long beard and a forbidding manner, was a specialist of Daniel's philosophical ideas. The other was friendlier. He was a poet, and on this trip he was helping Alla carry her props, the blown-up photographs with which she complements her lectures.

The discussion was about the forthcoming celebrations scheduled to commemorate Akhmatova's centenary. Would there be a monument to her built in Petersburg one day? Did she deserve one? In young Ludmila's view the festivities would not be giving the poet Nikolai Gumilev, Akhmatova's first husband, his due. The rediscovery in Russia of Gumilev, shot in 1921 as a counter-Revolutionary, was one of the most talked-about literary events of that spring. In our family, as in Nadezhda Mandelstam's circle, he had been regarded as an elegant poet, a craftsman, a Russian Parnassian with a passion for exoticism and pageantry; the notion that as an artist he might be equal or perhaps superior to Anna Akhmatova would have been greeted with skepticism, although Nadezhda Yakovlevna made a point of stressing the link between Gumilev and her husband, who like Akhmatova had belonged to the Acmeist school of poetry headed by Gumilev in Petersburg.

I ventured to say that perhaps Gumilev's taste for the

picturesque was a bit dated. In Ludmila's opinion, however, this was immaterial. She was writing her doctoral thesis on Gumilev and had an expert's knowledge of his works. Gumilev's regard for the Orthodox Church, his aristocratic view of life — which to my mind has more than a touch of fin de siècle pose — were what mattered. His were the values that needed to be revived in Russia. As an afterthought, casually, Ludmila added that Mandelstam and Pasternak, long overrated by the Russian dissident intelligentsia, were currently losing their popularity at the expense of Gumilev: today, readers yearned for truly Russian voices like his and Daniel's.

My aunt mentioned how much Daniel had loved Gumilev's poetry, and indeed Daniel had dedicated a remarkable poem to him. The bearded men were nodding in agreement. After all, the philosopher said, these two, Pasternak and Mandelstam, had not really loved Russia; their voices were the alien ones in the great choir of Russian poetry. Evidently he was alluding to the fact that these poets were of Jewish ancestry. I knew then that I was going to a Slavophile shrine in the company of a new breed of Slavophiles. Alla seemed vaguely aware of my discomfort, and yet evidently she shared her friends' convictions about what was truly Russian in poetry. In their lifetime, and despite the indignities inflicted on all independent-minded artists in the Soviet Union, Pasternak and Mandelstam, among the greatest in the Russian language, had been considered full members of the Russian literary community. But now in 1989 they were being evicted from it.

I tried not to look at my aunt. It was getting hot inside our train compartment. I was very angry. I was remembering Leonid Andreyev's activities at the turn of the century in defense of Russian Jews targeted by Prime Minister Stolypin's policies. Then the horrendous, racist propaganda that had marked my childhood during the German Occupation of France came to mind, making me feel even more uncomfortable.

To my relief, within instants we were in Abramtsevo. We clambered out of our stuffy compartment and onto a narrow platform that seemed lost in the woods. The bearded poet carrying my aunt's cumbersome props led the way. I was tempted to remain on that platform and catch the first train in the opposite direction which would take me straight back to Moscow. Yet at the same time I was fascinated. I made up my mind to go along with whatever might happen on this expedition, to observe rather than fight my aunt and her friends.

As we followed a narrow, meandering path through thick undergrowth, crossing a tiny river on a diminutive footbridge, I felt soothed. Perhaps I too was falling under the spell that, according to the Westernizers, had kept their Slavophile contemporaries in a fool's paradise as they basked in the beauty of rural Russia, ignoring the wretched poverty of her inhabitants. That day the early summer woods were full of wildflowers and birds. There is a description of Abramtsevo which dates back to the early eighteen-hundreds, even before it was bought by the Aksakovs, before the ravages of the Industrial Revolution reached that remote part of the world. Its rhythms herald some of Gogol's: "On the right bank of the river Vorya stands a manor house one story high surrounded by fruit-bearing trees. In the hot weather the river is three feet wide and one foot deep and in it swim pike, perches, and roaches. The water is good for people and cattle alike. The forest yields pine and fir for lumber, and for logs there is alder, maple, birch, and chestnut. Animals run through this forest — wolves, rabbits, foxes, squirrels. Birds fly above it — grouse, hazel hens, partridges, quail."

The manor house at Abramtsevo welcomed us with alder trees and lilacs in bloom and the hospitable coolness of its museum, yet another "house whose beauty was marvel once." As it stands today, this quadrangle of low, unpretentious wooden buildings framing a lawn and surrounded on all sides by trees remains a perfect *usadba,* the kind of sprawling, informal country house lovingly described by Pushkin, Tolstoy, and Turgenev.

We were met at the entrance to the house by an affable young woman, one of the museum directors, who offered to take us on a tour — we had a half hour before my aunt's reading was to begin. Not all of the house was open to the public, but those rooms that were restored filled one with nostalgia for an archaic, loving Russia that has disappeared forever, an *usadba* as it might have been in the days of the Aksakovs — if it ever existed.

The manor house, one of those where "comfort argues with simplicity," in Pasternak's words, had shiny, light-colored wooden floors, a few pieces of Empire furniture here and there, and windows opening onto a smooth bluish vista of wooded hills. Framed pencil portraits of the various members of the Aksakov clan were displayed against the parlor walls papered in a deep shade of green.

The dining room at Abramtsevo was evocative of the Mamontovs' years there. Here were the decorative ceramic tiles with stylized folk designs for which the estate was famous at the turn of the century, when a variety of craft studios run by the best-known artists of the time were scattered about the property. An oil by Valentin Serov — "Vera with a Still Life of Peaches" — hung in that spacious room whose verandah opened onto the distant view of the forest. Vera was one of the Mamontovs' children; her death as a young girl darkened her parents' late years, one in a series of disasters which all but destroyed Mamontov, causing him and his family to retire to Abramtsevo year round.

After our tour Alla recited fifteen or twenty of my uncle's poems for a tiny, rapt audience settled in the main parlor. With consummate skill she read poems full of richness. The sun played on the ancient furniture. My aunt looked beautiful standing against the open window, her tall figure silhouetted by the sparkling afternoon light. The summary of my uncle's philosophical concepts by the bearded philosopher, though not profound, was useful. I was trying to forget our morning train ride — it had to have been some failure of communication, a misunderstanding.

That evening our small group, chatting amicably, settled on the wooden railway platform to wait for the Moscowbound train. Knowing that Daniel's poetry was coming into its own in a renewed Russia, where the best of the old and the new might one day merge harmoniously, I felt at peace. But then, all of a sudden, Alla leaned toward me and said in a loud whisper, "A military dictatorship would be better than this."

"Than what?" I asked.

"This disorder, this anarchy . . ."

"What do you mean?"

"In town the stores are empty. Here the train is late," my aunt said. "This is anarchy. It's intolerable for us who have to live with it day in day out."

"What makes you think a dictatorship would help? Haven't you had enough dictatorship?"

"A military dictatorship under the sign of the White Eagle can save us," she said. "Daniel would have wanted it."

"The Romanovs?"

"The martyred Romanovs and their dynasty."

"How do you know Danya would have wanted their restoration?" I asked. "Does he say it in his books?"

"Well, not exactly, but I do know for certain that in the present situation he would want the White Eagle to save us."

"You really think the Romanovs should rule Russia again?"

"Yes. If they don't, some other inspired military ruler will."

The other members of our party had fallen silent, listening intently, but the roar of the approaching train put an end to the conversation. In any case, it was useless to argue with Alla. Evidently she had been converted. In the world where she lived when I first knew her, to be a monarchist would have been highly unusual. Her father, a distinguished physiologist whom I had met in his old age, had been an old-fashioned Moscow liberal. Although I found it far-fetched, the idea of a wide-ranging conspiracy came to mind. Clearly, Ludmila and the bearded men could not single-handedly have inspired my aunt with the notion that the White Eagle would one day save Russia.

On our way back to Moscow I found myself sitting in a window seat next to the prop carrier. He explained that like Ludmila he was a graduate student at the Gorky Literary Institute. Moving closer to me, he said in a confidential tone, "Olga Vadimovna, you must understand that not everyone in Russia wishes for a military dictatorship. What many of us would like is to have Alexander Solzhenitsyn come home and be an advisor to our government. Do you know his *Letter to the Soviet Leaders?* I read it not long ago in an émigré publication. Though written before Solzhenitsyn was driven out of Russia, it is a prophetic document. It says that Russia, Byelorussia, and the Ukraine, together with the Baltic republics, must unite with Kazakhstan to form a single, God-fearing, Slavic state. Our present leaders, what's left of the Communist apparat, may even stay in power as long as they are willing to give up Marxism, that deadly ideology, and take on Orthodoxy instead. Insofar as you are Russian, you must be sympathetic — that's what Alla Alexandrovna means by the return of the White Eagle. An orderly return to Russian pre-Revolutionary ways, preferably with the Romanovs back on the throne."

∾ 21 ∾
Lydia Korneevna Chukovskaya

A LMOST THIRTY YEARS after my first visit with Anna Akhmatova, another unforgettable Moscow spring was ending. Before I left San Francisco I had been informed by the Writers' Union that after a solemn gathering in honor of Akhmatova to be held in Moscow in the Column Hall sometime around her birthday on June 23, I was to join up with a group of Soviet and Western scholars with a special interest in Akhmatova's work. Together we would take a night train for Leningrad to celebrate the poet in her own city with scholarly meetings, readings, and sightseeing. But this program remained unconfirmed. I found it impossible to reach the Writers' Union on the telephone. On several occasions in mid-June I stopped by the Writers' Union on Vorovskaya Street.

The Writers' Union headquarters are located in a mansion there that is said to have served as an inspiration for the one in which Pierre Bezhukhov takes his Masonic vows in *War and Peace*. Nowadays, however, like the Filmmakers' Union Club, this mansion is more evocative of Bulgakov's literary institutions gone mad than of an elegant townhouse that Tolstoy might have visited. My inquiries there about dates and about the formalities needed for my visa to be extended went unanswered. No one could tell me anything about Akhmatova's centenary celebrations, though they were only a few days away.

Whenever I came by, sleepy, heavily made-up secretaries looked at me blankly, their indifference turning to hostility as they sized me up, an intruder bent on disturbing them. Literateurs with harried faces were rushing off to "important meetings in town" — at Party headquarters? In the Kremlin? They suggested I leave my telephone number with their absent assistants. Clearly, by 1989 the Writers' Union was in disarray. My one acquaintance there, Frieda Lourie, who had served as an interpreter for Arthur Miller and his wife when they were in Moscow, was away on a trip to the West.

I made up my mind to be philosophical: much as I wanted to go back to Akhmatova's city, nowadays such a visit could actually be postponed. My Moscow stay had been rich in insights and encounters. I was happy to have been there during part of the public rehabilitation of my uncle Daniel — I knew how much this would have meant to my father. However, I did long for some sort of symbolic reunion with Anna Akhmatova, who had posthumously played a benevolent part in getting me back to Russia. When Liusha Chukovskaya let me know through Anya that her mother, Lydia Korneevna Chukovskaya, though fatigued by the heat wave, was ready to receive me in the old Chukovsky apartment on Gorky Street, I postponed a date to go to the Taganka Theater with Oleg and Dima. Here was an occasion to converse with a writer who had devoted years of her life to chronicling Akhmatova's life with as much care as Boswell had Dr. Johnson's.

Moreover, since the entire Chukovsky family had been close to Solzhenitsyn before his exile in 1974, I took Lydia Korneevna's invitation to mean that despite the shadow Solzhenitsyn had sought to cast upon me, which had to be known to her, she had decided not to forsake the ancient friendship between her family and mine. In that quarrel, perhaps she was giving me the benefit of the doubt. Other considerations beyond the preservation of family ties may have motivated Lydia Korneevna as well. Perhaps she didn't fully share her daughter's wholehearted acceptance of Solzhenitsyn's public role in recent years. In 1989 Liusha was active in trying to secure Solzhenitsyn's official rehabilitation by the new Soviet government — she must have been unacquainted with the latest Russian version of his *August 1914*, with its ambiguous portrayal of the Jew Bogorov, a revolutionary who in 1911 had killed Pyotr Stolypin, the prime minister who had encouraged the intensely chauvinistic policies which marked that era in Russia.

But Solzhenitsyn was not mentioned on the afternoon of my visit. After I was shown by Liusha into a small, sunny room high above Gorky Street where Lydia Korneevna waited for me by an open window, a round table set for tea next to her, the talk was first about my uncle Daniel. As Lydia Korneevna expressed her satisfaction with his rehabilitation, I was struck by how healthy and energetic she looked. She had seemed older back in the sixties in Peredelkino, when she was sometimes a silent presence during my visits to her father. Striking especially were her eyes. Wide open, light blue, they were full of life.

During the long years that my family and I had known Lydia Korneevna, she had suffered from grievous problems with her sight. In the seventies my mother had regularly sent her a variety of ineffectual eye remedies through the few friends who traveled to Moscow in those days. But now, Lydia Korneevna explained, just as glasnost was beginning, the celebrated Soviet eye surgeon Dr. Fedorov, one of the most determined supporters of perestroika in the USSR, had operated successfully on her eyes, improving her vision to an undreamed-of degree. "Now I see everything," she said delightedly, and she went on to praise Dr. Fedorov and explain some of the methods that enabled him to return sight to thousands of Soviet citizens. Like Pasternak's heroine who personified Russia in his last work, *The Blind Beauty*, Lydia Korneevna had been cured of her near blindness by an intervention she considered miraculous. Although she had looked at truth directly throughout her entire life, her eyes were restored to her precisely when Russia was beginning to change, a country worthy at last to be viewed by people of conscience.

Wearing a pale blue summer frock, sitting very straight, her white hair carefully combed, Lydia Korneevna now had some of the majesty of her close friend and idol, Anna Akhmatova. And like Akhmatova in her time, she had every reason to hold her head high. With Pasternak and her father dead and Solzhenitsyn and Sakharov in exile, for many years she had been a living symbol of the Russian intelligentsia's honor, one of the principal keepers of its sacred flame. Many other intellectuals were no less brave than she, but none as scrupulous and unwavering, none as direct and eloquent. A writer who had expressed herself fearlessly through repeated public statements while the Brezhnev government was at its most repressive, she had been the Russian literary dissident par excellence — I knew this firsthand through Henry's and my work on behalf of imprisoned Soviet writers.

Sitting across the table from Lydia Korneevna I could not help but be impressed. In her eighties, like the frail Andrey Sakharov, whom I had seen on television that morning, she was a heroic presence embodying a democratic future in Russia. She and Sakharov had made it possible for young people such as the inhabitants of apartment 13 to be proud of their Russianness despite all that had happened to the preceding three or four generations. And indeed the conversation turned to the youth of Russia and to Anya. Though Lydia Korneevna, like her mentor Anna Akhmatova — and unlike her effusive father — abhors any show of sentimentality, she let me understand that she held my niece in high esteem.

Briefly we discussed Anya's future. Lydia Korneevna said that Liusha and she realized that soon Anya would have to leave the Chukovsky museum and give her full attention to her studies, at least for a while. The important thing was that she make the right decision as to her future career. And then, rather abruptly, Lydia Korneevna pulled some notes out of a drawer and asked me point-blank three or four questions regarding Akhmatova's visits to the West shortly before her death. She looked disappointed when I was unable to answer them on the spot — she needed to know right away, for the last volume of her *Conversations with Anna Akhmatova* was going to press before long.

As I promised to research these soon and send the answers through Anya, I was reminded once again about the perils of playing the role of intermediary between worlds isolated from each other. Lydia Korneevna seemed surprised that I could not identify at once a trivial comment about Anna Akhmatova made by a young woman journalist writing in *Le Monde* in 1965. I suddenly realized that for some twenty-five years that young woman had erroneously been linked with me in her mind, most probably by reason of age and nationality.

Lydia Korneevna must have sensed my dismay. From Anna Akhmatova, from her father and Pasternak, she has inherited an ability to turn a teatime visit into a dynamic literary happening — Pasternak was a Peredelkino neighbor with whom she had a lifelong admiring relationship, and her reminiscences about him, published in 1990, are exacting and yet poetic. In her small room overlooking Gorky Street, lined with photographs of distinguished literary contemporaries now departed, Lydia Korneevna remembered my parents and talked about the friendship that had linked them to the Chukovskys and to Anna Akhmatova.

Then Lydia Korneevna wished me well on my pilgrimage to Leningrad, which she felt certain was going to take place despite the inevitable bureaucratic hurdles — and indeed in the end the Writers' Union would prove to be an efficient and hospitable host. She herself had declined to participate in the festivities; the Writers' Union had at various times treated both Anna Akhmatova and Lydia Korneevna atrociously. Nevertheless, she was pleased to know that I would be going: several of Anna Akhmatova's friends planned to attend — the poets Anatol Neiman and Yevgeny Rein, the critic Lydia Ginzburg, and a friend from Peredelkino, Pasternak's son Yevgeny. Encouraged by the Chukovskys, Anya might be able to be there for a day or two.

I was ready to leave. Outside, Moscow was beckoning me: I was hoping to catch a glimpse of St. Basil at sunset on nearby Red Square. But there was one more ritual to fulfill before I left. I wanted to let Lydia Korneevna know that her example had given heart, year after year, to those abroad who were struggling to support the dissenters' cause. Lydia Korneevna had been heroic as she had taken on the Soviet authorities and particularly the KGB, a task that Solzhenitsyn and Sakharov had begun in 1973. But how to say this to a woman known for her dislike of sentimentality in any form? In a restrained voice I said a few heartfelt words. Lydia Korneevna smiled and shook my hand and assured me that she would be looking forward to seeing me again on my next visit to Moscow.

∾ 22 ∾

Russia's Muse

"TODAY I SEE YOU / a black angel in the snow, / and I cannot keep this secret to myself, / God's mark is upon you . . ." That was how the poet Osip Mandelstam described his peer Anna Akhmatova in 1910, at the beginning of her long career as a poet. She was a famous beauty with a great literary gift, which grew and flowered despite the calamities that Russia suffered in the twentieth century. For many Russians her poems, with their classical clarity, are second only to Pushkin's.

Born Anna Gorenko in 1889, at Bolshoi Fontan on the Black Sea near Odessa, the daughter of a marine engineer, Anna Akhmatova published her first collection of poems, *Evening,* at the age of twenty-two under the name of a maternal ancestor — her father had asked her not to use the family name as a writer. As Anna Akhmatova she quickly became the woman most admired in Petersburg literary circles just before the Revolution. She was married first to the poet Nikolai Gumilev, who was shot on Lenin's orders not long after they were divorced. After the Revolution she was relentlessly vilified by the Soviet authorities and by other writers as well. Her contemporary Vladimir Mayakovsky said about her (and about their elder, the

Olga Andreyev Carlisle

Symbolist Vyacheslav Ivanov): "Of course, as literary milestones, as the last born child of a collapsing structure, they find their place on the pages of literary history, but for us, for our epoch — these are insignificant, pathetic, and laughable anachronisms."

But Boris Pasternak praised Akhmatova, and so did Mandelstam, who considered her voice the purest in Russian poetry, and Marina Tsvetayeva, who called her "golden-mouthed Anna of all the Russias." Mandelstam dedicated many poems to her, including his dark "Preserve My Words":

Preserve my words forever for their aftertaste of misfortune
and smoke,
for their tar of collective patience and conscientious work —
water in the wells of Novgorod must be black and sweetened
to reflect a star with seven fins at Christmas.
(Translated by Robert Lowell with OAC)

Pasternak, remembering in 1928 her "Lot's Wife" in his poem "For Anna Akhmatova," recognized her rare ability to fuse personal fate with history:

In all our affairs, your liens throb
with the high charge of the world.
Each wire is a conductor.

In the late thirties Akhmatova's son, Lev Gumilev, and her husband, the art critic Nikolai Punin, were arrested. Except for an interlude during the Second World War, when Stalin exploited every patriotic impulse to help win the war, persecutions continued, notably with the infamous Zhdanov edict of 1946, named for its main enforcer, Leningrad's Party boss Andrey Zhdanov, which singled out Akhmatova and the popular satirical writer Mikhail Zoshchenko as pernicious and led to their exclusion from the Writers' Union, leaving them without means of support. To earn a little money over the years, Akhmatova did translations of foreign poetry, which she would ask editors not to include in collections of her poems. After Stalin's death she was slowly rehabilitated and allowed to travel to Italy, Paris, and Oxford, where she was given an honorary degree. But her works continued to be censored in the Soviet Union, and the émigré collections of her works remained incomplete.

At last, in the 1960s, Russia's greatest living poet, though censored, was no longer ignored in her own country. Shortly before she died in 1966, the poet Robert Frost called on her while on an official trip to the USSR. Akhmatova, witty to the end, described his visit to her small cottage in Kamarovo on the seashore near Leningrad — her words were recorded by Raisa and Lev Kopelev, the Moscow dissenters who had first introduced me to Solzhenitsyn:

And then the old man arrived. An American grandfather — red-faced, gray-haired, cheerful. We sat next to each other in wicker chairs. All kinds of food were served and wine was poured. We talked without rushing. And I kept thinking: "Here are you, my dear, a national poet. Every year your books are published, they praise you in all the newspapers and journals, they teach you in the schools, the President received you as an honored guest. And all they've done is slander me! Into what dirt they've trampled me! I've had everything — poverty, prison lines, fear, poems remembered only by heart, and burnt poems. And humiliation and grief. And you don't know anything about this and wouldn't be able to understand it if I told you . . . But now let's sit together, two old people, in wicker chairs. A single end awaits us. And perhaps the real difference is not actually so great?"

Today, as the gigantic scale of the war waged by Lenin and Stalin against the Soviet people is being revealed, so is the answering grandeur of Russian poetry of the early twentieth century. Boris Pasternak, Marina Tsvetayeva, Osip Mandelstam, Anna Akhmatova, the literary giants of twentieth-century Russia, were among the tyrants' victims. Like Pasternak, Akhmatova lived into her seventies, bearing testimony about her times, growing steadily as an artist. As centennials of Akhmatova's and Pasternak's births are celebrated and their works are published in their totality, the Russian public is astonished by the scope of their achievements, by the sheer beauty and abundance of their work.

The Requiem, describing how she stood in line day after day at the gates of the Kresty Prison, waiting for news of her son and her husband, has become Russia's most famous poem on the subject of Stalinist repression. It was composed between 1935 and 1940, but Akhmatova did not write it down until several years after Stalin's death; until then it was preserved only in her memory and in those of a few friends. When she recited parts of it to Pasternak on a visit to Moscow in the late thirties, he said that "after hearing her, I no longer feared death." This long work begins:

> *I wasn't under a new sky,*
> *its birds were the old familiar birds.*
> *They still spoke Russian. Misery*
> *spoke familiar Russian words.*
>
> *In the terrible years of the Yezhovshchina, I*
> *spent seventeen months in the prison lines*
> *at Leningrad. Once, someone somehow*
> *recognized me. Then a woman standing behind*
> *me, her lips blue with cold, who had of course*
> *never heard of me, woke up from the stupor*
> *that enveloped us, and asked me, whispering*
> *in my ear (for we only spoke in whispers):*
> *"Could you describe this?"*
>
> *I said, "I can."*

Then something like a smile glided over what was once her face.

(Translated by Robert Lowell with OAC)

English-language readers can look forward to Lydia Chukovskaya's *Conversations with Anna Akhmatova,* soon to be published in the United States. During the Revolutionary period in Petersburg, in a time of famine, Akhmatova gave her friend Chukovsky milk for Lydia. This was the gesture of a fairy godmother, and Lydia Chukovskaya was to live up to it. Her *Conversations with Anna Akhmatova* lies at the center of her life's work.

Not surprisingly in the case of two writers who refused to compromise, stern literary judgments abound in *Conversations.* The book is an encyclopedia of Akhmatova's insights into her own and others' work. Of confessional writing, which she detested, she said, "In Pushkin's day, poets never talked about themselves. But they said everything all the same — *everything,* to the end." She worshiped Dostoyevsky for his ability to chart the intricacies of the human spirit: "I was rereading *The Adolescent.* What a work! And not at all terrifying. It does not reflect real life, only the facets of Dostoyevsky's soul." On the other hand, her judgments of Tolstoy could be severe. A believer in women's right to self-fulfillment, she was offended by what she saw as his misogyny: "How disgusting his feelings for Anna [Karenina]! First he is in love with her, he relishes her, relishes the black curls on her neck . . . And then he begins to hate her — he even mocks her corpse. Do you remember — 'shamelessly stretched out'?" Nor was she kind to Chekhov, an attitude she may have inherited from her elders. Akhmatova's mother had been a revolutionary in her youth, an SR. In Russia at the turn of the century many revolutionaries considered Chekhov's vision of their country depressing, the ending of *Uncle Vanya* too bleak to bear.

Akhmatova loved Russia passionately. Her patriotic poems of the Second World War period are among the most beautiful ever written in that genre. Her love of Russia transcended politics and personal involvements. Here are lines from her celebrated "Courage," part of the cycle "The Wind of War" (1941–45), one of her most famous cycles of poems:

Victory stands at our door.
How shall we greet the longed for guest?
Women will lift their children high —
This is how we'll greet our guest!

∾ 23 ∾

Two Friends

I REMEMBER VIVIDLY my first meeting with Anna Akhmatova. Once, in the spring of 1962, during one of my almost daily visits to Nadezhda Yakovlevna Mandelstam, she announced that the next day she would take me to meet Akhmatova, who had recently arrived from Leningrad on one of her semiannual visits to the capital. Nadezhda Yakovlevna had spoken to her about me, and Akhmatova expressed her readiness to see me. It turned out that she remembered my mother and father warmly — she had met them the year before in Leningrad. I was both delighted and awed at the prospect of meeting Anna Akhmatova. With the death in 1960 of her friend Boris Pasternak, she had become the unchallenged dean of Russian poets.

The following day was one of the hot, luminous days that made my first spring in Russia so wonderful. Even before leaves had opened on the trees, the air was filled with a faint smell of sap. The last patches of snow were fast disappearing from the sidewalks, and puddles shone in their place. Russian Orthodox Easter and the First of May were only days away; that year they were occurring within the same week. Whether they were going to honor the Christian festival or the international Labor Day or both, busy Muscovites were scurrying for holiday supplies. At that time the shops were relatively well stocked in Moscow. No one in the capital knew or cared very much if they were empty in the provinces. The Soviet Union was still a mighty colonial power. Khrushchev's resounding economic failure, which was eventually to cost him his leadership and mark the end of a period of political and cultural détente, had not yet been felt in Moscow. The ordinarily dour, passive crowds were full of new energy.

Lines of Pasternak's came to my mind as I walked from my hotel to Nadezhda Yakovlevna's that morning. In all of literature there was no greater celebrant of spring than Pasternak; the poem he dedicated to Akhmatova in 1928 made the thought of meeting her seem less forbidding; after all, she was a friend of friends, a part of that Moscow spring:

> *I hear the soiled, dripping small talk of the roofs,*
> *the students' black boots drum eclogues on the sidewalks,*
> *the undefined city takes on personality,*
> *is alive in each sound.*
>
> *Although it's spring, there's no leaving the city.*
> *The sharp customers overlook nothing . . .*
> (Translated by Robert Lowell with OAC)

In my memory Akhmatova's own lines to Pasternak answered:

> *And now, like molten diamonds,*
> *Puddles are glistening, ice seized with longing . . .*
> *Moscow's languor burns us again.*

I was calling for Nadezhda Yakovlevna at the home of the Shklovskys, with whom she was staying. The family of the avant-garde literary critic was living next door to the Tretyakov Gallery of Art, in the very heart of Moscow. From there it was a brief walk through narrow, ancient streets to the Ordynka, where Akhmatova was visiting with Victor Ardov, a popular Moscow playwright, and his family. That section of the city, which subsequently has been much rebuilt, was full of charm then, a bit of old Moscow with its low, stucco townhouses and its white-washed churches with their many cupolas. That morning in the sunshine, despite years of neglect, they looked like huge snowdrops. As we neared the Ordynka, Nadezhda Yakovlevna told me that this street, running eastward, was once the beginning of a highway linking Moscow to the encampments of the Tartar Horde. It was along this road that, for centuries, Muscovites traveled to deliver their tribute to their Asiatic masters.

My apprehension at the prospect of meeting Akhmatova mounted as we walked down the Ordynka, but before I knew it we had reached our destination: we were crossing a muddy courtyard, climbing several flights of stairs, ringing the Ardovs' doorbell. Akhmatova herself opened the door. She embraced Nadezhda Yakovlevna and greeted me with a smile and a handshake. But despite her affability I found the poet even more intimidating than I had feared.

At seventy-three, Akhmatova was tall, portly, and extremely handsome. She was wearing a slightly worn but becoming robe of black silk edged in purple. Her movements were slow and full of nobility. The expression on her face was a mixture of dignity and kindness, and one or the other of these moods dominated at a given moment. But most striking was the intelligence reflected in her eyes, which marked every sentence she uttered in a slow, slightly muffled tone. The deep, harmonious voice was immensely attractive. She was simple yet majestic, self-absorbed yet perceptive. The trademarks of her youth, when she had been a famous St. Petersburg belle — the willful profile, the dark bangs that are part of pre-Revolutionary Russian literary lore — had vanished. The Akhmatova whom Osip Mandelstam had recognized years before had emerged, the one with "God's mark" upon her.

Nadezhda Yakovlevna elected to leave me alone with

her friend soon after our arrival: she had errands to run in the neighborhood. Discreetly Akhmatova's hosts had retired to another part of the apartment. Akhmatova and I sat down alone, rather stiffly, in the Ardovs' sitting room. She occupied a Victorian couch upholstered in dark red velvet which stood near the window; I sat facing her across an oval table on which stood a small bunch of anemones in a glass. It was very warm in the apartment. Maple branches lightly dusted with green swayed outside the open window; the gusts of fresh air which came in seemed to ask us why we were indoors on such a beautiful day.

Unable to recall any of the questions I had planned to ask her if I ever met her, I was silent as Akhmatova spoke at length about Acmeism, the poetic creed of her and Mandelstam's youth. She elucidated for me some of the Acmeists' complex relationships with the other literary groups of that era, and notably with the Futurists, to whom Pasternak had been linked. Her desire to share her knowledge, to preserve the past, was deeply moving, but on that day Acmeism, which Mandelstam had once defined as "a nostalgia for world culture," seemed remote.

Then Akhmatova mentioned her own recent work and the fact that she was experiencing a new surge of creativity. Because of the terrible, artificial isolation in which Russian writers had been kept for decades, she feared that Western readers had taken on face value the Soviet critics' allegations that she, as well as Pasternak and Mandelstam — poets whom she considered the greatest of that age — had lost their poetic voices early in the twenties. What had happened, of course, was that they and many other first-rate writers had continued to write in increasingly difficult circumstances. Under the threat of instant arrest they were prevented from publishing or even circulating their works.

Now, in a more tolerant age, Akhmatova was honored even by those in the world of official Soviet letters who had called her "half nun, half whore" after the issuing of the postwar Zhdanov edict. Sorrow was reflected in her face as she spoke of that period. I was able to reassure her as to Western readers' growing understanding of these years. By 1962, following the publication of *Doctor Zhivago,* there was an awareness in the West that a world of unpublished contemporary Russian writing was about to be revealed. Soon afterward, Akhmatova's *The Requiem,* published in Munich in 1963, demonstrated that Akhmatova had not been silent in the thirties and forties, that as an artist she had outgrown even the marvelously melodic, intensely feminine love poems of her youth.

My shyness was beginning to fade as Akhmatova invited me to follow her into a back room: she wanted to recite some poems to me and found that room more tranquil than the sitting room, where the telephone occasionally rang. She shut the door and sat at a tiny writing table, placing me across it, very close to her. Her eyes half shut, her head bent to one side, she recited magnificently in that monotonous yet musical manner which is a tradition with Russian poets. She seemed to listen to her own voice with her whole being. To hear her "Muse" in Akhmatova's interpretation was overwhelming. Clearly, the Muse was an essential presence in her life, the one whose assiduous visits had made this gifted, beautiful woman into a major artist.

After a while Nadezhda Yakovlevna tapped lightly at the door. We moved back to the sitting room. The conversation became lighthearted. The two women discussed the literary news of the day and Akhmatova's forthcoming recording session: for the first time the poet had been asked officially to make a record of some of her poems.

In addition to affection, sparkling humor marked the exchange between the two friends. In difficult times Akhmatova and Nadezhda Yakovlevna had looked after each other. After Mandelstam's death his widow and his intimate friend and fellow Acmeist had shared many dark hours. Now they were savoring better days. As they conversed, Nadezhda Yakovlevna's impulsiveness and biting wit complemented Akhmatova's dry intelligence and serenity. Even now in old age their looks were a happy contrast: Akhmatova, the beauty renowned throughout her life for her stately carriage and her elegant, Bourbon profile; and Nadezhda Yakovlevna, petite, vivacious, blue-eyed, described in her youth by Anna Akhmatova as *"laide mais délicieuse."*

As far as my acquaintance with Akhmatova was concerned, Nadezhda Yakovlevna's magic had worked. From that day on, Akhmatova treated me as a friend. She declared to Nadezhda Yakovlevna that despite my foreign birth I was a true Russian. Whenever I called on her alone, she bestowed on me the greatest honor and gave me the greatest pleasure: she read aloud a few poems out of her various collections of verse. In addition, I saw her occasionally with Nadezhda Yakovlevna. These visits, full of gaiety, were primarily social: we participated for a while in what Pasternak had called an "Akhmatovka." Sounding like the name of a railroad station, evoking noise and confusion, the word referred to the stream of telephone calls and visits which took over whenever Akhmatova stayed in Moscow.

That year, 1962, it was hard for me to leave Moscow when June came. My friends were sad also; no one wanted that season to end. We all somehow knew that, in the USSR, too many obstacles and vested interests stood in the way of a lasting political springtime. And indeed, hopes for a genuine liberalization of Russia were fading when I saw Akhmatova again, in 1965. The pattern of my visits with her remained the same as in 1962. A rather distant, thoughtful exchange on literary topics, in which I was primarily the listener, was followed by Akhmatova's reciting a few poems.

After these meetings I remember trying to understand what it was that gave Anna Akhmatova her powers as a writer and as a person. It seems to me now that it was her total, absolute self-respect which made her different from any other woman artist I can think of and which enabled her to experience her feelings, analyze them, and then describe them with extraordinary objectivity. I remember a conversation we had about Freudian psychology. Akhmatova said, "What was true for Vienna in the late nineteenth century need not be true elsewhere, in another time. Why do people assume that they are determined to such an extreme degree by social and biological patterns? How *can* they abdicate their responsibility to themselves so readily, and thus lose the gift of freedom?"

Many talented women are emotionally splintered by their own talent and by outside pressures. But Akhmatova knew how to resist all pressures, including political intimidation. Never losing touch with what she felt, she devoted her life to recreating her feelings through writing. Today, as her fame in Russia grows, we see that those feelings are universal — little wonder the all-controlling masters of the country regarded her as dangerous. Like Pasternak, she was telling Russians that regardless of what was said by those in power, they mattered as individuals.

∾ 24 ∾

Anna Akhmatova's Museum

NOW, IN 1989, it was in Fontanny Dom, the Baroque Sheremetiev Palace elegantly poised along a peaceful canal in Leningrad, that I felt Akhmatova's presence most keenly. In the twenties she had moved into a room there with her husband, the Modernist art critic Punin, and had remained for years after their estrangement; her room was now being inaugurated as a small museum. Anna Akhmatova herself had disliked museums established in famous writers' homes — she found such places contrived. She had been displeased with the one installed in Pushkin's apartment, evocative as it is of the great poet for even the non-Pushkinist visitor. But Anna Akhmatova was an ardent, uncompromising student of Pushkin's life and works and was critical of other, more academic Pushkinists. Most probably she would have been critical of her own museum as well, yet on that day, recognizing many faces of friends in the crowd, perhaps she would have relented. The day was special, her birthday, a radiant June 23.

In the courtyard of the palace, lost in the middle of a crowd of worshipful poetry lovers, waiting for my turn to go into the newly opened museum, I reflected that nothing in Anna Akhmatova's life had been accidental. The opulent curving grille enclosing the palace courtyard, the view of the canal, the mirrored halls inside, even the azure June sky seemed to have been preordained by her. She made these splendors hers; through her poems they are forever a part of her literary persona. Now, on her hundredth birthday, though absent, she was being enshrined in her own palace, as befits a queen.

Inside, on the second floor, her room, which had been part of a communal apartment while she lived there, was freshly painted a deep green. Outside, very close to the window, the maple tree often mentioned in her poems was moving its freshly opened branches ever so softly. There were several well-known portraits of her on the walls, and two or three objects that had belonged to her had been placed in the room — I recall a small wooden box, a few books. A couch and a plain table were the room's only furnishings. Gone were Anna Akhmatova herself and the fear, the wartime abandonment, the penetrating cold that Lydia Korneevna makes so tangible in her *Conversations with Anna Akhmatova.*

In that sparse room where one of Russia's greatest poets had lived for such a long time, partly by choice and partly through desperation, I recognized many acquaintances from the past filing by in silence — the poet Anatol Neiman, an intimate of Anna Akhmatova's in her late years; Koma Ivanov, who as a child had met Akhmatova at the Pasternaks' in Peredelkino; Professor Victor Erlich from Yale, the son of my grandmother's friend Sophia Erlich; Pasternak's son, Yevgeny, with his wife, Alena; Vladimir Kornilov, a poet from Moscow, a favorite of Nadezhda Yakovlevna's on whom I had called on several occasions in the sixties.

But these people I had known in their youth looked now as if they had been bleached out, their faces and postures altered almost beyond recognition, like those of the guests at the party at the end of *Remembrance of Things Past*. Like Proust's hero, away for many years, I had come back to a gathering of survivors, a group of admirers lingering now in the green sunlit room as if wishing to slow the passage of time. Among them were many young people unknown to me, even a few children. I wished that my father, my uncle Volodia, and my aunt Ariadne, with their ardent love of Russian poetry, could be there. Then with a happy start I remembered that Anya was on her way to Leningrad that night, and that perhaps Dima too would be coming, though his hospital duties made his arrival uncertain.

A recording of Anna Akhmatova reading her poems was playing, hushing conversation. Her verses were about the devastations of the twentieth century, yet the steady, solemn delivery spoke of redemption, echoing the motto inscribed at the entrance of Fontanny Dom, *"Deus conservat omnia"*:

All is despoiled, abandoned, sold;
Death's wing has swept the sky of color;
All's eaten by a hungry dolor.
What is this light which we behold?

Odors of cherry blossom sigh
From the rumored forest beyond the town.
At night, new constellations crown
The high, clear heavens of July.

Closer it comes, and closer still,
To houses ruinous and blind:
Some marvelous thing still undivined,
Some fiat of the century's will.

(Translated by Richard Wilbur with OAC)

Later on, in the courtyard, a woman in her middle years to whom I had been introduced that morning was speaking about the kind of monument to Akhmatova which might be erected one day on the quay above the Neva facing the

Kresty Prison, where according to *The Requiem* Akhmatova had wanted one built. Should it be made of granite or marble or bronze? A friend standing next to her said that in her opinion the monument should be a joint one, to Akhmatova and to Gumilev, her first husband, as good a poet as Akhmatova, the friend said, if not better. I suggested that perhaps the one sketch that has been preserved out of the sixteen Modigliani made of Akhmatova could serve as a model for a memorial. It is so resemblant and monumental, like a study for a sculpture.

My new acquaintances disagreed: it stood to reason that Akhmatova, a Russian patriot, would have wanted to be portrayed by a Russian artist, not by some Italian member of a derelict bohemia. It had been said that the Writers' Union would soon be organizing a competition for the best design for a memorial on the bank of the Neva. I inquired whether in these new times there were also plans to honor the following year's centenarian, Boris Pasternak, with a monument in his native Moscow. The women doubted it. "Pasternak isn't quite as Russian as Akhmatova," one of them said.

During that week of celebrations, first in Moscow and then in Leningrad, for hours on end while the gorgeous weather summoned one outside, critics and scholars gravely presented their insights into Anna Akhmatova's poems. Often they merely set forth their own tastes in music and in art, their opinions about Pushkin, about the Revolution, about emigrating. Time and again participants quoted the opening lines of *The Requiem,* which are sometimes used to denigrate émigrés; in fact, it slowly emerged through scholarly discussions that those lines came out of a very personal wound inflicted on Akhmatova by a man whom she had loved and who left her behind forever when he emigrated: "I wasn't under a new sky, / its birds were the old familiar birds . . ."

On the evening of our departure for Leningrad, the lavish birthday celebration in the Hall of Columns in Moscow had been a sampling of everything Anna Akhmatova detested, or so it seemed to me. On the stage stood oversized vases of gladiolas and arums and a gigantic portrait of her next to the figure "100" written out in red on a white panel. Actors declaimed her verse; opera singers sang poems set to music. Women in folk costumes danced on stage and sang. Literary officials, each of whom alluded to having had a special relationship to the dead poet, eulogized her at leisure. Clearly this was the beginning of a new era in Russian literary scholarship. Now there would be a growing tribe of Akhmatovists, as there is of Pushkinists.

Nonetheless, many of the events that unfolded in the course of almost ten days, first in Moscow and then in Leningrad, would have pleased Akhmatova. In Leningrad, St. Nicholas on the Sea, the dazzling blue and gold Baroque church, was decorated with birch boughs for the long memorial service. Before that, in Moscow, Yevgeny Pasternak made a moving speech on the subject of his father's friendship with Akhmatova, as did poets who had known her personally. Her poems resisted trivialization. Read aloud for hours on end, they remained fresh, redeeming the duller lectures delivered in Pushkin House, the central literary archive, and from the podiums of stately concert halls, and in buses on excursions to what are now known as "Akhmatova's places."

The excursions proved a privileged way to sightsee and to learn more about Akhmatova. I learned, for instance, that before Akhmatova moved into Fontanny Dom with Punin, she had been an emancipated woman who had lived in other rooms in town with other men. We were reminded that Anna Akhmatova had been flirtatious — "an aged Columbine," she had said of herself toward the end of her life. I thought back to Nadezhda Yakovlevna's naughty tales out of the twenties, about Pasternak and Akhmatova kissing in the stairs on their way to the Mandelstams' apartment. In enormous diesel-powered buses that afforded an unimpaired view of prodigious cityscapes, we were taken to the Summer Garden, which Akhmatova had celebrated, and to St. Isaac's Cathedral, where she had singled out for all eternity the sculpture of a black angel, and to Tsarskoye Selo, where she had lived as a child.

At Tsarskoye Selo, Akhmatova's son, Lev Nikolaevich Gumilev, an anthropologist of great renown, spoke in front of the small house that Akhmatova and her family had occupied when she was an adolescent. I was taken back in time, moved as I had been when Yevgeny Pasternak spoke in Pushkin House — Yevgeny Borisovich had sounded exactly like his father. As for Lev Gumilev, a white-haired elderly man, he resembled to a remarkable degree Anna Akhmatova in her late years. His muffled voice had some of Anna Andreevna's intonations. He had spent decades in camps. Lev's arrest, hoping for news of Lev, waiting for Lev's release, year after year, had been central motifs in *The Requiem* and in Anna Akhmatova's life — and, by extension, in the lives of those close to her, notably Lydia Korneevna and Nadezhda Yakovlevna, not to mention those of innumerable Russians at home and abroad. In *Conversations with Anna Akhmatova,* I found a reference to my parents reading *The Requiem* for the first time on a visit to Akhmatova in 1962. The poet expressed some uncertainty regarding this work; then, according to Lydia Korneevna, she added, "I had it typed and shared it with Olga and Vadim Andreyev . . . Those who read *The Requiem* do cry."

Like the city itself, Anna Akhmatova's "blessed cradle," and like the ancient parks that in 1989 were still miraculously well maintained, Akhmatova's poems reasserted themselves again and again. No English translation does full justice to them: the secret of her greatness, like Pushkin's, is her flawless use of language, her tone, which Mandelstam had singled out from all others. More often than not, Akhmatova's verses sound banal in translation. Richard Wilbur has come closest, I think, to capturing their tone. The poem "Lot's Wife," quoted many times during her centennial, is expressive of Anna Akhmatova's fate and *sounds* like her:

The just man followed then his angel guide
Where he strode on the black highway, hulking and bright;
But a wild grief in his wife's bosom cried,
Look back, it is not too late for a last sight

Of the red towers of your native Sodom, the square
Where once you sang, the gardens you shall mourn,
And the tall house with empty windows where
You loved your husband and your babes were born.

She turned, and looking on the bitter view
Her eyes were welded shut by mortal pain;
Into transparent salt her body grew,
And her quick feet were rooted in the plain.

Who would waste tears upon her? Is she not
The least of our losses, this unhappy wife?
Yet in my heart she will not be forgot
Who, for a single glance, gave up her life.

(Translated by Richard Wilbur with OAC)

Akhmatova's verse makes one think of a classical drawing, by Claude Lorrain perhaps. Andrey Sinyavsky, in *A Voice from the Choir*, a book written while he was in camp, perhaps best conveys Akhmatova's style:

Anna Akhmatova's poetry resembles a pond or a lake edged with trees, or a mirror in which everything seems less real, yet stands out in sharper relief than in actual life. A bright sky and glittering clouds are reflected, becoming brighter still, in a dark and haunted pool, but on the surface there are neither ripples nor lapping of water: all is bathed in the silence of unseen depths, illuminated by a dark, subaqueous light, like the first coating of paint on a canvas: white on black, a strange effect of blackness coated in whiteness; a background smooth, deep, and funereal, like a mirror, in which objects are sharply outlined and have a hint of something disturbing and magical — where can this come from, you wonder, when there is really nothing there?

Add to this the deep, velvety timbre of her voice, so resonant when she read, and her dress — neat-fitting and austere. Also: her love of tradition, her attachment to the classical mirror of poetry in which she peers intently at herself and where, on the still background of the lyric poetry of centuries past, both the present day and the living melody of its speech are solemnly and magisterially reflected like the streets of Venice in its canals. Her poetry conveys the impression that others have just passed by before her — the same as when you suddenly glance at a mirror and have the feeling that someone has flitted past a moment ago and things are still nervously alert to a presence which has been and gone . . .

In the diamond mirror of mute waters
shine the living shapes of clouds . . .
(Translated by Max Hayward)

∽ 25 ∽

In Search of the Constituent Assembly

I N LENINGRAD — soon to regain its old name, St. Petersburg — I spent my days at the Akhmatova lectures and my nights exploring the city alone or in the company of one or another among my Akhmatovist acquaintances. At the end of a long scholarly day, my friends Victor and Isa Erlich were usually ready to cover on foot some of the great stretches of historic Petersburg. As adolescents in 1939, they had fled Warsaw, going to the United States by way of Russia and Canada. The Erlichs are amusing and kind, and when we lived in Connecticut Henry and I saw them often. Victor's mother was born in Russia, the daughter of the great scholar Simon Dubnov, author of the first Russian-language history of the Jews. Sophia Dubnova Erlich had been a poet, a protégée of Chukovsky's in Petersburg during the Revolution. In later years in emigration, she became my grandmother's closest friend. I had loved her. During the time that I was not allowed to go back to Russia her small apartment near Columbia University was a Russian enclave where I was welcomed as a member of her family.

Victor's erudition, the Erlichs' joy at being in the city where Victor's mother had lived as a young woman, their vitality, their faith in the happy outcome of glasnost made them ideal after-hours companions. Having spent many years of our friendship commiserating about the evils of Communism, we now avoided discussing unpleasant pros-'pects, notably the anti-Semitism that seemed to be rising ever closer to the surface of Soviet life. However, as I talked with the Erlichs, I became increasingly aware of yet another troublesome subject — the place of émigrés in the Russian literary imagination.

Like my family, the Erlichs are émigrés with a complex background. Victor's father was a well-known Polish socialist, Henrich Erlich, who in 1939 was seized in the Metropole Hotel in Moscow and shot while the Germans were invading Poland. Now that the Soviet Union was becoming a better informed society, would the émigrés, once despised for their allegedly cowardly flight abroad, be reintegrated into Russian culture? The Akhmatova conference suggested that they might, if gingerly.

Sometimes, having rested for an hour or two in the late afternoon, I went out again alone. These walks usually turned into somewhat surreal explorations of my family's past in Petersburg — imaginary visits with Leonid Andreyev, with my mother's SR friends, with Akhmatova, and, of course, with Pushkin, with whom a great many Russians feel an intense personal kinship.

My father had often told me about the June White Nights, when because of its northern latitude the sun never sets on Peter's capital. To be there on the eve of a new age for Russia, wandering through the city of his youth, bathed in that season in a light that turns from lemon yellow to a scarlet dawn, was dreamlike. With its canals painted with shimmering reflections, Petersburg is to this day as beautiful as Venice. Like Venice it is emblematic of the death of a culture. A living city still, it speaks also, however tentatively, of salvation. Mandelstam's vision of it was inspired by the waters surrounding it:

Olga Andreyev Carlisle

A radiance travels at a prodigious height,
Is it a star there, shining?
Transparent star, wandering light,
Your twin, Petropolis, is dying.

A transparent spring over the black Neva,
The wax of immortality has melted.
O should you be a star, Petropolis, your town,
Your twin, Petropolis, is dying.

The Writers' Union had assigned me a room in the sprawling October Hotel at the end of Nevsky Prospect. The hotel was undergoing repairs, the water flowed brown out of the faucets, and I had to lock myself up against the drunken black marketeers encamped next door. To get to my room I walked miles along corridors across a variety of obstacles — missing floorboards, drunkards, prostitutes on the prowl, barricades of discarded furniture. However, when I reached my room and bolted the door behind me I was rewarded. My window opened onto a view reminiscent of Rome in the late afternoon light — a view of the Nevskaya Lavra monastery, to which the relics of Alexander Nevsky had just been returned. Nevsky, of Prokofiev and Eisenstein fame, was one of the great warrior-saints of Holy Russia, who in 1242 had stopped the invading Teutonic Knights.

A trolley running along Nevsky Prospect brought me from my hotel to the Neva River in a matter of minutes for my evening walks. The celebrated thoroughfare, which runs through Petersburg as it runs through so many of Dostoyevsky's and Gogol's stories, was thick with people and traffic at any hour of the day or night. Since it was dusty and noisy I had no desire to follow it on foot. But the broad river and the Summer Garden nearby, the bridges, the blue-green Winter Palace crowned with oversized statues, tempted me in every direction at once.

To the left lay Senate Square. There the Decembrists, the

first Russians openly to demand a constitution, had been dispersed one December night in 1825. For decades afterward the tzar continued to persecute them, unwilling to consider the reforms that might turn Russia into a modern state and ensure the long-term survival of his dynasty. The failure of that rebellion, of that muffled and yet momentous confrontation between the tzar and the people, between the tzar and progressive Europe, happened in one night on the bank of the Neva, but from that time on Russians everywhere knew that autocracy could be challenged. The moral qualities of the Decembrists confirmed that the struggle for freedom was possible and that it was noble.

The Decembrists were the idealistic young officers enamored of the Enlightenment, who believed that Russia could be reformed — serfdom abolished and a constitutional monarchy established. Several of them had been friends of Pushkin, the flower of the Russian intelligentsia of their day. For their daring, ill-timed show of force on Senate Square, those who were not executed were punished with torture, humiliation, and lifelong confinement in Siberia.

To this day Senate Square, like so many Petersburg vistas, looks like an immense stage set. At the river's edge just beyond it, Peter the Great's equestrian statue leaps forth, taking flight toward the Neva. This awesome statue, the homage of one autocrat to another — from Catherine to Peter — is the ultimate symbol of the merciless, self-serving state that has dissolved with such astonishing rapidity. Still, where else but in Petersburg can one see an equestrian statue — Pushkin's "Bronze Horseman" — that continues to speak for a sense of national identity, however fractured?

Late one afternoon I followed the granite quays of the Neva upstream to the east. I wanted to see the Smolny Institute, where in 1917 the Bolsheviks had plotted the October coup d'état. The embankment leading there was fit-

tingly named for Robespierre, who had served as a source
of inspiration for Lenin in his revolutionary struggle. At
the end of the embankment, near the Smolny Institute, I
would find the Tauride Palace, built by Catherine the Great
for her favorite, Potemkin. There, a hall that had originally
been an immense winter garden, the Constituent Assembly, the only fully democratic and multinational political
body ever convened in Russia, held its one meeting on January 18, 1918. The populist Socialist Revolutionaries had
been an overwhelming majority in this elected body,
whose gathering was the culmination of a relentless struggle against tzarism by four generations of revolutionaries,
from 1825 to 1917. After a session that lasted a day and a
night, during which the Assembly voted a number of reforms similar to those which are now being proposed in
Russia — notably the distribution of the land to the peasants and the proclamation of a Democratic Federation of
Republics, each of them sovereign — it was disbanded on
Lenin's orders, the minutes of the meeting immediately destroyed.

Even before the Assembly gathered on a gray winter
morning, the Tauride Palace had been occupied by heavily
armed, drunken Red Army men and sailors. When the session ended at dawn the following day, many delegates and
their supporters were arrested on the spot. My maternal
grandfather, Victor Chernov, an SR of peasant origin specializing in agrarian matters who had been elected president of the Assembly on that fateful January 18, managed
to walk away from the palace: he used a side door to elude
the Red Army men assigned to seize him. A seasoned revolutionary, he had lived underground for long stretches of
time under the tzarist regime.

The year before, following the February 1917 revolution, Victor Chernov had returned from a long European
exile to become a member of the Provisional Government
led by another member of the SR party, Alexander Kerensky. He arrived in Petersburg a month after Lenin, having

refused to take advantage of the safe passage through Germany offered to him by the Kaiser's government as it had been offered to and accepted by the Bolshevik leader. Appointed minister of agriculture, Chernov had pushed for immediate land reform; in forced emigration in Europe after the 1905 revolution, he had spent over a decade working on this desperately needed change. The land was never given to the peasants, however. The Bolshevik Red Terror started right after the disbanding of the Constituent Assembly — years of unrecorded annihilation by the Bolsheviks of entire social classes throughout what would become the Soviet Union.

The Tauride Palace turned out to be a serene and elegant classical building which in no way evokes the drama that unfolded there. It was freshly painted a light yellow typical of eighteenth-century St. Petersburg. But when I crossed Liteyny Prospect near the palace, I remembered one of the stories about the Revolution which had enthralled me when I was a child — my mother's tales about her mother. My grandmother Olga Kolbassin, Victor Chernov's wife, an SR herself, had worked for months in the provinces, helping organize the elections for the Constituent Assembly. Before the opening of the Assembly she had participated in a huge, peaceful demonstration by workers and soldiers supporting the Assembly, who marched along Liteyny on January 16, 1918. The unprovoked shooting that occurred along the way was the prelude to the suppression of the Assembly, a signal to the country that the Bolsheviks' rule, like the tzar's, would be violent.

In her memoir, *Cold Spring in Russia,* my mother described revolutionary Petrograd in the winter of 1917–18. Clearly the instigators of the August 1991 coup neglected to learn from Lenin about the danger of sending Russian soldiers against the Russian people.

Thousands of demonstrators coming from various sections of town were converging on the Tauride Palace, which was their rallying point. They were singing old revolutionary songs and carrying red banners endorsing the Constituent Assembly and promising the peasants a prompt distribution of land. Mother walked with a group of Socialists along Liteyny Boulevard. Suddenly their way was blocked by a Red cavalry detachment. An order rang out: 'Back!' and then at once: 'Fire!' The cavalrymen opened fire into the crowd of unarmed demonstrators. A young man, walking next to Mother, a flag in his hand, fell. Bullets whistled and several women near Mother dropped to the ground. Red stains appeared and spread on the trampled snow around them. The demonstrators turned back and started to run; horses caught up to them, tumbling them down to the ground and crushing them. The Bolsheviks had planned this dispersal beforehand, placing armed troops and weaponry at crossroads, in order to terrify and disband the Assembly sympathizers.

The Bolsheviks started using violence and police methods even before the delegates gathered at the Tauride Palace. The direction of these tactics was left to Uritsky, the chief of the Bolshevik police in Petrograd. The Constituent Assembly's fate was sealed before it ever convened. To stifle it, Lenin used all possible means. They included not only the Red Army and the police but also whole regiments of Latvian sharp-shooters, briefed and instructed beforehand. These Latvians, who did not know Russia or the Russian language and who did not care whom they were to shoot, played a decisive role in this event. Lenin, an amazing organizer and strategist, was also an excellent psychologist. He realized that Russian soldiers, many of whom were of peasant background, might, if appealed to by other Russians, suddenly turn against the Bolsheviks. To prevent such a possibility, Lenin made concentrated use of the Latvian divisions. Bolsheviks were to use them time and again afterward to put down rebellious Russian peasants and workers.

But this was summertime in 1989, seventy-one years later, and Liteyny was a lively avenue filled with cars and passers-by, including many tourists in bright resort clothes. The weather was still warm, and people lined up on the sidewalk were buying ice cream and cherries and bunches of roses.

In 1989 the Smolny Institute, at the end of Liteyny, still housed a museum of Bolshevik history. Back in the summer and fall of 1917, from their headquarters established in a finishing school for the daughters of the nobility, the Bolsheviks had used modern means of subversion against the Provisional Government — telephone eavesdropping, intensive propaganda, and, above all, acts of terror. In July an attempted coup against the Provisional Government failed. In October another coup, meticulously planned, succeeded. The Bolsheviks took over the government, moving it to Moscow five months later. The working-class population of the city, like the personnel of the nearby Kronstadt navy base, though heavily propagandized, was considered restive and potentially threatening to Lenin and his comrades. And in fact the repression of the revolt of the Kronstadt sailors in 1921 proved to be one of the bloodiest episodes in the bloody history of the Bolsheviks' conquest of the Russian empire following the October takeover.

When I had last been in Leningrad, in 1967, the Smolny convent and the church, adjacent to the institute, were closed, unapproachable behind a high barbed wire fence. But now in the distance Rastrelli's architectural wonder, a turquoise Baroque church flanked by buildings and gardens that were once part of the Smolny finishing school, looked pristine. The fence was gone, and it seemed as if there never had been a revolution in Petersburg, as if young women in open carriages and officers on horseback were about to ride out of the gates of the convent gardens. As I got closer, the church appeared ethereal in the twilight. Sounds of music were floating toward me. At a small wooden kiosk by the main entrance tickets were for sale:

the event was not a church service but a concert of sacred music. I bought a ticket and went in.

A group of thirty or forty singers in flowing robes were assembled in the center of the church. All around the nave enormous windows admitted streams of brilliant daylight even at that hour — by then it was past eight o'clock. The choir was performing nineteenth-century religious compositions inside a space whose acoustics let the singing soar and reverberate. It was hard to believe that next door to this building echoing with heavenly voices, Lenin had started his methodical subjugation of the Russian empire.

While the momentous political events for which Petersburg has served as a stage since its founding seem to be all but forgotten, the literary life that flourished there in the nineteenth and the early part of the twentieth century has been lovingly recorded. Akhmatova's judgment notwithstanding, I discovered that the museums devoted to Pushkin, and to Pushkin's counterpart during the so-called Silver Age at the turn of the century, Alexander Blok, are both instructive and poetic. They are located in the quarters once inhabited by these poets, the leading artists of their respective ages. Modest as Pushkin's apartment on the Moika Canal may seem, it is situated at the heart of aristocratic Petersburg, while Blok's, also overlooking a canal near the estuary of the Neva, is at the edge of what was a working-class neighborhood. Akhmatova's poem about her meeting with the most beautiful and gifted among her literary elders is suggestive of that apartment as it stands today; the poem is also a fine example of the restrained yet candid eroticism of Akhmatova's early lyrics, which her contemporaries found so seductive:

I came to the house of the poet.
Sunday. Precisely at noon.
The room is big and quiet.
Outside, in the frosty view,

hangs a raspberry-colored sun
over ropes of blue-gray smoke.
The gaze of my watchful host
silently envelops me.

His eyes are so serene
one could be lost in them forever.
I know I must take care
not to return his look.

But the talk is what I remember
from that smoky Sunday noon,
in the poet's high gray house
by the sea gates of the Neva.

(Translated by Stanley Kunitz)

One day as the Akhmatova centenary conference was drawing to its end, I asked Pasternak's protégé Koma Ivanov, a fellow participant, what that poet's feelings about Petersburg might have been, beyond his celebration of Pushkin's art in *Themes and Variations*. Ivanov reminded me of five poems in the collection *Beyond the Barriers*. They are about the harshness of Petersburg, an industrial city originally willed into existence by a man possessed by an imperial vision. Under Petersburg's beauty Pasternak had recognized the antihumanistic vision of its founder:

Who are you, who are you? Whoever,
This city is your invention.
Streets rush forth like thoughts to the harbor
Like a black river of manifestos,
Even in your grave, even shrouded,
You are finding no rest.

And indeed Pushkin, who in *The Bronze Horseman* had denounced Peter the Great's ruthlessness, was killed there in a duel at the age of thirty-seven, most probably with the connivance of the tzar, and there Akhmatova had led a life of fear and deprivation, as did the Mandelstams until they were forced to leave for Moscow and Voronezh. Yet Osip

Mandelstam never ceased to long for Petersburg as he had known it as a child, a world of harmony which was later to betray him, where hundreds of thousands were destroyed in the early years of the Revolution and again in the thirties. Shortly before he was arrested he wrote:

Petersburg, I do not want to die,
I still have the telephone numbers
That will find the voices of the dead.

∽ 26 ∽

Remembering the Emigrés

JUST BEFORE AKHMATOVA'S conference ended, as a
farewell, Anya came to spend a couple of days in town
with me. Together we went to look at the Tauride Palace. Behind its formal façade I was still hoping to capture
some echo of the turmoil of that forgotten day in January
1918. As we walked around the city I told Anya as many
family stories about the Revolution as I could remember,
especially the events of January 18, about which Victor
Chernov, her great-grandfather, said in his memoirs, "It
was a horrible night, decisive not only for Russia but for
Europe and the world as well."

The closing session of Akhmatova's centenary was held
in Pushkin House. The palace on Vasilevsky Island had
been a stronghold of intellectual independence even in the
darkest days of the Bolshevik Revolution. Now, in the
peaceful atmosphere of June 1989, during that last meeting there, foreign guests of the conference — those like
myself who had given no scholarly lecture — were invited
to say whatever we wanted to about Akhmatova. Surrounded by close friends of the poet and by scholars of
formidable erudition, I had no intention of speaking, but
by midmorning I changed my mind and notified one of the
organizers of the conference.

During my wanderings in the Erlichs' and Anya's company through a city that is a memorial to Russia's past, I had begun to feel that too much of that past was in fact forgotten. At a gathering celebrating Akhmatova, a poet who had been condemned to what was contemptuously referred to by the Soviet press as "internal emigration," why not say something about a related subject — about the "external émigrés" of Russia? These people, long reviled, had been the country's God-given gift, helping Russian culture survive in exile while it was being destroyed at home. They had supported their country in time of war. Marina Tsvetayeva, Alexey Remizov, Nikolai Berdyaev had loved Russia no less than Anna Akhmatova, and despite what some Soviet critics maintained, she knew this and honored them for it.

I walked up to the podium with some trepidation. Trying to locate in the audience the friends who might be sympathetic to what I had to say, I recounted how through the three years that I had been acquainted with Anna Akhmatova, I had noticed a transformation in her attitude toward emigration. Little by little she had recognized it as the tragedy it was for those who were caught in it. Her friendship with my parents may have played some role in her change of heart. Knowing them she understood how dreadful it had been for Russians passionately attached to their country to be forced to leave under penalty of prison or death — and to be treated as traitors for some seventy years afterward. In conclusion I said, "Forced emigration once divided Russian culture in two halves. If we want it to have a future worthy of its past, scholars in this country must wholeheartedly return all the works of exiled writers and artists to Russia." Finding Anya's face in the crowd, I knew I had been right to speak up.

Though the political climate was said to be freer in Leningrad than in Moscow, at that time, 1989, glasnost was less than two years old; it appeared that no one there had yet addressed this issue in public. As I finished speaking, some of the participants and journalists attending the conference came up to ask about the fate of various Russian writers who had lived in Paris or the United States. They wanted to know about Poplavsky and Khodasevich, and also about Balanchine and Stravinsky. Then, after another round of eulogies to Anna Akhmatova, the conference ended with a copious luncheon interrupted by toasts to the future of Akhmatova scholarship.

As speakers followed each other I had the impression that we were celebrating the end of an era unique in the history of literature — the end of seventy years during which the writers of the Soviet Union had been both subsidized and controlled by the state to a degree unprecedented anywhere else in the world. Now, sooner or later, they would be free of both the controls and the material support. Were the writers of Russia ready for competition, for a free literary market? What lay ahead for Russian literature? I thought back to a comment I had overheard earlier that day at the conference, the grumbling of a gray-haired man who must have been a friend of Akhmatova's: "It was so in Anna Andreevna's days — there are many talented poets in Russia, but even more bandits and charlatans. I fear they'll win out." It seemed as if one could be sure of one thing only. Like Pasternak's legacy in Peredelkino, Akhmatova's would not be forgotten in her "blessed cradle," regardless of whether a monument to her would one day stand on the banks of the Neva.

After the luncheon Anya and I took a trolley back to the Hotel October. From the nearby railway station my niece would be taking the train back to Moscow that evening. I was spending one more day in Leningrad and would then fly to the United States directly. On my last afternoon with Anya, there was a great deal I wanted to tell her, about Victor Chernov and his bright hopes for a Constituent Assembly in 1918, and about my experiences with Solzhenitsyn, a subject I had often touched upon in conversation with her but never fully recounted. That story had always seemed too long and complicated to tell, unsuited to the happy days at hand.

Dodging the black marketeers haunting the corridors of the October, we reached my room. I locked the door behind us, and we settled by the window with the serene, distant view of the domed Nevskaya Lavra. I was about to start the tale of my adventures as Solzhenitsyn's trustee when the phone rang. *Fifth Wheel,* the television program that had presented my aunt Alla's readings of Daniel's poems, wanted to tape a program about the poets of the Parisian emigration — was I not the Olga Carlisle who had once published a book that included their works? Someone in the office had a copy of it, they'd bring it by the hotel. They wanted to build a program around it. *Fifth Wheel* planned to film the program in what had been Andreyev's apartment during the Revolution — the last one he had occupied in the city, at the corner of Moika and the Field of Mars. They'd come for me at the hotel early in the morning, since I would be leaving at dawn the following day.

Then someone from Moscow telephoned to ask whether I would consider lecturing on émigré literature at the Literary Institute in Moscow the following year. I was surprised and flattered, but Anya said soberly, "Don't you realize that the battle for the return of émigré literature is being launched? Right now it's a favorite subject of conversation among intellectuals, and not only in apartment 13. I do hope you'll accept the teaching job; that would bring you back to Moscow." And indeed this prospect made saying goodbye to Anya a little less difficult.

Nonetheless, I felt a mounting sadness. It seemed to me that everything that I, the oldest representative of our émigré family, had wanted to pass on to my Russian niece remained unsaid. I was no longer ready to start describing our work for Solzhenitsyn in what seemed like another life. Outside, the view of the Nevskaya Lavra was taking on a Roman glow. Anya and I decided to take a last walk.

On an earlier exploration alone, following details I remembered out of my mother's tales of the Revolution, I had been able to locate a small palace on Gallernaya Street a block from the Neva to the west of the city, where the Chernov family had stayed in the spring and summer of 1917 until the October coup had forced them underground. I was thrilled; my mother's description had been rather vague. Now I wanted to show it to Anya — there was just time enough before her train left. My aunt Ariadne, her grandmother, had lived there as an eight-year-old. Various SRs and their families had occupied the palace, including Alexander Kerensky, whom the young Chernov girls had found a bit ridiculous because of his self-importance and the white paramilitary tunic he liked to wear. The SRs, like the Bolsheviks, their erstwhile Socialist comrades, were as a rule quite restrained in their habits and dress.

Before the February revolution, the palace on Gallernaya Street, lavishly built in what the French call "modern style," had belonged to a relative of Nicholas II, the Grand Duke Andrey. Now in ruins, it was surrounded by chestnut trees in bloom and sagging fences, which gave it a ghostly look. But even in its state of extreme disrepair the grand duke's residence looked quite French, like the townhouses beyond the Etoile in Paris, a reminder of how removed from Russian traditions the Romanovs had been before World War I.

For a long time we studied the Grand Duke Andrey's palace. We strolled back and forth along Gallernaya Street, which is around the corner from Blok's house by the "sea gates of the Neva." The sun, reflected in the half-broken windows, was turning red, drowning the palace and its garden in an otherworldly light. Anya was lost in thought.

All of a sudden she looked quite grown up. Remembering a glimpse I had had on television the week before of Sakharov's exhausted face, I made a silent wish: "Let not the new democratic yearnings of Russia go the way of those earlier bright dreams."

THREE

1990

∽ 27 ∾

Return to Moscow

ON A SPRINGLIKE DAY in San Francisco at the
end of February 1990, the telephone rang. Clear
as a bell I heard Anya's voice at the other end —
I had not spoken to her since our time together in June.
She was calling from apartment 13, she told me. Trying to
control the intensity in her voice, she said, "Don't worry
about the rumors — there are no pogroms in Moscow at
this time. I know some are reported in your newspapers,
but they're false rumors. It's only Pamyat, trying to force
Jews to emigrate, using scare tactics. I'm really calling to
tell you and Henry that I'm engaged. To Vitya. You remember him, from apartment 13, the young violinist from
the Moscow Soloists chamber orchestra? He's Jewish, but
I know that everything will be all right. They say that two
days ago Bush spoke to Gorbachev about stopping the
anti-Semitic provocations in our country. If that's true, it's
bound to help. In the meantime, please don't worry. Alla
Alexandrovna said you might be coming in March. We'll
be celebrating Oleg's birthday then. A big party in apartment 13 — you're invited."

Before I knew it she had hung up, before I could tell her
how much I appreciated her call or congratulate her on her

engagement. I did remember the dark-eyed, mild-mannered Vitya, whom I had met shortly before I left Moscow. And the reports about impending pogroms had me thoroughly alarmed, though the American press took pains to stress that the notorious Pamyat Society stopped short of physical violence against Jews, seeking instead to intimidate them with threatening telephone calls or slashed tires.

With each month that fall the mails from the Soviet Union had become more irregular. By December they stopped altogether. No New Year greetings from Moscow ever reached us in 1990. My exchange of postcards with Dima, which had been uninterrupted since my uncle Volodia's illness in the late seventies, ended. Then in March, shortly after my telephone conversation with Anya, I received a registered letter from Moscow, an invitation to teach a seminar at the Gorky Literary Institute there. Its director, Professor Smirnov, was requesting a series of lectures on Russian émigré literature, to be given in April of that year.

A letter from my aunt Alla arrived around the same time, mailed from Europe. She was urging me to stay with her while I taught at the institute, where I'd be paid a small salary in rubles. In the cold season commuting there from apartment 13 was out of the question: it was too far. The institute's budget made it impossible for the school to provide me with independent lodgings. However, Alla wrote, her apartment near the Kremlin was only a three-minute walk to the school. I'd be comfortable there. I later gathered that her goddaughter, Ludmila, a teaching assistant at the institute, had played a part in securing my invitation there.

Encouraged by Henry, I decided to accept both the institute's and Alla's invitations. It seemed wonderful to be able to go to Moscow in time to glimpse the long-awaited reunion of émigré and Soviet literatures. Some years before, in 1986, at the University of Iowa's Writers' Workshop, where Henry had taught for a semester, I had given a seminar entitled "The Literary Uses of Exile." It was based on readings out of Kundera, Nabokov, and Solzhenitsyn. Now I could devise a course that might include the works of other exiles as well, unavailable in English translation, such as Alexey Remizov and Boris Poplavsky. I could share my firsthand knowledge with students and see the inhabitants of apartment 13 again.

But at that time I had yet another reason to accept the institute's invitation: I was determined to find out more about the Russian chauvinists, whose provocative activities were being reported more and more often in the Western press. The new twists given to the old "Russian Idea" were disquieting. Researching a study of the rebirth of Russian national sentiment in the Soviet Union, I was interested in finding out about Solzhenitsyn's future in his country. Now that all his works were being published there, was he coming home? The possibility of his return was viewed by some as being decisive for the future of Russia. I had not forgotten my conversation on the train from Abramtsevo with that bearded poet friend of Alla's, nor what she herself had said about her hopes for the restoration of the Romanovs.

Accepting my aunt's invitation, I let her know that I was taking on another assignment that I would be working on while living at her place — an article for the "Arts and Leisure" section of the *New York Times* about the first festival of Jewish films ever to be held in the USSR, scheduled to take place in Moscow in the spring of 1990. It would be a test of glasnost: the USSR had not yet recognized Israel diplomatically. Alexander Askoldov had given his support to the event.

The festival's organizers were Janice Plotkin and Deborah Kauffman, two dedicated young women from Berkeley, who hold a yearly Jewish Film Festival in San Francisco. They had befriended Askoldov in the summer of

1988, when he was there with *Commissar*. Now the Jewish Film Festival was headed for Moscow, seeking to acquaint moviegoers with aspects of Jewish culture forgotten in the Soviet Union, to inform them about Jewish issues throughout the world. It would travel there with an American entourage of almost eighty people, filmmakers and backers of the project. Many of the visitors had parents or grandparents who had been born within what became the Soviet Union. For them it would be a symbolic homecoming and perhaps an opportunity to establish contacts with Soviet relatives.

Knowing how hectic Moscow would be once I got there, I tried to prepare myself for my assignment by viewing ahead of time some of the films that would be shown at the festival. I saw Louis Malle's *Au Revoir les Enfants*, which seemed to come straight out of my French childhood during the Occupation; the uncompromising and yet lighthearted *Rouge Baiser,* dealing with fractured émigré lives in postwar Paris; and the humorous *Crossing Delancey,* about Jews in New York today.

Before I left the Bay Area I met with Janice and Deborah to show them some of the newspaper clippings I had collected about the activities of Pamyat in the Soviet Union. The festival had been agreed upon many months before — before the Soviet national problems had begun to come to a head, notably in Baku and Vilnius; before chauvinistic publications of every kind had multiplied throughout the country in the absence of formal censorship; before an increase in the number of Jews allowed to leave the Soviet Union had caused popular resentment against them to soar. At that time, non-Jewish Soviet citizens were not allowed to emigrate.

But Janice and Deborah would not be deterred. Glasnost was in full swing; Soviet chauvinism had to be challenged. The festival had the support of the American Soviet Kino Initiative, a Los Angeles–based joint venture between

Soviet and American moviemakers, and of Andrey Smirnov, the president of the Soviet Filmmakers' Union at that
time.

Landing in Moscow on a dusky afternoon in March
1990, I knew that a second visit there after glasnost could
not be anything like the first one, filled as it had been with
recognitions and discoveries. The man sitting next to me
on the plane helped set the mood for a difficult journey. A
dour Frenchman, most probably a Communist traveling
on some undefined political mission, he made no mystery
of his disgust with the new Soviet Union, an agreeable
country gone mad. Did I have essential foodstuffs in my
luggage? Otherwise I might starve. Somberly he admon-
ished me not to take cabs in this *"pays de sauvages,"* as I
would run the risk of being robbed or even killed.

That winter the new Russian revolution was taking an
alarming turn. Some days before, hoping to rule more ef-
fectively a state that was beginning to disintegrate, Gorbachev had had himself elected president of the Soviet
Union — by that Soviet Parliament which he himself had
created, rather than by universal suffrage. The Soviet people, with the exception of a few intellectuals, were beginning to detest him for his inability to give them the "normal life" they yearned for. Perestroika was failing; stores
in the Soviet Union were emptier than ever. Some weeks
earlier there had been a huge pro-democratic demonstration in Moscow, a warning to Gorbachev that there could
be no going back on reforms. The new president had responded by selecting an advisory committee, a Presidential
Soviet of "wise men," several of whom, like Valentin Rasputin, a Siberian member of the so-called School of Village
Writers, were known to be aggressively nationalistic. One
or two were avowed hard-line Communists.

At the airport the cold was penetrating — it was beginning to snow. There were no customs officials anywhere in
sight. Passports were barely looked at by distracted men in

civilian clothes. To my relief my two suitcases crammed with gifts and especially with books — all that were needed to teach a six-week course on a long-forbidden subject — were there right away. So were my aunt Alla and her goddaughter Ludmila, both full of greetings and welcoming smiles. They had with them an attractive young woman, a professor from the institute, who was carrying a bouquet of red carnations. A car sent by the school was there as well, ready to take us to Alla's apartment.

And here, long enough for a hearty bear hug, was Anya, looking smart in a Western-style sports jacket. With her was Vitya, just as I remembered him, a slender, shy-looking twenty-six-year-old with a charming, sudden smile. Anya and Vitya had come to the airport to renew their invitation for me to help celebrate Oleg's birthday in apartment 13 at the end of the following month. Very politely they declined my aunt's invitation to come back to her house for tea. They disappeared before I knew it.

I will never forget that first wintry evening in Alla's kitchen overlooking an illuminated, snow-dusted Kremlin. I was shivering; perhaps I was coming down with the flu. As in 1989, there was a touch of the fantastic, an eeriness out of *The Master and Margarita* to my visit. Surely I did not believe that should a pogrom suddenly be provoked in Moscow my presence there would make the slightest difference. But I recalled the day in 1940 when the Germans took away the Jews of Oléron in open trucks. My cousin and I had gone to the village square to say goodbye to a school friend. There was nothing we could do to prevent his being driven away, though instinctively we knew that the truckload of people was doomed, that we would never see them again. In part it had been this obscurely remembered day which had brought me to my aunt's in Moscow that spring.

Over tea in the cozy kitchen I hastened to tell Alla in detail about the forthcoming Jewish Film Festival, which would occupy part of my time in Moscow — I was not due to begin teaching at the institute for a while. Janice and Deborah and their party would soon be arriving at the Hotel Rossiya on the other side of Red Square. Polite and evasive, Alla and Ludmila smiled and served delicious homemade cakes. Obviously they regarded my *New York Times* assignment as a caprice, too bizarre to discuss — perhaps I had taken the assignment for purely financial motives. My aunt, as affectionate as ever, made it clear that she trusted me completely. Above all she wished to make my Moscow stay a fruitful one. Of course my friends from Berkeley or anywhere else were welcome to visit me at her apartment, and the telephone was mine to use at any time of the day or night. After tea she moved us into her small painting studio. We sat for a while under my uncle Daniel's photograph, the one my father had on his desk when I was a child. The serene, familiar face strengthened my resolve to look after the integrity of the Andreyev legacy.

When the young professor from the institute had left and we were preparing to go to bed, Ludmila, who now was permanently settled at my aunt's, showed me a pile of newspapers and magazines lying atop the refrigerator in the kitchen. "These may help you understand why, on the eve of its spiritual rebirth, the Russian community is worried about Jews and Freemasons," she said in a matter-of-fact tone. "They still rule the Soviet Union, the small nation bent on destroying the great one. Supported by the West under the guise of so-called perestroika, Jews are seeking to appropriate the little that Communism has not annihilated in Russia — her natural resources, her art, her national pride."

I was outraged. I felt that I could not stay another minute under Alla's roof without saying exactly what I thought of her and Ludmila's ideas, and I did, vigorously, while the two women exchanged knowing, saddened glances. I told

Alla that one of my reasons for being there was precisely to report on what was currently happening to Jews in Moscow. I was a journalist as well as a member of the Andreyev family, which for almost a century had considered anti-Semitism evil and had actively fought against it.

But though as cordial as ever, Alla was now firm. I had to understand that Russians living in Russia would have the last word on matters that touched their country's future: the Jews had to go. With their cooperatives and black marketeers and overnight millionaires, they were sucking up what was left of Russia's energies. "However," she said sanctimoniously, "unlike certain other peoples, Russians are fundamentally a nonviolent Christian nation. We will not harm Jews. All we want is for them to leave the Soviet Union as quickly as possible. For everyone's good."

I became ill that night. I had indeed caught some kind of flu — I had a temperature, an earache. Alla gave me her own room, the best in her three-room flat. Over my bed hung a color lithograph of the late Nicholas II with a saint's halo. The last Romanov and his family had recently been canonized as martyrs by the Russian Orthodox Church abroad. I tossed and turned and stayed awake through the night, an otherworldly Kremlin shining outside my window. Finally I put on my reading light. Under the tzar's vacuous gaze I leafed through some of the newspapers and journals from the pile on my aunt's icebox. The articles I looked at — in *Molodaya Gvardia* and especially in *Nash Sovremennik* — reminded me of the French newspapers toward the end of the Occupation with their relentless anti-Semitic allusions.

Several articles I read that night called for the immediate return of Alexander Solzhenitsyn to the Soviet Union, vilifying in passing that contemptible Russia-hater, Andrey Sinyavsky. Solzhenitsyn alone had the stature to inspire Russians along the difficult path ahead. His *Letter to the Soviet Leaders* was quoted. His high regard for Orthodoxy would lead Russia out of the abyss, and his understanding that for Russians, morality was more precious by far than democratic institutions. Was it all said without his knowledge?

I had no choice but to confront my aunt. We would have to have a showdown. The alternative — giving up teaching at the institute and going back to San Francisco — was impossible. As long as Alla was warned that I would not, in private or public, condone her ideas, my presence in her house was all to the good, putting her on notice that the Andreyevs' name, including Daniel's, was not hers to involve in some murky intrigue that she herself might not be fully aware of.

I spent the next few days in bed fighting the flu and getting ready for my course at the institute. I had built all around my bed a protective wall of books. Nabokov, Poplavsky, Berdyaev, and Remizov sheltered me from the goings-on in Alla's apartment. At all hours friends of Ludmila's from the institute and priests serving in the church nearby dropped in, as did enthusiasts of Daniel's works, often calling on my aunt unannounced. Alla was almost never alone. Nonetheless, she found the time to be a caring, attentive nurse. She made special soups for me, trying her best to make me as comfortable as possible. I marveled at my aunt's equanimity, at her ability to maintain a friendly demeanor in the face of what she must have recognized as intense censure.

Whenever Anya or Aliosha came by, sometimes bringing supplies from the free market, I would get up, and we would converse amicably with Alla in the kitchen. During these visits, the future of Daniel's literary works was the principal subject of conversation. Alla was involved in bringing out *The Rose of the World,* that monumental cosmology, through a nongovernmental, cooperative publishing house. She told us that Igor Shafarevich — he of *Russophobia* fame — was writing a text about *The Rose* for the journal *Moskva*. Every day came new requests from journals and magazines for unpublished poems by Daniel, and for Alla there were readings to be given all over the country; one in Kiev was scheduled for early April.

My temperature would not go down. Doctor Oleg made house calls, bringing me hard-to-obtain medicines that were not very effective and fresh gossip from apartment 13. I tried to repay him with English lessons. Oleg was hoping to be able to study in the West for a couple of months and needed urgent help with the language. His visits were a breath of fresh air, a reminder that I would one day recover from the flu and escape the ambiguity of my situation at Alla's.

In the meantime I tried to assuage my sense of guilt through daily confrontations with Alla, usually in the late morning at breakfast while Ludmila was away at school. It became a ritual: I would tell my aunt that even if she harbored some of the feelings toward the Jews expressed in the journals she collected, she might want to learn to keep them secret. In the West after the Holocaust the notions concocted by the Nazis — such as the alleged Judeo-Masonic plot against Aryan nations — were considered obscene. Should their rebirth in Russia become known to the rest of the world, such views would put the country beyond the pale of civilized nations when it most needed their support.

To this my aunt would quietly reply that this was in fact one of the aims of these publications — to repel Western interference once and for all. Responsible Russians did not want the evils of capitalism to penetrate their already devastated country. If these incontrovertible insights into the harm the Jews had inflicted on the Russian nation since the nineteenth century would keep Western profiteers and speculators away, these journals would have played a beneficial role.

At this point I would stand up and tell Alla that she had

better not forget that these were *her* ideas — not the Andreyevs', not Leonid Andreyev's or my father's, not Daniel's, not those of our family friends. Then I'd retreat in silence behind my barricade of books, seeking comfort in the company of Professor Pnin and of his circle of memorable eccentrics. I wished that my aunt's eccentricity was of the kind that could be laughed off, perhaps even enjoyed, like that of Nabokov's immortal creations. Outside it would snow lightly. A pale gray dusk would last late into the evening. Days were getting longer; soon it would be April. Guessing my distress, and despite the fact that communicating between the United States and the Soviet Union was becoming ever more difficult, Henry managed to reach me on the telephone almost every morning, giving me news of San Francisco where weeks before a beautiful spring had arrived.

∞ 28 ∞

A Spring Slow in Coming

I STAYED INDOORS for several days. Oleg was firm: as long as I had a fever I was not to go out, except perhaps to his birthday party and to those film festival functions that were absolutely indispensable to my article. From the wide double window in my room, whenever I ventured beyond the barricade of books, I watched the five golden cupolas of the Dormition and the brick watchtowers take on surprising, ever-changing hues. The spring in 1990 was slow in coming; in the daytime the outlines of the Kremlin were often blurred by snow flying in circles outside my window. I recalled lines from Pasternak:

> *Do you remember that life — the flakes like doves*
> *Thrusting their breasts against the howling,*
> *The storm swirling them, fiendishly*
> *Dashing them to the pavement?*

Day after day, whenever their telephone worked, I was able to communicate with Janice and Deborah encamped with their staff of American volunteers and their guests in the huge circular compound of the Hotel Rossiya. They were so close, and yet they in their fortress-like hotel and I at Alla's seemed to inhabit different planets, coming to-

gether only once in a while on matters concerning the festival. One morning, unable to reach me by phone, the two
young women stopped in at the apartment unexpectedly.
They were received graciously by Alla and offered tea in
the kitchen. My aunt's anti-Jewish sentiments were recently acquired and, apparently, quite theoretical, but this
did not reassure me. I had known others during the war,
impressionable people whose naïveté had been manipulated by propagandists into fanaticism.

From the beginning the festival's organizers were subjected to minor harassments very much in the style of the
KGB, such as the disappearance at the airport of the festival posters and the repeated breakdown of the telephone
in their hotel suite. Meeting with the Moscow municipal
authorities to discuss the details of the events scheduled to
begin the following week, they were told to come back —
in June. There were enough Jewish events in town as it
was, they said; whereas in fact one lone dance company
from Israel was performing there that week. Then, omi-
nously, the movie theaters originally assigned to the simul-
taneous festival screenings became unavailable overnight.

Taken aside by various Russian officials, Janice and
Deborah were told in hushed tones that a Jewish film festival in Moscow could be divisive, perhaps even dangerous. Security might be difficult to maintain. They should
desist. In fact, a large gathering of Jewish visitors at the
Rossiya was in itself provocative. Mercifully the great majority of the festival's American guests remained unaware
of these interferences, swept up as they were in a brisk
round of sightseeing and visits organized by local well-
wishers. As for the festival's officials, both the Americans
and their Soviet counterparts were determined to proceed,
although everyone in town knew about a recent meeting
of liberal members of the Writers' Union — participants
had been roughed up and the group disbanded by loud,
menacing hoodlums armed with bullhorns. Among the vis-

iting filmmakers I talked with, Paul Mazursky, whose *Enemies, a Love Story* was to be shown, was not taken in. When he realized how distressed I was he tried to comfort me: "How could it be otherwise, with Russia's past? We have to accept the fact that it will never change," he said — which made me feel even worse than I already did.

From a practical point of view, the failure of this particular undertaking would have been a catastrophe for the Soviet filmmakers looking for new prospects and for support in the West. It could easily have signaled the end of future American-Soviet collaboration in film. Rustram Ibraguimbekov, a portly, jovial Azerbaizhani screenwriter who was a vice president of the Filmmakers' Union at that time, was pressed into action.

Rustram was on his way from Los Angeles to his native Baku, which was then the scene of bloody confrontations between the native population and Russian settlers. Hoping to catch up with Rustram, with whom I was slightly acquainted, I took a subway to the Filmmakers' Union Club, which turned out to be as noisy and crazy as ever, with familiar faces coming in and out of focus — here was Yevtushenko, buttonholing me about *his* film, the best ever made. He vanished before I could tell him about the difficulties of the First Moscow Jewish Film Festival, which he, the author of "Babi Yar," would certainly have taken to heart.

Now I was sitting in the club's upstairs dining room across the table from Rustram Ibraguimbekov, a platter of pickles and smoked fish between us, which reminded me all too vividly of the meal I had shared there with Askoldov the year before. Defiantly setting up my pocket tape recorder on the table — though the din in the room was such that nothing could possibly be recorded — I told Rustram, as forcefully as I could, about the embarrassing details I would have to report in the *New York Times*, should the festival be canceled or run into trouble.

I felt sorry for my host. He was taken by surprise. The only other time we had met was at the dinner given by Tom Luddy when I had first arrived in Moscow in 1989. Now my feverish intensity must have seemed strange to him — he could not know about my life at Alla's. But Rustram never lost his optimistic composure; he was no less hospitable than Askoldov, pouring red wine for me and ordering the best entrees. Having heard me out he promised to intervene at once.

As for Janice and Deborah, they appealed to Alexander Yakovlev, one of the main architects of glasnost and Gorbachev's most liberal supporter at the Ideological Section of the Central Committee of the Communist Party. They also alerted two California politicians, Senators Cranston and Wilson. Miraculously, the three cinemas scheduled for the festival's screenings became available on the day of its opening.

Late that afternoon I went out with Anya, whom I had asked to come to the opening party with me. I was still a bit shaky, but it was invigorating to stroll in the cool Moscow twilight arm-in-arm with my niece. We crossed Red Square, where, according to Mandelstam, "the earth is roundest":

> The earth is roundest in Red Square,
> Slanting down, open and wide . . .

On our way to the Rossiya we made a loop past St. Basil, walking down to the river quay below, catching a whiff of spring from the trees along the bank. As we walked, I asked Anya more about what she had told me when she phoned the previous month. Had she heard any new report of harassments of Jews in Moscow or elsewhere? Was Vitya's family of Petersburg musicians all right?

Anya said that as far as she knew, the harassment was occurring mostly in provincial towns — and as a rule it was intimidation rather than physical attacks. Her Jewish friends in town, including Vitya, preferred not to discuss the situation, especially distressing and even somewhat humiliating at a time when the country was ostensibly starting on a new liberal political course. In her opinion, Anya told me, the country was moving toward a new dictatorship, that of the far right, a secret alliance made up of KGB officials, Communist functionaries, and chauvinistic Village Writers like Rasputin, Belov, and Astafiev. Now past their artistic prime, these men wanted their share of political power — Rasputin had just become advisor to President Gorbachev.

From the sadness in Anya's voice I knew that my questions were painful to her. She said, "Vitya as a Jew and as a brilliant musician has good reasons to want to emigrate someday. I know one thing — I wouldn't want to bring up children here, where things are so far from normal. Recently I talked it over with my father. You know what a patriot he is — he himself will never leave Russia, but he had to admit that it might be different for me, especially if I want children. Now let's go to the party."

And we did, to a lavishly catered and yet somewhat strained affair in a very large public room of the Rossiya overlooking the Moscow River. There the two courageous friends from Berkeley, their vast entourage, and a few Soviet guests led by the unflappable Rustram were trying hard to appear cheerful. Back in San Francisco I had helped draw up a guest list for the opening of the First Moscow Jewish Film Festival, and I found it strange that none of the dignitaries who had been invited had come, though they were all avowed film lovers. Where were Mikhail and Raisa Gorbachev, Voznesensky, Bella Akhmadulina and her husband, Boris Messerer, the theater director Yuri Lubimov, the magazine editor Vitaly Korotich, and the deputies Yuri Karyakin and Yevgeny Yevtushenko? It was quite possible, of course, that their invitations had never reached them.

Munching on delicacies which neither of us had tasted in a long time, Anya and I were introduced to an energetic-looking, handsome, dark-eyed woman, Aviva Kempner, who had produced one of the three films inaugurating the festival that night. I had seen a tape of *Partisans of Vilna* before I left San Francisco, a documentary about the ancient Hanseatic city once known as the Jerusalem of the North. It is a chronicle of the development of the Jewish resistance in Vilnius during World War II, and of its complex and sometimes dramatic relationship with the Red Army. Aviva was wondering whether her visa for Vilnius would still be honored now that Lithuania had declared its independence — as it turned out, it was, a day or two later.

Then we encountered Askoldov's wife, Svetlana — Askoldov was out of town, but Svetlana had with her a guest from New York, the human rights activist Cora Weiss. And here was Irina Ehrenburg, the writer's daughter, an old family friend whom I had not seen since 1967. At over seventy, she was a testimonial to the staying powers of the old Moscow intelligentsia. She was full of good humor and declared herself optimistic about the ultimate fate of her country. To my remarking that Valentin Rasputin seemed like a cynical choice as advisor to Gorbachev at that particular time, Irina pointed out that Chingiz Aitmatov had also been elevated to that post. He is the Kirghiz writer with liberal leanings who had hosted the first legendary Forum of intellectuals in Issyk-Kul in 1986. That Forum, which inaugurated glasnost, was an event out of "A Thousand and One Nights," a mixture of Oriental splendor and political ambiguities.

As we parted, Irina said with a sly smile, "At least in our country the president consults with writers, even if they are not always the right ones." I remembered that the previous year when I met Voznesensky at the Writers' Union Club he had told me delightedly that Mikhail Gorbachev knew a great many of his poems by heart. Well, perhaps Irina

was right, and all was not lost. I trusted the political acu-
men of Ilya Ehrenburg's daughter, although like most
Moscow intellectuals at that time she was dismissive of
Gorbachev. She was especially critical of his early campaign against alcoholism — the gratuitous destruction of
thousands of acres of vineyards in Georgia had infuriated
her: "Stupid and counterproductive, what a way to begin
the reconstruction of Russia!"

For me what turned out to be the most poignant moment of the festival came later that night, at a screening of
Uri Barbash's *Beyond the Wall*. This film from Israel was
that country's biggest box office success ever. Anya said
afterward that it had some of the impact of *The Gulag
Archipelago*, which she was reading at that time. But in
fact *Beyond the Wall*, despite its gritty realism, is far more
optimistic than the dark, enormous *Gulag*. It supports the
notion that Arabs and Jews may find friendship even in the
most horrific of situations, inside a maximum security
prison — that retribution is never a solution in human affairs. During the movie's last, exhilarating prison scene, I
could feel Anya's emotion; in the dark she was wiping her
eyes.

Despite the lack of publicity other than word of mouth,
despite the sense of threat that could be felt in the city,
with its three theaters running simultaneously in different
parts of Moscow, the festival was attended by more people
in Moscow than it had in all its years of existence in San
Francisco. It was sold out. Every day my friends from
apartment 13 and their friends phoned to ask for tickets
that could not be had. An authentic Soviet-American joint
effort, the First Moscow Jewish Film Festival was proving
a silent, almost subterranean success. As far as I know, it
was never reported in the media in the Soviet Union, perhaps for fear of the Pamyat hoodlums who were said to be
roaming the streets.

Involved as I was with émigré literature just then, I was

especially interested in films dealing with exile. I remember the anguished faces of the people walking out of *Enemies, a Love Story* on the last night of the festival. Isaac Bashevis Singer, whose story inspired Mazursky's film, is little known in the Soviet Union, but he was suddenly becoming an object of fascination. His tales are about the life that awaits the Soviet citizens who will emigrate. They are timeless evocations of the surreal no-man's-land which greets every man or woman brave enough to leave home in search of a better life elsewhere; more often than not they prophesize a lonely future for them.

∾ 29 ∾

Fear in Moscow

SENDING OFF MY ARTICLE to the *New York Times* proved to be a difficult undertaking, though reporters from the newspaper's Moscow bureau tried to be helpful. Communications between the Soviet Union and the West were ever more erratic. Finally one night at 3:00 A.M. Moscow time I was able to phone in my piece directly to Michael Leahy of the "Arts and Leisure" section of the paper. He had it in time to run it on the appropriate Sunday in April, in a softened version. "We can't have this read like an Op-Ed article about Russian chauvinists," Michael said. It seemed sensible to go along with the changes he proposed, even though the new version did not fully reflect my dismay at the way the festival had been handled in Moscow.

Now I had to prepare for my triweekly classes. I kept thinking of a Russian proverb quoted in my family: "The wise man likes to learn, the fool to teach." As the day when I was to report to the institute was nearing, I was feeling more uncertain. As an instructor I had dealt only with students who were aspiring writers — American writers. But now I would be lecturing in Russian, about Russian literature, to aspiring Russian writers enrolled in a four-year graduate program. My students were certain to know more than I about every aspect of Russian literature, except perhaps émigré literature, though, judging by my experience the previous year in apartment 13, they might be able to teach me a thing or two about Nabokov and Tsvetayeva as well.

Sometimes in the middle of the night I would wake up with a start. The illuminated brick walls of the Kremlin outside my window cast a reddish glow over every object in the room. My aunt's mirrored dressing table, the old upright piano, the portrait of Nicholas II over the bed seemed to be smoldering, ready to burst into flames. It looked like the beginning of some great fire, like the one described at the end of *The Possessed,* a fire heralding the arrival of the "true twentieth century," in Akhmatova's words:

Like a man possessed of demonic fever,
on a dreadful night reflected in mirrors,
refusing to recognize himself —
while along the fabulous embankment
oblivious of the world calendar,
the true twentieth century edges in.

In 1990 in Moscow the twentieth century's ills were festering. I had been struck by a remark of Ludmila's at breakfast: "You'll see, Olga Vadimovna, you'll love the institute, though it is still a Jewish institute."

"What do you mean?" I asked.

"Well, there are still a few Jewish instructors there, but soon they'll be gone."

Could Ludmila be taunting me, or had she not taken seriously what I had said on my first evening at Alla's about racism? She made me fearful. Fear was something that I had caught in Moscow. Despite glasnost, everyone I encountered there, with the exception of a few stable, exceptionally busy individuals like Oleg or my cousin

Aliosha, appeared once again to be experiencing fear of one sort or another. For many it was the fear of a return to Stalinism under the leadership of the hard-liners in Gorbachev's government. For all but a few privileged families there was fear of hunger. Basic foodstuffs were still available in government-run stores at controlled prices, but certain items such as cheese or sugar or matches would suddenly disappear, not to reappear for months, if at all.

For those who were set on emigrating, like Dima's neighbors on the tenth floor of 144 Leninsky Prospect, there was the fear of having to go to Israel rather than the United States, where the family wanted to live. I was acquainted with several other friends of Oleg's and Dima's who were ready to leave the Soviet Union — but only for a country where life would be "normal." The idea of going to Israel, viewed as a militarized state under siege, horrified them. Yet American emigration regulations were changing. With the closing down of the Gulag, the United States no longer conferred automatic refugee status on emigrating Jews.

For me, there was the dread that people like Valentin Rasputin, whom Alla often quoted, those who had helped inspire her with her ideas, would gain greater power in the Soviet Union: I had doubts about avowals of Christianity and nonviolence. "There can be no neutrality in Russia," Rasputin had declared in an interview. "You are either with it or against it. The motherland is in danger. Tomorrow we could wake up in our beds and it won't be Russia anymore. Everything around will be the same, but it will be foreign." And about Jews: "We tried to acculturate them, but they remained without love of country. They are out of harmony with the soul of Russia."

As I lay in the reddish darkness of my room I had fantasies of being aboard a plane flying westward, back to Paris and San Francisco, a blessed afternoon that would take me away from this country which felt like my own and yet was so unsettling. I thought about my mother and her sisters in 1919, confined for weeks in the National Hotel, only a few hundred yards from where I was now. I thought about my grandmother, who had spent almost three years in prison during the Revolution, released thanks to Gorky's intervention. But there was no Gorky in Russia now, not even a Pasternak, who, threatened himself, had intervened time and again, hoping to protect friends in trouble. I tried to imagine how Pasternak had dealt with fear, remembering a story of a fantastic telephone conversation he had had with Stalin, about Mandelstam's merit as a poet. Nadezhda Mandelstam liked to recount that story over and over again, always pointing out that Pasternak had spoken truthfully, that the notion that he may have hurt her husband was absurd.

According to Anya, to whom I confided my state of mind, it was the death of Andrey Sakharov the previous December, less than three months before, that had opened the floodgates of fear for many Russians. She had felt it on the day of Sakharov's burial. "Once again we are left unprotected," Anya said. "The country was orphaned while its democratic future was far from resolved. People feel vulnerable, old terrors are returning. I myself do not believe in pomp or rituals, especially when these concern someone I did not know personally. What I did on that day last December when Sakharov was buried was to babysit Clara's grandchild. Clara works at the Chukovsky museum. That day it was very comforting to be with her five-year-old grandson."

Clara, Anya told me, had gone to take some flowers to Elena Bonner. The funeral had turned out to be a tremendous event despite the cold and falling snow. That day Elena Bonner told Gorbachev that he had lost his best adversary. "It's what we Russians have lost that's scary — the only honorable leader Russia, and the Soviet Union, have ever had," said Anya. "I'm afraid he has left no heir.

There is simply no one around who has even remotely his intelligence or his bravery. No wonder we're scared."

That afternoon Anya and I were alone in Alla's apartment. My aunt had gone off for a weekend in Kiev, where she was giving a recital of Daniel's poems. "To an audience of Russians," she had said before leaving, "because nowadays there are practically no Ukrainians left in Ukraine. People who say otherwise are lying. By now nearly everyone there is Russian." To my relief Ludmila also was away — she was in another part of the city visiting her young son, who lived with her mother. Outside, the five cupolas of the Dormition, caught in a shaft of sunlight between squalls of wet snow, were all shiny, like golden apples. From the free market Anya had brought some potatoes and a basket of real, red apples, along with a bunch of anemones, the kind I had seen when I first met Akhmatova at the Ardovs'.

At last I was beginning to shake off the flu. In the sunshine the Dormition suddenly looked not like an embodiment of power but like a beautiful object, a symbol of hope and order. The apples Anya had brought smelled delicious — I had discovered that apples were a fine antidote to insomnia. Perhaps because Anya was with me, a member of my family with whom I could share my anxieties, I no longer felt quite as depressed.

A day or two later, after a breakfast of kasha with milk, Alla and Ludmila walked me to the institute. I was to give my first class that afternoon, about Nabokov. It was once again a very cold day. Bundled to our eyes we followed slippery back alleys to the Tverskoy Boulevard, where the Hertzens' family mansion that houses the Gorky Literary Institute is located. We were received in the director's office, where Professor Smirnov and several other faculty members greeted me with a mixture of warmth and curiosity — a foreign granddaughter of Leonid Andreyev is an object of interest in Russia.

But I felt a certain aloofness on their part as well, an attitude that week after week my students were never to lose. My being invited to the institute through Alla's and Ludmila's efforts might have been the reason for the students' unwillingness to befriend me. There were Jewish pupils among them, and my being introduced by people determined to see to it that their school would cease to be a "Jewish institute" could not have been reassuring to them.

I, too, remained reserved with my students. A political shift to the right was likely to occur sooner or later, and I did not want to run the risk of compromising them. Still, I was sorry that the mass of books I had brought in my luggage did not include *Shield,* a 1906 collection put together by Andreyev and Gorky in defense of Jews persecuted in tzarist Russia, and which contains entries by such writers as the famous Symbolist poet Vyacheslav Ivanov. I would have liked to read from it to my pupils. A number of its contributors, like Ivanov and Andreyev, eventually became exiles.

As it was, I was left with *Lolita* and *Pnin* and *Speak, Memory,* and with Tsvetayeva's émigré poems, and those of Boris Poplavsky. Because the school owned no copying machine for duplicating the texts I had brought with me, we usually read aloud the text under study and then analyzed it. My students were sophisticated in their literary judgments and remarkably well read. They were responsive to the materials we discussed. Except for the fact that they were careful not to interject anything personal in our exchanges, our literary discussions were no different from those which would have taken place at Yale or in Iowa. Current politics were not touched upon, even though the Writers' Union, upon whom the institute depends, was at that time caught in an ugly anti-Semitic campaign by its chauvinistic members against their more liberal colleagues, some of whom were Jewish. Opposed to any kind of liberal reform, these writers were spreading crude anti-Semitic slogans. Hideous cartoons resembling those disseminated by the Third Reich began circulating in Moscow.

When the time came to read some of Solzhenitsyn's works written in emigration — his *Lenin in Zurich, August 1914, Our Pluralists* — my students let me know discreetly that they would much rather learn a little more about Parisian émigré poets than discuss the Vermont recluse. I was happy to comply, though I had to borrow some books from Dima for that part of the course. It turned out that, like Dima, several of my students had an expert knowledge of the works of Khodasevich and Georgi Ivanov, although these poets were forbidden in the Soviet Union until 1989.

Perhaps in part because of the unspoken tensions within the institute, I emerged from class exhausted. It would still be daytime — the days were getting longer quickly in Moscow's northern latitude. What to do? To go back to my aunt's apartment, where Ludmila would be having a late lunch with a group of her schoolmates, was not an inviting prospect. I did not have the energy to contact my old Moscow friends. Apartment 13, more than an hour away by subway with a twenty-minute walk afterward, seemed all but inaccessible in the cold weather; taxis were now almost impossible to find. But then one afternoon in the courtyard of the institute, a rundown eighteenth-century mansion embellished with a heroic statue of Gorky, I found myself face to face with the poet N.* He was an acquaintance who almost thirty years before had taken me on an unforgettable excursion to the monastery of St. Sergius in Zagorsk.

N, now in his mid-sixties, is what is referred to in Russia as a "war poet" — a poet who fought in World War II. He is a man of integrity, though he was never a dissenter. He

---

* N's real name is omitted here to protect him from possible pressures from right-wing colleagues.

had steadily grown as an artist despite the pressures of the Brezhnev era; over the years from time to time I had come across collections of his verse, which were becoming stronger with each publication. At first I did not recognize N, who wore a big fur hat over his graying hair, but he, a visiting writer, had heard that I would be teaching at the institute. He greeted me and offered to take me for a ride — his own class was over and his small car was parked nearby. I accepted. After only a few minutes in N's company I discovered that this man, who had always considered himself Russian, who had fought for Russia against the Germans, who was one of the well-known Russian men of letters of his generation, was on the verge of a nervous breakdown because of the abrupt realization that he no longer had a country. For N is Jewish — one of the writers Ludmila hoped would soon be thrown out of the institute.

The harm that Alla and those who shared her beliefs were doing to Russian society — to Russian culture — struck me with renewed force as I spent time with N. From then on, he occasionally took me for a ride after class. He had always been in love with Russian Orthodox antiquity, and now he drove me to shrines which allegedly were no longer a part of his rightful inheritance because of his Jewish origins but which somehow had become mine. Our roles had reversed since the sixties, when I would have been considered an outsider and he a Russian. It would all have been ridiculous were it not so disturbing.

I soon realized that to question N about the events at the Writers' Union would be tactless. He was persuaded that it was only a matter of months before a huge pogrom against Jews and their liberal supporters would be unleashed throughout the Soviet Union. He predicted a coup orchestrated by Stalinists in alliance with the Pamyat Society. Civil war might follow, though the government's tanks might eventually put an end to it.

When I had last seen N, blond, blue-eyed, and athletic, he was one of the idealistic young men who, in the Khrushchev era, had wanted to believe that "Communism with a human face" would prevail in the Soviet Union and its satellites. If he had had doubts about this, he never discussed them with me. He was a Party member. He had put his faith in Communist ideals and in Russian goodness. But now, almost thirty years later, he was a prospective enemy of the people. His best hope for survival was to be put, together with his family, on a plane bound for Israel, though he said that in fact he would never leave Moscow, even for the sake of his wife and children.

Nothing I said could reassure N — and in truth I had no reason to believe that his apprehensions were unfounded. Still, I reminded him over and over that nowadays the Soviet Union needed the support of the West, which would not tolerate persecution of Jews; that a vast majority of Soviet citizens yearned for a normal life, not for pogroms; that the campaign against alleged speculators and cosmopolitan writers was being plotted by a very small group of individuals hoping to use anti-Semitism as a rallying cry to arouse a populace that would in fact not be moved. N would look at me sadly and remain silent.

Then I would try to divert him. I reminisced about our excursion in 1962 to the monastery of St. Sergius, Russia's holiest shrine, a symbol of Russian resistance to subjugation by Tartars, Poles, French. Ghia Margvelashvili, a Georgian editor in love with Russian literature, who had succeeded that year in publishing Mandelstam's verse in *Literary Georgia,* thereby opening the way for future publications of Mandelstam in the Soviet Union, had been along on that expedition. Did N remember which poems by Mandelstam we had taken turns reciting on the way to Zagorsk? Did he recall the small, lace-curtained restaurant near the monastery where the three of us had lunch? The drive back to Moscow at sunset?

One afternoon N took me to the Novodevechy cemetery, that eccentric and rather unsettling necropolis where
Russian notables have been buried since the nineteenth
century and which is part of the great Novodevechy monastery to the west of the city. We found Chekhov's tomb
there, moving in its simplicity, and near it Chaliapin's,
which shows the great singer life-size, weightily reclining
on an oddly shaped couch. And here was a childhood
friend of my mother's, Gorky's son Max, in fashionable
1920s clothes. He had been killed shortly before his father,
left to freeze in a ditch after a drunken binge in the company of NKVD operatives.

N helped me find my grandmother Alexandra Mikhailovna's plain grave only a few steps from the tall white
marble bust of Alleluyeva, Stalin's wife, whom he is said
to have killed with his own hands in a fit of rage. Daniel
Andreyev is buried nearby, next to his mother. On that icy
late afternoon in early April, his tomb was covered with
fresh flowers. I recited for N a poem of Daniel's that I had
memorized. Written in 1952, it seems to speak about our
times:

> *As we wait for tomorrow*
>   *we weep and cry and protest.*
> *Yes, it will be harsh and bloody,*
>   *a day of reprisals, of trials and storms.*
> *Yet that day is the door, the threshold — a border*
>   *between true brotherhood*
> *And the prideful empires*
>   *that are falling, never to rise.*

Wherever we went on our afternoon excursions, there
was always something along the way to remind us of Russia's hard fate. Once N took me to see Kolomenskoyo, an
exquisite, tent-shaped seventeenth-century chapel high on
the bank of the Moscow River. We sat in its shadow for a
while, gazing at the misty, faraway view of the city. At N's

request I told him a little about my adventures with Solzhenitsyn. When we got up to go N said, "Of course you do remember that Kolomenskoyo is a monument out of Russia's short-lived Renaissance? The chapel was built to commemorate the birth of Ivan the Terrible. Russia would never quite recover from his reign of terror. It was he who laid the foundations for the tyranny that is about to reassert itself."

On our last excursion, a day or two before I was to leave, N took me to Peredelkino "to say goodbye to Pasternak," his favorite poet of the revolutionary era. We walked around the cemetery, which was still leafless and wintry and quite melancholy. When we came to Pasternak's grave I remarked that his white tombstone with the elegantly carved profile had recently been cleaned. "Didn't you know?" N said. "The carving was defaced. It happened earlier this winter, just before his centenary celebrations here in Peredelkino. The stone was smeared all over. After all, Pasternak was a Jew."

I was speechless; I thought of Anya. So as not to distress me, she had told me nothing about this malevolent act, which she knew I would find shattering, an affront to Russian honor.

᧞ 30 ᧞

Farewell to the Soviet Union

THAT SPRING, reading and rereading what Alla had
saved of my uncle's works, I became convinced that
Daniel had powerfully expressed the complexity
and magnitude of Russia's suffering under Stalin. This of
course would be the reason for his ardent popularity.
Hearing Alla recite his poems, I remembered that my uncle
was said to have loved her deeply — by all accounts theirs
was a great love. I remembered also that there is no evidence whatever, either in his works or in the facts of his
life, that Daniel was anti-Semitic. Before leaving Moscow
I investigated this question. There still are people in Moscow who knew him personally, including Aliosha, who
had met my uncle in the late fifties.

Alla, younger than Daniel by some ten years, had been
my uncle's beloved, his friend, his feminine Other, his support. She is bright, warmhearted, impressionable, stubborn, and highly capable in day-to-day matters, but although he dedicated many beautiful poems to her she was
never her husband's intellectual guide. Now I wondered:
did Alla's service to Russian literature give her the right, so
many years later, to speak for Daniel on philosophical
matters?

In her public performances, whenever I was present, Alla let the facts of Daniel's life and art stand for themselves, without interjecting her own beliefs. I was grateful for her restraint. However, in the conducting of his publishing affairs she appeared to be influenced by a variety of people. The ones I knew were Ludmila and the bearded philosopher who had presented an outline of my uncle's ideas in Abramtsevo — eventually this man went on to write a disappointing, simplistic introduction to one of Daniel's masterworks, *The Iron Mystery*. The publisher of that book turned out to be Molodaya Gvaradia, a house associated with a magazine by the same name, which, for a number of years, has been one of the Soviet Union's most aggressively chauvinistic publications.

For my part, I was not certain whether I had the right, or indeed perhaps the obligation, to explain to those who take an interest in Russian culture that Daniel was a literary mystic in the tradition of Alexander Blok, that there is nothing in his biography or in his works that would link him to the political stance of the editors of Molodaya Gvaradia or to the ideas put forth by Igor Shafarevich in his *Russophobia*. Should I be writing about this? I planned to seek advice from my family and knowledgeable friends — until I heard Vadim Kozhinov speak at the institute in April 1990. After that I made up my mind to speak out.

It happened early in my teaching assignment at the institute, when I had not yet fully recovered from the flu. Ludmila had insisted that despite the blustery weather I come with her to a noonday lecture. The celebrated literary activist Vadim Kozhinov had agreed to speak at the school. It was an event I should not miss. Had Alla been home that day she would most probably have dissuaded me from going, not only because of the bad weather but also because she had come to realize that I was not about to be converted to the views of the new Russian far right.

But as it turned out, wearing my warmest hat and a huge woolen scarf over my coat, I let myself be guided by Ludmila along snow-covered back alleys to the institute, to what must have been the main conference room there.

That room, once the scene of many propaganda speeches and of Marxist-Leninist indoctrination seminars, now had an abandoned air. Yellowed political posters from the pre-glasnost era were still tacked to the walls; portraits of Gorky and Lenin hung there, looking forlorn. Beyond the old-fashioned double windows, swaying leafless trees created a desolate background for a man with close-cropped hair sitting against the light, leaning on a large desk. There were a number of students settled at desks around the room. I recognized no familiar faces here, although one or two of those present might have attended my class.

The lecture was about to begin when, in her usual conspiratorial manner, Ludmila, who had first sat next to me, started to move about the room, conversing in whispers with the teacher who was introducing the speaker and then with some of the students scattered around the room. When she finally sat down again, Vadim Kozhinov, a swarthy fifty-year-old man who had the emaciated, unsteady hands of an addict, began speaking in a feverish voice. Listening to this man of letters, a much-publicized journalist who had been a Party member and was said to be an expert on the nineteenth-century poet Tyutchev, I recognized the intonation of the German leaders I had heard on the radio as a child. Kozhinov must have studied the delivery of Dr. Goebbels, Hitler's minister of propaganda. He spoke in a steady, hypnotic voice, insisting that Jews have no claim to the Russian soil, that in the Old Testament they portray the Holy Virgin as a prostitute. I could not believe my ears.

Addressing himself to the concerns of his audience of future Russian writers, Kozhinov said that the prompt reinstatement of censorship was their best hope as artists. His own work had withstood that test in earlier days. As an authority on Tyutchev, a writer who had served as the tzar's censor, he knew what he was talking about: Russia could not survive without censorship. In the past, literature had flourished because of it. Order was what was needed in Russia now. Discipline. Love for the church. A strong state. The rhetoric was fascistic, just as Shafarevich's views on the historical role of Jews are fascistic. It was all very familiar and frightening.

The audience of about thirty sat there in silence. Vadim Kozhinov's delivery was mesmerizing. For a brief instant I myself believed that indeed perhaps in the Bible the Virgin's holiness is doubted — Kozhinov spoke with such absolute certainty. I do not know how many in the audience actually believed the speaker's allegations. We did not look at each other sitting stiffly at our desks. My impression was that the great majority thought that they were confronted with a cobra ready to strike, that it was safer not to move or say a word. The institute might not remain Jewish for long, and it would be imprudent to attract attention to oneself, especially if one were a Jew — and there must have been some in the audience. I, too, remained silent. Kozhinov's diatribe brought back childhood memories too painful for words, memories of friends destroyed by the Nazis.

Toward the end of his hour-long lecture Kozhinov launched into a passionate eulogy of Alexander Solzhenitsyn. Here was a true servant of the Russian earth, who would soon be returning to the motherland to help rule it, a patriot who had successfully resisted the corrupting influences of the West and the attacks of depraved cosmopolitans like the Jew Andrey Sinyavsky. I wondered whether Solzhenitsyn knew what kind of apologists he had in Russia. Did anyone in Moscow report to him about the use made of his name? Did the Chukovskys know, or his official representative, an editor of the magazine *Novii Mir?*

When his speech was over Kozhinov was asked to join the students for "informal conversation in the hallways." He declined. A car was waiting for him; he was to give a speech elsewhere shortly. I had the impression that Kozhinov's presence at the institute was part of a propaganda effort orchestrated from outside the school. Quickly, with a clipped military step, he walked out of the conference room without another word.

I was silent on my way back to Alla's apartment, too offended to say anything to Ludmila. She, however, was determined to start a conversation. She asked me point-blank: "Well, Olga Vadimovna, what do you think of Vadim Kozhinov's ideas? You must realize that they are those of the mainstream Russian intellectual elite right now. Nor do they differ very much from those of Solzhenitsyn."

"Ludmila," I said, "I think I've told you before how I feel about anti-Semites."

"Olga Vadimovna, you are so wrong. Vadim Kozhinov is not an anti-Semite."

"How can you say that?" I asked. "Didn't you hear what he said just now?"

"Yes, I did, Olga Vadimovna, and I can say with absolute certainty — Kozhinov is *not* an anti-Semite. The best proof is that his wife is Jewish. By the way, so is Alexander Solzhenitsyn's. I was told this by someone who knows the family intimately.

"As for Kozhinov, all he wants to do is save Russian culture. The destructive role played by the Jews in Russia is a matter of historical record. We've had a Jewish dictatorship here ever since the revolution. Before that, Jews brought down the empire. They tried to destroy our church, killed millions of believers, appropriated our land. Do you know, for instance, that it has recently been established beyond any doubt that the head of the Cheka, Felix

Dzherzhinsky, was a Jew from Taganrog masquerading as a Polish aristocrat?" Ludmila was so caught up in her proselytizing that she was oblivious of my reactions. Her anti-Semitism was visceral. Alla's, on the other hand, was a new creed that secretly thrilled her.

Those still alive who had known Alla and Daniel as a couple were shocked by her evolution. Some days later I had a long conversation with Irina Nikolaevna Ugrimova, a close friend of our family, now in her eighties, who had known my uncle since childhood. The Ugrimov family, exiled for some years, had been arrested upon their return to Russia in 1948. The case made against them had to do with their acquaintance with Daniel.

"With the passage of time and all the horrors — the interminable years in prison — Danya did become somewhat strange," Irina Nikolaevna said, "though all his life he remained a courteous, fascinating, loving man — how sad that you never met him! By the way, I do not think that he resembled your father that much, though their physical likeness was striking. Danya was far more eccentric than Vadim. For instance, he would prefer not to stay in town because he liked to go barefoot so as to remain in touch with the earth. There was a luminous, saintly quality about him. I can assure you that Alla's current ideas would have struck him as deranged. Such ideas were anathema in the Dobrovs' household, with which I was familiar in my earliest years."

In pre-Revolutionary Russia, anti-Semitism was quite widespread in the upper layers of Russian society and among the uneducated, but it was unacceptable to the Russian intelligentsia. The intelligentsia's enthusiasm for Dostoyevsky, for instance, was dampened when, after his experiences in the House of the Dead, he embraced the tzarist authorities' religious and social positions. Without the intellectuals' acceptance of Jews as equals, Russian culture would not exist as we know it — without the painters

Bakst and Levithan, without the poets Pasternak and Mandelstam, without the Rubinstein family of musicians, without the writer Babel and the filmmaker Eisenstein and the religious philosopher Shestov. Today, Joseph Brodsky is Jewish, and the composer Alfred Schnitke and the painter Eric Bulatov are half Jewish. The future of Russian culture is impossible to imagine without Jewish participation.

Once Alla took me to a soirée honoring a younger member of the school of Village Writers, a friend of hers called Leonid Borodin. The reading was held at a former political club in a working-class section of Moscow, Krasnaya Presnya, and the evening was a revelation for someone like myself who had never attended a Pamyat-oriented assembly before — though ostensibly this was not a Pamyat meeting but a literary event. First my aunt recited some of Borodin's poems, which sounded quite beautiful, in part because of her talent as a performer. Then the author himself, an attractive blond man of about forty-five, read one of his stories, a typical Village tale of the betrayal of a peasant family by corrupt city dwellers. Borodin had spent several years in a labor camp on charges of anti-Soviet activities, and his second story, the more successful of the two, was about the gulag in the seventies.

However, what was so remarkable about the evening was the second half of the program, when five men sitting in a row on stage took turns praising Borodin and damning Andrey Sinyavsky! As far as I remember, there was a young editor there from Molodaya Gvaradia and a literary critic named Yuri Bondarenko, and they all performed like puppets, calling for Alexander Solzhenitsyn to lead Russia and berating the moral depravity of Russia-haters. It was a flow of shrill clichés that seemed to have been well rehearsed — this, like Kozhinov's lecture, had to be an event organized from the outside.

This second part of the program, which went on late into the evening, was enthusiastically applauded. It reminded me once again of Brecht's genius at capturing the use of demagoguery and the behavior of people under the spell of totalitarian ideology. It was out of *The Rise and Fall of Arturo Ui,* which dramatizes the rise of Hitler in Germany before World War II. The evening ended peaceably enough, except for the fact that Alla's tape recorder, a gift from my brother which Ludmila had brought along, was stolen. The audience dispersed without confrontation; no one challenged the wound-up propagandists on stage — and for good reason. In the back of the small auditorium, wearing a yellow polo shirt, the notorious Pamyat strongman Vassiliev was sprawled in his seat, a pudgy goon who, Alla allowed, wasn't at all a nice person and shouldn't have been there in the first place.

Complete isolation from the outside world is a Soviet legacy. It may well be that Solzhenitsyn knew nothing of the strident following he commanded in Moscow before the August 1991 coup. Back in Vermont he would have been busy reworking his 1973 *Letter to the Soviet Leaders,* turning it into a proposal for the future management of the USSR which, unlike its earlier versions, no longer relied on the inclusion of the Baltic states into the Union. He was to release this document in the late summer of 1990. The empire was falling apart, but, like Gorbachev, Solzhenitsyn did not seem to be fully aware of it. He was proposing the creation of a Slavic Soviet Union, reduced in size, encompassing Russia, the Ukraine, and Kazakhstan but without the other Asiatic Soviet republics. Politically speaking, this was a dangerous proposal, since it would have put the Soviet Union's Islamic lands directly under the influence of fundamentalist Iran, across the border from the Soviet Union. Equally provocative was Solzhenitsyn's declaration, made at that time, on the subject of Israel. While berating the West's corruption, he praised "the Hebrew cultural revolution," which he said had set the example for nations "not to capitulate before American cultural imperialism and its by-product, Western intellectual waste."

But only in part was my stay in Moscow in 1990 darkened by what I witnessed at Alla's. There were happy occasions during which I felt proud to be Russian. One evening Aliosha invited me to dinner with some of his close friends, whom he had known when he had studied and then taught mathematics at Moscow University. Several of them, now in their early fifties, had been members of Sakharov's circle of dissenters; two had spent time in the gulag in the eighties. Now they were all coming into their own, working as scientists again, active in newly formed democratic groupings. That evening they were celebrating because the KGB candidates who were expected to win municipal elections a few days before had in fact lost everywhere, except for one lone sector to the north of Moscow.

Aliosha's friends were interested in a redrafting of the Soviet constitution, using as a basis for their proposals the project Andrey Sakharov had completed before his death. As we talked about it, no one among us foresaw that less than eighteen months later, there would no longer be a central government in the Soviet Union that would play the constitutional function of the USA's federal government. Establishing a new constitutional order under these conditions is proving a complex if not altogether impossible task.

Another happy occasion that spring was Oleg's birthday party. This was my homecoming to apartment 13, where I was greeted as a member of the collective and asked to move in for the rest of my stay in Moscow. I was tempted. The messy apartment felt like home, safe from the demonic Bulgakov atmosphere at Alla's. That morning she and I had been filmed there for a television show called *Families,* about the three Andreyev men of letters — Leonid, Vadim, and Daniel. Alla had been at her most assertive, objecting to my wearing a red dress for the occasion. Still, I had to decline Dima's invitation. My schedule would have made commuting to the institute by subway too strenuous, given the half-melted snowdrifts that still marked this remote section of Leninsky Prospect.

But everything about Oleg's birthday party I took in with delight. Doctor Oleg and Doctor Dima's admirers in the neighborhood and at the hospital had provided the makings of a sumptuous buffet set up in the kitchen — gargantuan offerings of vegetables and fruit, meat and cabbage pies. And here was Oleg's mother's specialty, pickled green tomatoes, a favorite of mine since 1989. Sipping Georgian wine, I mingled with the guests, filled with a fresh sense of awe. It was a relief to be among these young people after being with the diffident students at the institute. Here was a crowd of free-thinking, free-speaking men and women in their twenties from a spectrum of professions. As I talked with them I felt hopeful. They were passionately interested in what was going on in the West, hoping to travel there but not necessarily planning to emigrate. My gift to Oleg of several American paperbacks by Nabokov, the fulfillment of a year-old promise, was welcomed by the whole company, who would take turns borrowing them.

For seventy years Russian literature survived in exile, to be welcomed back to Russia as one of its most important and revealing branches, a mirror image of the mother country as well as a window on the outside world. Teaching Nabokov I discovered that, for young writers, whether in Iowa or Moscow, he was the most inspiring of models. Eclecticism remains the best hope for the survival of Russian culture. Over the centuries it has flourished thanks to its ability to incorporate foreign and native elements. Russian architecture would not exist without Italian masters; early Russian painting was based on French prototypes, as was the ballet. Later Diaghilev's Ballets Russes enjoyed their greatest triumphs on stages in Paris and London.

I became convinced that not even the political wizard Mikhail Sergeevich Gorbachev nor the grim prophet from

Vermont could turn the Russian clock back to the isolation and fear of the pre-glasnost days. And in fact Oleg's friends were among the young people who in August 1991 would help defend the democratic future of Russia on the barricades set up to protect the Moscow White House.

A little more than a year later, in 1992, Aliosha, with whom I met in Paris — he was the guest of the Institut des Hautes Etudes Scientifiques — told me that indeed the inhabitants of apartment 13 had bodily stood by Yeltsin during the August days, as had his own mathematician friends. As for Aliosha himself, he had been lecturing at the University of Tartu that summer, where to his intense disappointment "nothing at all happened." "By the time Lena and I came back to Moscow," he said, "the third Russian revolution had been won. Without us, damn it!"

No less memorable than Oleg's birthday party was the concert to which Victor Yerofeev took me on my last night in Moscow. Yerofeev, a writer whom I had first met in California, is a literary critic and a novelist who is a contributor to the liberal magazine *Ogonek*. I was delighted to be invited to a gala at the Conservatory in honor of Alfred Schnitke, a composer who is half Jewish, half German by heritage, a musical heir to Shostakovich, and, in my opinion, one of the great contemporary Russian artists. Three of his compositions often performed in the West were at last being premiered in the Soviet Union, where he had been ignored throughout the Brezhnev years.

A day or two before the concert, Schnitke was awarded the Lenin Prize, which he turned down because "he did not approve of the name of the prize," Yerofeev reported, though no one was supposed to know this yet at the time of the concert: turning down a Lenin Prize was at that time a bold gesture of defiance. But of course everyone in the audience knew, and this turned the gala, attended by the Moscow cultural elite, into a triumph. There were colossal bouquets of white and red roses on the stage of the venerable Conservatory, and guests in black tie and evening dresses sat in the front rows. Each piece was given an ovation, and when Schnitke came up on stage at the end — middle-aged, shy, with the long hair of a Romantic — the audience went wild.

But what was truly unforgettable about that concert were the tragic expressiveness of the compositions performed. They spoke directly of the Soviet people's sufferings in the twentieth century. But then, like Ludmila, I was becoming obsessive: the fact that the artist being celebrated that night was partly Jewish filled me with heightened satisfaction.

My most poignant farewell was with the poet N. Though he knew of Alla's sentiments he came up to see me at her apartment on my last afternoon there. N would not stay for tea at Alla's, but he offered to take me for a last ride through Moscow. We went first to the Hippodrome, where, not that many years before, N had played the horses — now a sad-looking, neglected enclave waiting for the entrepreneurs of the nineties to give it new life. From there we drove to the Novodevechy monastery, to the high bank above the pond that adjoins it. This spot offers a view of the seventeenth-century ensemble of churches, convents, and cemeteries, and of the swans gliding on the pond.

The day was mild and hazy; spring was in the air. Easter had just been celebrated — every day in Alla's part of town dozens of people stood in line outside to be baptized in the small church behind her house. This was a bewildering sight, but here one came face to face with the serenity of the Greek Orthodox spirit. From the distance Novodevechy has a grace that reminded me of Zagorsk as N and I had seen it in 1962 — except that across the road from where we stood on that high bank above the convent, there now was a very expensive cooperative restaurant. Customers were pulling up to its entrance in Mercedes cars, brash

Soviet *nouveau riches* whose coarse manners and lavish clothes were in painful contrast with the lyrical view of the monastery below.

N was sadder even than usual, and once again I tried to cheer him up. "Do you remember that in 1962 Ghia Margvelashvili invited us to visit him in Tbilisi?" I asked. "Why don't we take him up on his invitation a year or two from now? It should be possible for me to come back then. I'm friends also with the filmmaker Abuladze, whom you must know as well. Wouldn't it be a wonderful trip?"

N belongs to that group of Russian poets from Pasternak to Bella Akhmadulina who have been in love with Georgia and Georgians all their lives — N's translations of modern Georgian poetry into Russian have become classics. But the thought of a trip to Georgia did not interest N. He looked at me disconsolately. "Don't you understand, Olga Vadimovna, that in a year or two not only Russia but Georgia as well will be engulfed in civil war?" he said. "The Soviet Union will never be a democracy. Don't you understand? We have not yet even begun to pay for Russia's imperial past."

As I relate these experiences I think of my friends from apartment 13. Anya and Vitya now live in southern France. From their home in Montpellier, Vitya travels on concert tours, while Anya commutes to Paris, where she is writing a doctoral thesis on Nabokov. At present they have no plans to live in Russia. Both Doctor Oleg and Dima spent some months of medical training in Vienna, but they are now back at apartment 13, working in the pediatric hospital on Leninsky Prospect. I remember my walk with Oleg and his admonitions against my rosy Western views of Russia's post-Soviet future. Nonetheless, during my two recent visits to Russia, I had deepened my understanding of this land that does not yet know its name or its future, a country locked in an age-old conflict between two aspects of herself, nationalism and a humanistic tradition, both deeply rooted in her past. Threats from the Red Browns intensify from day to day, the economic collapse accelerates. Reflecting on the fact that the country's destiny lies ultimately in the hands of my young friends and their generation, I was most pleasantly surprised by a recent message from Dima, in keeping with his romantic view of life.

"Life here has become so damn interesting, it truly would be a great shame to die now. Paris in the twenties could not have been more breathtaking."